Exploring the Heritage of American Higher Education

The Evolution of Philosophy and Policy

by
E. Grady Bogue
and
Jeffery Aper

AMERICAN COUNCIL ON EDUCATION
ORYX PRESS
Series on Higher Education
2000

The rare Arabian Oryx is believed to have inspired the myth of the unicorn. This desert antelope became virtually extinct in the early 1960s. At that time, several groups of international conservationists arranged to have nine animals sent to the Phoenix Zoo to be the nucleus of a captive breeding herd. Today, the Oryx population is over 1,000, and over 500 have been returned to the Middle East.

© 2000 by The American Council on Education and The Oryx Press
Published by The Oryx Press
4041 North Central at Indian School Road
Phoenix, Arizona 85012-3397
http://www.oryxpress.com

Published simultaneously in Canada
Printed and bound in the United States of America

∞ The paper used in this publication meets the minimum requirements of American National Standard for Information Science—Permanence of Paper for Printed Library Materials, ANSI Z39.48, 1984.

Library of Congress Cataloging-in-Publication Data
Bogue, E. Grady (Ernest Grady), 1935–
   Exploring the heritage of American higher education : the evolution of philosophy and policy / by E. Grady Bogue and Jeffery Aper.
      p. cm. — (American Council on Education/Oryx Press series on higher education)
   Includes bibliographical references and index.
   ISBN 1-57356-310-2 (alk. paper)
   1. Education, Higher—United States. 2. Education, Higher—Aims and objectives—United States. 3. Higher education and state—United States. I. Aper, Jeffery. II. Title. III. Series.
LA227.4.B66 2000
378.73—dc21   99-049294

This book is dedicated to four professors/academic administrators who among them have contributed a century and half of devoted service to Louisiana State University and the University of Tennessee, respectively: Dr. Martin D. Woodin and Dr. Huel Perkins, Louisiana State University; and Dr. John Prados and Dr. Otis Stephens, the University of Tennessee.

CONTENTS

PREFACE

Whether viewed from a philosophical or political perspective, the investment Americans have made in their colleges and universities is rich. The extent and quality of that investment has been most obvious in the latter half of the twentieth century. That investment of both faith and finance has created a splendid heritage of imagination and innovation that is widely regarded both nationally and internationally.

While American higher education owes much of its structural and philosophic heritage to Europe, and especially England, higher education in the United States is a distinctive construction widely admired. Enriching this heritage are new voices and ideas from cultures over the world. American colleges and universities are extraordinary organizations that hold hands with the past even as they reach for the future. Cultural curators and cultural critics, colleges and universities are expected to nurture a reverence for history and heritage while challenging conventional wisdom. That Americans have been willing to politically and financially support an enterprise with the avowed mission of criticizing and evaluating their society is a matter of marvel and wonder.

The scope of the enterprise is a tribute to academic, civic, and political leaders; the faith of Americans in the power of education; and their willingness to fund and support a system of promise and diversity. The first college in this nation was established in 1636, and Americans moved to create new colleges before they had established a system of elementary and secondary schools. From less than a dozen institutions prior to the American Revolution, the U.S. now has approximately 4,000 institutions, including two-year community col-

leges, specialized schools such as theological seminaries and schools of mortu-
ary science, private liberal arts colleges with religious affiliation, public comprehensive universities, and public and private internationally recognized research
universities.

American higher education is a system of multiple chances and choices. It is
a system of both privilege and opportunity. It is a system with two major
categories of institutions: public institutions depending upon government
support and subject to government regulations; and private institutions experiencing both the risk and the freedom of independence. Each system offers
complementary strengths to the goals of access, innovation, and quality. It is a
system in which the principle of autonomy, so essential in the search for truth
and in the nurture of democracy, is in dynamic tension with the principle of
accountability, which is antidote to professional arrogance and intellectual
narrowness. It is a system in which debate over educational purpose and
curriculum constitutes a form of ideological conflict, and the metaphors of war
are often used to describe these debates. How does an organization simultaneously conserve and critique the heritage of the society of which it is a part?
American higher education is a system with built-in organizational tension in
its missions. It is a system too powerful and too important to our personal,
social, economic, and political welfare for its purpose and performance to be
left entirely in the hands of those who give primary voice and meaning and life
to the university. It is, therefore, a system with complex governance structures
in which lay boards of trustees play an important and critical role, an organization in which collegial/consensus principles of organization contend with
hierarchical/bureaucratic organizational principles. It is a system in which
many agencies external to the campus have an influence on the campus—
alumni, accrediting agencies, government. It is a system of shared authorities
that works but is easier experienced than described.

Americans are justifiably proud of their colleges and universities and we
often extend a significant salute to this historic sector of our society. However,
there is also a public disaffection with higher education as we approach the
twenty-first century. Contemporary and compelling issues of focus, trust, and
accountability currently face American colleges and universities. And for many
the heritage of American higher education is unfamiliar and often misunderstood.

American higher education, a distinctive and important civic instrument,
has come under frequent and critical assault as we approach the twenty-first
century. While these years are by no means the first season of criticism for
higher education, traditional assumptions and principles are being contested in
professional and public forums with considerable frequency and intensity. Each
year of the past decade has seen at least one major book-length critique of
American higher education, including Bloom's *The Closing of the American*

Mind, Sykes' *Profscam*, Anderson's *Imposters in the Temple*, Smith's *Killing the Spirit*, Roche's *The Fall of the Ivory Tower*, Solomon and Solomon's *Up the University*, and Kors and Silvergate's *The Shadow University*. The charges in these books are extensive, but one theme that emerges in almost all is that some American faculty are in flight from their most fundamental responsibility, teaching, and are moving to other more lucrative and selfish pursuits. In another paradox, the criticism falls heavily on American research universities, which attract both national and international regard.

The values mission of the academy has also come under scrutiny. A 1996 book by David Patterson with the forbidding title *When Learned Men Murder* reminds us that formal education does not always ensure that conscience guides our competence. Of the fourteen men gathered at the 1941 Wannsee conference in Berlin to design and plan the Holocaust—the intended eradication of an entire people—eight held doctorates from some of Europe's most prestigious universities. A 1993 essay entitled *An American Imperative: Higher Expectations for Higher Education* suggested that American colleges and universities are neglecting both to teach and to exemplify those values that undergird human dignity and democratic society. Other essays and commentary in the professional and public press lament the neglect of management and educational integrity in our colleges and universities and challenge long-held traditions and views on such themes as access, quality, and tenure.

For public higher education, state and federal government agencies have developed more assertive voices in shaping higher education purpose, influencing higher education policy, and evaluating higher education performance. For private higher education, a certain ferment, and occasional outright conflict, have characterized relationships between private institutions, boards of trustees, and associating/sponsoring organizations—especially in the case of colleges and universities with religious affiliation. An issue of historic origin, the conflict between the tradition and teaching of religious faith and the unfettered search for truth continues in the modern religiously affiliated college and university.

This paradox of confidence and criticism, this confluence of salute and suspicion presents American higher education and society with important leadership challenges. How do Americans revere and respect the best philosophic, scientific, artistic, and moral traditions of higher education and simultaneously work for reform and renewal? This is a dance of tradition and change that is difficult to choreograph and perform.

THESIS AND PURPOSE OF THE BOOK

Surely there is much about American higher education that requires reform and renewal. However, challenges to higher education tradition, mission, and performance are not necessarily signs of pathology. An institution whose mission embraces the unswerving search for truth, whose methods include the adversarial testing of ideas in a public forum, whose spirit embraces a certain irreverence, and whose best work is done when its graduates exit with sustained curiosity and with the competence and courage to ask "why," may count it a measure of success when those graduates turn their curiosity to the academy itself. Higher education is not excluded from critical scrutiny. There is no need to demean the past, however, as we search for ways to improve the future servant role of American higher education.

Our thesis in this book can be divided into three parts: (1) American higher education is at once a powerful, imaginative, yet often misunderstood instrument of our democratic society; (2) the celebration of the rich political and philosophical heritage of colleges and universities is appropriate as we approach the twenty-first century; and (3) the debate over the purpose and performance of higher education is both a natural and a necessary consequence of its mission complexity and political/moral context.

Reaching for the future via reform and renewal of higher education begins with an understanding of whence we came. Thus, the authors propose to make an unfamiliar heritage familiar. In realizing that goal, the first intent is to paint in broad stroke some of the important historic moments in the evolution of American higher education, giving the reader access to the arguments that have both shaped and stressed colleges and universities. The second intent is to explore some of the major philosophical principles and traditions that undergird the American academy and to bring those principles under critical review and scrutiny. Ralph Waldo Emerson once noted that it is in our best interest to throw ourselves on the side of our assailants to see what we might learn from them. We intend to do this, so that both academics and civic/political friends might benefit from the discourse and the journey. The third intent is to examine the issues that currently challenge the academy, and to think about pathways to the future. While taking this journey, we hope to point the reader to some of the key historic and contemporary literature associated with higher education purpose and performance. We will also furnish data points and profiles that will leave the reader with some sense of the scope of the American higher education enterprise.

Understanding any organization is a complex work, and certainly no less so for colleges and universities. One cannot take one large expository bite and hope to find it intellectually digestible. There are several possibilities for organizing this book. The historian might use a time-sequence organizational approach, exploring multiple themes as time and history unfold. One might also organize the discussion around leadership issues and challenges facing an organization. We have elected to organize the chapters in this book around the following series of questions concerning higher education purpose and performance, with the aforementioned goals in mind.

1. What is the scope of American higher education?
2. What are the missions of higher education?
3. How are colleges and universities governed?
4. What is taught and who decides?
5. How is quality defined, developed, and demonstrated?
6. Who finances and who benefits from higher education?
7. Who does and who should attend college and how do students and colleges influence each other?
8. What are the issues in faculty role and responsibility?
9. What is the relationship between intercollegiate athletics and academics?
10. What leadership challenges confront higher education in the closing years of the twentieth century?

Another advantage of this approach is that it allows the treatment of particular themes in some depth rather than spreading the attention over several chapters. We believe that it is useful to see the unfolding of higher education mission in one engagement. Here the reader can gain an understanding of not only what the diverse missions are, but how they have historically developed and what issues have accompanied the evolution of higher education mission. The same approach holds true for other themes, such as curriculum philosophy, quality assurance, and student life. Some friends questioned whether a chapter on intercollegiate athletics was needed or appropriate. If the reader is to understand the heritage and character of American colleges and universities, then clearly the presence of athletic programs is a distinctive feature that should not be ignored. Whether seen as complementary or corrupting to the higher education purpose, the conversation deserves attention in any work that purports to bring a fuller understanding of higher education heritage.

Whether via analysis or argument, experiment or artistic interpretation, document study or observation, higher education is an instrument of our inclination to wonder, an instrument of our collective curiosity, an instrument that offers a glimpse into multiple truths. And there are multiple truths concerning the purpose and performance of higher education. We believe the reader may gain a clearer understanding into the nature of the enterprise by engaging the questions we have framed. While we have attempted to build a sense of flow into the chapters, the reader may also gain understanding from independent reading of any chapter.

INTENDED AUDIENCE

Exploring the Heritage of American Higher Education is intended to serve four reading audiences. First, the book may serve as a basal or complementary text for courses in higher education graduate programs. Second, the book may serve as a useful and informing guide to faculty and college administrators interested in a more thorough acquaintance with the heritage of the enterprise in which they serve. Third, the book should prove informing to international students and friends interested in learning about the heritage of American higher education. Finally, the book may enrich the understanding and appreciation of civic and political friends holding the policy and financial health of higher education in trust, including members of governing boards; legislative, executive, and judicial officers having responsibility for higher education; journalists and other media professionals who interpret higher education to the public; and civic and corporate friends furnishing support for higher education through their gifts of money, caring, and time.

ACKNOWLEDGMENTS

The authors would like to acknowledge the support and assistance of the following friends and colleagues who reviewed the manuscript and offered helpful suggestions: Greg Blimling, Allen Edwards, Joni Finney, John Folger, George Keller, Malcolm McInnis, Robert Saunders, Betty Siegel, Ron Simpson, and William Troutt. And we would like to acknowledge the supportive assistance of Denise Howell, Sharon Merryman, and Mike Carvella in preparing and correcting the manuscript. Finally our thanks go to our editor Lori Kennedy and other colleagues at Oryx Press for their support in strengthening the manuscript and moving it to publication.

CHAPTER 1

Portraits in Diversity

The Scope of America's Investment in Higher Education

Americans often engage in behaviors that at first defy conventional understanding, but in retrospect, turn out to have beneficial effects. Who, for example, would construct a government with three branches, each to keep an eye on the other? It may seem inefficient at first, but upon further investigation, it's not a bad way to keep power in check. Who would create a governmental partnership so that some of the more fundamental obligations of a society, such as the education of its people, were entrusted to individual states rather than to the central government? However, it's not a bad way to keep this fundamental societal responsibility close to the feet of the people.

Higher education in this nation reflects some of that same lack of neatness in its structural and philosophical architecture. Who, for example, would think of starting colleges in a new land before an obvious structure for education at the earlier levels was set in place? But Harvard was chartered in 1636, well before the idea for elementary and secondary schools. Indeed it would be 200 years before Americans had established high school as a pervasive expectation for its young men and women.

Consider the sweep and scope of the collegiate enterprise. From Stanford University in the West to Samford University in the South, one can see the beauty of a private system of higher education, largely unfettered by government regulation and intervention. Two beautiful campuses are represented—one a major research university of historic reputation that has, over the years, contributed ideas and talent to national life; the other, a small, comprehensive university with religious affiliation, also making a contribution to the leadership talent of our nation. And both campuses are direct beneficiaries of the financial largess of Americans, who have great faith in the power of education and are willing to invest their money in these and other institutions of higher education.

From the University of Michigan in the North to the University of Montevallo in the South, we move from one of America's larger public research universities to one of America's smaller public liberal arts colleges. Though these institutions vary widely in mission, there is an excellence particular to each of them; and they constitute different but strong threads in the colorful fabric of American higher education.

From Central Piedmont Community College in the East to Maricopa Community College in the West, we touch an American educational invention, the two-year college. Community colleges offer the options of relatively quick insertion into the work force or transfer to a university. Who can place a value on what the community college movement has made to the social, economic, and cultural life of the people and the nation? More than 40 percent of first-time freshmen entering college in our land do so in American community colleges—colleges of the people, bringing educational opportunity and excellence within physical and fiscal reach of most every American.

From Antioch College in Ohio to the Air Force Academy in Colorado, we can touch the heritage of an older and inventive private college and the heritage of a newer institution devoted to a single purpose—the preparation of military leadership. There are, interestingly, 10 different degree-granting institutions operated by United States military services—institutions that include the aforementioned Air Force Academy; academies for the Army, Navy, and Coast Guard; and other specialized military colleges such as the Naval Postgraduate School and the Air Force Institute of Technology.

National Technological University has offices in Fort Collins, Colorado, but has no campus. It is a television network offering graduate engineering education over the nation. Sullivan College in Louisville, Kentucky, offers a four-year degree in business and a two-year degree in culinary arts. It is a regionally accredited proprietary college in business to educate and to make a profit at the same time.

Who can appreciate and adequately communicate what it means to walk the halls of a 400-year-old internationally recognized university such as Harvard and study with scholars known the world over for the power of their ideas and scholarship? Who can understand and convey what it means to walk the halls of Dalton College or Darton College and to be lifted from the poverty of the commonplace by bright and caring teachers who may never be known beyond the Georgia communities surrounding these two-year colleges?

Our aspiration in this opening chapter is to furnish some perspective on the magnificent financial, political, and philosophical investment that Americans have made in higher education.

A CLASSIFICATION OF INSTITUTIONS

As we close the twentieth century and anticipate the dawn of the twenty-first century, the number of colleges and universities in the United States has grown to 4,000. Some historic perspective on this number may be gained by noting that more than 200 years ago, prior to the Revolutionary War, there were only nine colleges established in this nation. Included in that number were Harvard College, College of William and Mary, Yale College, Dartmouth College, College of New Jersey (now Princeton University), Kings College (now Columbia University), College of Rhode Island (now Brown University), Queens College (now Rutgers University), and College of Philadelphia (now the University of Pennsylvania). Enrolled in the 4,000 contemporary American colleges are approximately 14 million students. One way to understand the complexity and diversity of these institutions is to examine them from different perspectives, through lenses of control: governmental (public control) and independent (private control). The most informing and widely known classification system is one published by the Carnegie Foundation for the Advancement of Teaching (1994). Table 1.1 is adapted from that organization's 1994 publication and presents a profile of American colleges and universities by mission and control.

TABLE 1.1

ENROLLMENT AND NUMBER OF INSTITUTIONS BY TYPE AND CONTROL: 1994

Institutional Type	Enrollment (thousands)			Number		
	Total	Public	Private	Total	Public	Private
Doctorate-Granting	3,981	3,111	869	236	151	85
Master's Colleges	3,139	2,291	848	529	275	254
Baccalaureate Colleges	1,053	275	777	637	86	551
Associate of Arts	6,527	6,234	292	1,471	963	508
Specialized Colleges	548	145	404	693	72	621
Tribal Colleges	15	15	0	29	29	0
TOTAL	15,263	12,072	3,191	3,595	1,576	2,019

Source: Adapted from *A Classification of Institutions of Higher Education: 1994.* The Carnegie Foundation for the Advancement of Teaching.

One of the most fundamental and distinctive marks of American higher education is the existence of dual systems of higher education, private and public. Public institutions are directly and operationally supported by public tax funds and governed by local, state, and national government entities; whereas private institutions are supported primarily by student fee and endowment income and are governed by boards that have no political or governmental connection. The United States has approximately 2,300 private institutions and 1,700 public institutions, but almost 80 percent of enrollment is in public institutions. Of the 2,300 private institutions, approximately 600 are proprietary, or "for profit" institutions.

American private colleges and universities offer educational programs centered in deeply held values, usually linked to supporting religious bodies. These institutions exhibit curricular initiatives that can move with greater speed than many public institutions because private schools are relatively unencumbered by government regulation. Private colleges often offer students a keener sense of community and closeness in fellowship.

One of the complementary strengths of public colleges is the offering of educational programs where wonder and curiosity are unencumbered by the confines of religious orthodoxy. These institutions serve as public forums for the testing of social and scientific ideas and for experimentation in arts and cultural expression. They also offer the power and promise of ideas put to work in great programs of public service.

Private and public institutions of higher education share the mission of furnishing the minds and hearts of students with what scholar Gilbert Highet (1976) identified as the four pleasures of an educated human being: learning, loving, serving, and creating.

Institutions may be classified by highest degree offered, with subcategories in each of the primary degree classifications. For example, research I universities award 50 or more doctoral degrees each year and annually receive $40 million or more in federal support, whereas doctoral universities offer fewer degrees in fewer fields. Within the "specialized" classification are theological seminaries, medical schools, schools of art, music, and design, and separate professional schools in fields such as law, engineering, teaching, business, and psychology.

Consider the variance in number of institutions by state as further evidence of the diversity in American higher education. New York and California have the largest number of institutions, with 314 and 328 respectively. Nebraska, Delaware, and Nevada come in with 9 each, and Alaska has the fewest, with 8 institutions.

Furnishing some perspective on the growth in American higher education, Table 1.2 gives an idea about the investment Americans have made in higher education. The number of colleges in this nation has almost doubled within the last half of the twentieth century. The number of two-year colleges has tripled from approximately 500 to more than 1,500 in that same 40- to 50-year period and reflects again the contribution of junior and community colleges to the richness of American higher education. And in the last quarter century, the number of doctoral-granting universities has grown from approximately 100 to almost 250.

TABLE 1.2

GROWTH OF COLLEGES AND UNIVERSITIES IN AMERICA

Year	Number of Institutions
1700	2
1800	23
1900	977
1950	1900
1960	2000
1970	2600
1980	3100
1998	4000

Sources: Kurian, G. T. (1994) *Datapedia of the United States*. Thwing, C. F. (1906) *A History of Higher Education in America*. Tewksbury, D. (1965) *The Founding of American Colleges and Universities before the Civil War*. Almanac Issue, *Chronicle of Higher Education*, August 28, 1998.

It is certainly informing, but also potentially misleading, to examine higher education by state. It is misleading because the number, pattern, and governance arrangements for higher education in one state may give little clue to the patterns in other states. It is informing, however, because diversity in heritage and mission is the distinctive, common theme in American higher education.

The authors exhibit an understandable but perhaps forgivable bias in using the state of Tennessee as an example of the diverse heritage that can be found in almost every state of the union. Within a 40-mile circle of Knoxville are the oldest and newest colleges in the state: The University of Tennessee at Knoxville, a research I university with an enrollment of 26,000, and Tusculum College, a private liberal arts bachelor's degree college with an enrollment of 1,000, were both founded in 1794. The newest college in the state is Pellissippi State Technical Community College, established in 1974.

In Tennessee, there is a rich pattern of both public and private institutions. Of the 83 colleges and universities in the state, 58 are private and 25 are public. Within that pattern are 29 two-year schools and 54 senior institutions (*Almanac Issue, Chronicle of Higher Education*, 1998). Not every state enjoys this tradition in the presence and proportion of private colleges.

There are six colleges/universities located throughout the state that are historically black institutions. They include Lemoyne-Owen College in Memphis; Lane College in Jackson; Tennessee State University, Meharry Medical College, and Fisk University in Nashville; and Knoxville College in Knoxville. Many of these and other historically black colleges over the nation were established in response to mean and prejudicial motives that kept African-American men and women from being admitted to and attending white colleges. A nation built on the principle of liberty and human dignity kept a people in slavery for more than 100 years, and we are still at work cleaning up the bitter outcomes of that unhappy political and social legacy.

From both personal and organizational life, history teaches us that from apparent evil and mean intent may arise outcomes of more noble proportion. Historically black colleges across the nation have made central contributions to American higher education. While Tennessee private institutions operate under separate institutional governing boards or boards of trustees, the 25 public institutions in the state are operated by two public governing boards—the University of Tennessee Board of Trustees and the Tennessee Board of Regents. We will further consider governance arrangements in chapter three.

Tennessee has three research I universities: two of the institutions are public, the University of Tennessee at Knoxville and the University of Tennessee Health Science Center in Memphis. One institution, Vanderbilt University in Nashville, is private. There are 22 baccalaureate colleges in the state of Tennessee, and they are all private in governance control. Eighteen of these 22 colleges have founding dates in the nineteenth century, the earliest being Maryville College, just outside of Knoxville, with a founding date of 1819. Most of those 22 baccalaureate colleges have some connection with or support by church and religious bodies. There are more than a dozen different religious fellowships represented in the heritage of these colleges. If one looks at the curricular patterns and the celebratory events on the campuses of Carson Newman College, Knoxville College, Lee College, Maryville College, and Tusculum College—all private colleges in East Tennessee—one can appreciate firsthand the cultural heritage, innovative spirit, values commitment, and profound influence of religion in American higher education. This religious connection is, as a point of historic interest, another distinctive mark of American higher education. The first American colleges were established to prepare religous leaders and educate clergy. The curriculum was composed of the trivium of grammar, rhetoric, and dialectic; the quadrivium of arithmetic, geometry, astronomy, and music; and the classical languages of Latin and Greek. Admission was based on ability to read and write Latin and Greek. The statutes of Harvard provided this statement of admission qualification and mission:

(1) When any Scholar is able to Read Tully or such like classical Latin Author ex tempore, and make and speak true Latin in verse and prose suit (ut ainunt) Marte, and decline perfectly the paradigms of Nouns and verbs in the Greek tongue, then may he be admitted into the College, nor shall any claim admission before such qualification. (2) Every one shall consider the main End of his life and studies to know God and Jesus Christ which is Eternal Life. John 17:3 (Hofstadter and Smith, 1961, p. 8).

This is a relatively unambiguous statement of both entry and exit expectations. The extent to which this earlier emphasis on religion in American colleges and universities has been replaced, primarily in the late twentieth century, with what George Marsden calls "established nonbelief," is found in *The Soul of the American University: From Protestant Establishment to Established Nonbelief* (1994).

Those interested in further statistical portraits of American higher education will find the following annual publications of interest: *The Condition of Education*, published by the U.S. Department of Education; *The Almanac Issue of the Chronicle of Higher Education*, published by the Chronicle of Higher Education; and *Fact Book on Higher Education*, published by the American Council on Education (ACE) and the Oryx Press.

A DEVELOPMENTAL PANORAMA

Satellite technology is still relatively new. But if the technology had been available in 1950, and one could have taken snapshots from space every 10 years, the following panorama is a highly generalized picture of what one might have seen in the development of higher education over the nation. On the first pass in the 1950s, one might have seen one or two major state universities offering a few doctoral degrees. Generally, the state universities would have been located away from the state's major population centers so as not to distract the life of undergraduates with the "evils" and "degradation" of the city. A small number of former "normal" schools for the preparation of teachers would have been scattered over the state and perhaps some of them would have become state colleges offering work beyond education, but not yet venturing into graduate work. Depending on the state, there may have been some expression of two-year colleges. But for many states, two-year colleges would not have existed at this time, with the possible exception of some private two-year colleges. Perhaps one might have found venerable private institutions, both doctoral universities and religiously-affiliated liberal arts colleges. Veterans from both World War II and the Korean War would have helped enrollments swell and become the impetus for a long trend of diversifying enrollments in age, gender, and ethnicity.

In the 1960s, one would have seen the awakening of state colleges and the first wave of the World War II baby boom increase college enrollments. Major expansions of former teachers' colleges would have been underway, with dramatic growth of physical plants and academic programs and many institutions moving to master's and doctoral level work. Political tensions in the state would have been heightened as these rapidly-growing schools competed with the state's major public university, or universities, for resources. New branch campuses would have been established, and some new universities would have been created. Many states would have established coordinating commissions as academic referees and given these commissions responsibility for master planning and financial allocation, while other states would have moved to a single governing board as a solution. The federal government would have made major contributions to research, physical plant expansion, and financial aid.

The decade of the 1970s would have shown the rapid emergence/expansion of two-year technical and community colleges designed to bring access within physical and financial reach of citizens in the state. State universities would have continued their growth in buildings, enrollments, faculties, and programs. Many of these newer state universities would have been established and/or expanded to serve the metropolitan areas of the states because, as we earlier noted, the older state universities were often located some distance from the cities. Doctoral programs would have continued to grow to furnish the large number of new faculty needed to serve the expansion of the 1960s and 1970s. Newly emerging programs of continuing education would have been developed to serve the lifelong educational interests for both personal and professional development.

In this same decade and in the previous decade, many states would have begun adding new professional schools in medicine, law, and veterinary medicine. Clinical centers in medicine would have been found in new places in the state. And during this and the previous decade, some private colleges would have been transformed into public colleges. Within a contiguous four-state region, for example, we could have seen the following developments: in Georgia, Armstrong College, a private two-year school in Savannah, was transformed into Armstrong State College, a campus in the University of Georgia system; in Alabama, Athens College, a private liberal arts college with religious affiliation, became Athens State College, a senior public campus; in Tennessee, the University of Chattanooga, a private liberal arts campus with religious affiliation became the University of Tennessee at Chattanooga, a campus in the University of Tennessee system; and in Charleston, South Carolina, the College of Charleston, a private liberal arts campus, retained its name but became a senior public campus in that state. Similar transformations would have been found in other states.

In the 1980s, major public institutions of higher education would have continued their growth in enrollment and programs, though the beginning pains of retrenchment and reallocation would have hit many state systems as some states began to experience revenue reductions due to a downturn in various state economies. Enrollment growth would have continued in many two-year colleges; and, contrary to some predictions made in previous years, the number of private institutions would have showed a rather dramatic growth, from approximately 1,500 to 2,000 from 1970 to 1990. The enrollment of women in higher education would have outdistanced that of men, and women would have entered formerly male-dominated professions such as law, medicine, and pharmacy in increasing numbers. Minority enrollments would have grown among all ethnic groups, especially for Asian Americans, but still not have reached parity for African Americans and Hispanic Americans as compared to their proportion in the general population of the nation.

In the 1990s, state systems of higher education would have settled into some maturity and the full effect of cost containment pressures would have hit many campuses, causing a rethinking of organizational and program patterns and a reexamination of mission priorities. Some of those new medical schools established in the 1960s and 1970s would have experienced enrollment declines. Campuses would have experimented with new forms of distance learning, utilizing the technology of television, computers, and satellite communication. Branch campuses of two-year colleges would have sprung up in small towns not too distant from the home campus, making it not unusual to find a community college operating several branch campuses—mini systems of higher education. Private colleges would have been manifesting a vitality that might not have been predicted in the 1960s and 1970s.

If the satellite could peer into colleges and universities today, it would show that the number of faculty serving in these 4,000 colleges and universities would have grown from less than 250,000 in the 1950s to more than 600,000 in the 1990s. A snapshot of financial records would reveal that educational expenditures for higher education as a percentage of gross national product would have grown from around 1 percent in the 1950s to more than 2 percent in the 1990s. It would also reveal that income for colleges and universities would have grown from approximately $2.5 billion in the early 1950s to almost $200 billion in the 1990s. This is indeed a magnificent investment in the presence and promise of higher education in America.

What had begun in the seventeenth century as an elite system for the training of clergy has evolved into a system of advanced education brought within financial and physical reach of almost every American. With its public and private systems of elementary and secondary education, the nation's systems of public and private colleges and universities constitute a major operational expression of faith in the power of education for a democratic society. As it stands today, there are 4,000 university/college campuses, 600,000 faculty members, 14 million students, and $190 billion in revenues.

The numbers that detail the financial investment Americans have made in higher education are impressive, and the development of American higher education within the last half of the twentieth century is even more astounding. The numbers themselves hide an incredible diversity of institutional size, mission, and heritage; and the numbers fail in communicating other investments Americans have made in their colleges and universities.

Let's take a qualitative walk through one of our state research universities. A brief glance at a cluster of quantitative indicators will convey something about the activity and achievement of the university:

- Enrollment profiles mark an overall stabilized enrollment around 26,000, but with growth in graduate enrollment
- Aptitude profiles reveal growth in ACT/SAT and GRE scores
- Faculty tenure ratios reflect the aging of the faculty
- Exponential curves portray growth in computer capacity
- Exponential growth patterns mark success in attracting federally funded research funds
- Dormitory occupancy rates detail a 10-year decline
- Faculty salary profiles carry the sad news of the state's economic recession impact
- Intercollegiate athletics revenue profiles herald a highly successful and winning year in all major sports of the university
- Library holdings mark the slide in rank of the university library in its holdings compared to other major universities of the nation

But this is only one way to sense what gives meaning to this state research university. Early in the morning, we begin the walking journey in the old speech and drama building on the north side of the campus, noting that the seats in the drama theater, built in 1928, still have hat boxes underneath the seats. An interpretive production of *Macbeth* will be held here during the coming week, a black-tie affair with the governor in attendance. A short walk away is the more modern music building where in early morning, a student wind ensemble may be found rehearsing for a performance scheduled later in the month.

In the natural history museum, specimens of birds and insects from over the world are found. Faculty and student caretakers labor away in quiet devotion over their flying and crawling repository, thinking little of *Macbeth* drama and Strauss sonatas. At the head of the quadrangle constituting the heart of the campus is the library, home to several million volumes, where a student can, at the touch of a finger, access the accumulated history of human knowledge.

Down one side of the quadrangle on a lower floor are the editorial offices of a distinguished literary journal, and here faculty editors are at work early in the morning, reviewing submitted manuscripts.

Fewer faculty are at work in the math building, but the early morning student population reflects another important feature of American higher education, its international attraction. A large number of students, mostly graduates from Asian countries, gives evidence of sizeable enrollments in mathematics of students from Korea, Japan, and China.

A pass through the geology building reveals the complex instrumentation for an earthquake center, and students pouring over maps taken by satellite in search for clues to new oil fields. Meanwhile, over in the agriculture center, extension agents and research faculty are busy planning major new centers for growing and harvesting catfish—and also coping with the threat of catfish rustlers, a new version of the old West being played out with a somewhat different critter.

Mid-morning brings us to the university press, devoted to scholarship with a special focus on publications of regional cultural interest. Here we find a prominently displayed copy of a Pulitzer Prize-winning novel initially rejected by every major publishing house in the United States but eventually published by the University Press. An interesting story in the valuation of writing as an art form.

In the biology building a department chair conducts a personal tour of all six floors. On the top floor, rats with brain implant electrodes wander their cages, furnishing the basis for experimentation on neurological research.

Over in chemistry and engineering, cooperating faculty are busy planning the construction of a new multimillion dollar particle accelerator for electrons. With bending magnets furnishing the accelerating kick, the electrons will yield X-rays that can then be extracted at various points around the circumference of the accelerator and used for research into micro devices, health diagnostics, and microchips.

In the business building, the dean puzzles over how to compensate for the recent loss of half of the accounting faculty, who had taken jobs at other institutions because of several years of stable faculty salaries associated with the state's economic doldrums. He could manage some smiles, however, at the recent endowment of $2 million chairs in his college.

Coming back from the south side of the campus, the sound of basketballs thumping the floor in the university assembly center are heard as the university men's basketball coach, without question the best-known personality in the state, puts his team through its practice paces. Spring warm-ups have begun for the university's baseball team that would later go to the college world series. In the football offices, the coaching staff frets the impact of the university's new admissions policy on their recruitment season. And in another nearby office, the athletic director studies the elements of a lawsuit recently filed by several women athletes—the suit claiming that the university is in violation of Title IX, a federal act requiring gender equity in intercollegiate athletics programs.

This is just one qualitative journey that could unfold in 4,000 variations and stories that reflect the memories and meanings Americans attach to their colleges and universities. There is a sense of place, stability, pride, and belonging—that lingering of alma mater—that remains after one has departed with degree in hand. It brings alumni back to campus for reunions. It energizes a philanthropic impulse that has funded entire campuses, brought gifts from $1 to more than $250 million to campuses, and produces annual private giving to colleges and universities of more than $20 billion every year. Each year thousands of people invest time and caring in service on college and university governing boards, usually without pay.

It would be important and appropriate to note that the memories of fun and friendship remain following the undergraduate years as well. The undergraduate who departed from his dormitory for the holiday season and returned to find a Volkswagen Beetle residing in his room, said Volkswagen disassembled in the parking lot and reassembled in the dorm room by a team of playful and mischievous engineering undergraduates, will likely hold in heart and mind this incident more than the equation for mass and energy exchange in physics or a supply and demand curve in economics.

Across the nation, faculty members open their office doors each day to aspiring and curious men and women from a wide range of generations. Pursuing study for a degree, searching for expanded options in their lives, hoping to upgrade a skill or credential, experiencing only the joy of continued learning—students bring their hopes and aspirations, their questions and anxieties into these faculty offices. Behind their quiet smiles and their pleasant demeanor, these students may mask whatever pains of family, finance, health, or home they may be carrying; and they come seeking feedback on that last book review or research paper, advice on their plans of study, or evaluation of their thesis or dissertation plans.

Sharing in the fellowship of what scholar Gilbert Highet (1976) called *The Immortal Profession* and the "joys of teaching and learning," the authors also visit with students, prepare for evening classes, and glance out the office windows at the University of Tennessee and see the finishing construction moves, as giant cranes put in place final steel work for a 10,000-seat addition to Neyland Football Stadium. This addition will make the stadium a 100,000-seat Saturday celebration center. The 300-piece University of Tennessee marching band will lead a parade across campus, playing "Rocky Top" to the cheers of fans just finishing their tailgate parties. The football Volunteers will race onto the field in front of 100,000 emotional fans to battle Alabama,

Florida, Georgia, or other opponents in the Southeastern Conference. Where are the numbers to explain and capture the "Big Orange" fervor that grips the campus and city, the puzzling configuration of athletics and academics on the American college and university campus? When the "wave" sweeps around the football stadium on a sunny fall afternoon, who would believe the alliance between what takes place in this stadium, the field of athletic contest, and in the house of intellect that surrounds, the forum of ideological contest, exists?

And who would believe the difference in scope and setting between what takes place in athletics and academics on the 26,000-student campus of the University of Tennessee, and what takes place on Saturday at the 1,000-student campus of Maryville College just 30 miles away, founded in 1819. While 100,000 fans occupy Neyland Stadium, a few hundred fans sit on concrete and aluminum bleacher seats as the NCAA Division III nonscholarship football team of Maryville College takes on the visitors from Centre College. There is no television coverage for the Maryville game, and the athletic budget at Maryville College is a tiny fraction of the athletic budget at the University of Tennessee. There are no master's or doctoral programs on the Maryville campus, but a caring faculty invests their undergraduate students with a thoughtfully constructed and delivered undergraduate curriculum.

THE PARADOX OF PUBLIC ESTEEM AND PUBLIC CRITICISM

Even as we celebrate the rich philosophic heritage of American higher education and admire the investment Americans have made in their colleges and universities, we must recognize that many of the principles, policies, and practices that constitute that heritage are under examination and assault as we stand on the threshold of the twenty-first century. Authors George Land and Beth Jarman (1992) have written of "breakpoint" moments in the life and change of organizations. American higher education is facing one of those breakpoint moments. Ways of doing business that worked in the past may not work in the future. Evidence of this transitional moment abound.

There has been a shift in the climate and context in which colleges and universities operate. In recent years, state and federal governments have implemented policies designed to bring greater public accountability to higher education. More than two-thirds of the states now have some requirement vested in state law that requires assessment, and many states now require colleges and universities to make annual reports on a cluster of performance indicators. Other states have policies in which some portion of appropriations to state colleges is linked to performance measures rather than enrollments.

Cost-containment pressures, to be detailed in chapter six, are causing states to ask new questions of their colleges and universities—questions of mission and method, policy and productivity. State and federal revenue patterns may no longer permit the expansion mentality that higher education enjoyed for so many years. Reallocation and retrenchment are terms familiar to both corporate and collegiate America. There is pleasure and pain in contending with increasing enrollment pressures without the promise of enhanced financial support.

For example, California is known as one of the leading states in the nation for the quality of its higher education system and the extent of opportunity represented in a vast system of 9 campuses in the University of California system, 22 campuses in the California State University system, 106 community colleges and 72 private colleges and universities. For years California had one of the most admired mission systems in the nation. An article appearing in the May/June 1996 issue of *Change Magazine* detailed the high reputational standing of the University of California's campuses and programs (Webster and Skinner, 1996, pp. 36–40). Released at virtually the same moment was a special publication of the California Higher Education Policy Center entitled *Shared Responsibility: Strategies to Enhance Quality and Opportunity in California Higher Education* (1996). This report indicated that higher education in California would experience an increased enrollment demand of almost 500,000 students in the next 10 years, that this enrollment demand would ordinarily call for an additional expenditure of $5 billion—but that the probability of this much additional support becoming available approaches zero. How to reconcile the demand for educational sources and the ability of the state and higher education to meet that demand becomes a challenge of imposing and complex proportion—but not necessarily one of impossible proportion. Meeting this challenge will require choice and imagination. A University of California academic department that lost all of its senior faculty to an attractive early retirement program finds that a nationally and internationally recognized academic program for more than three decades has been decimated overnight. What had been the hope of a vital center of both teaching and policy research excellence was reduced in a moment to empty echoes in a hallway with closed faculty office doors.

Other evidences of a change in context and a transitional moment for higher education include public and professional press coverage detailing depressing and disappointing stories of presidents and professors, deans and directors, taking their students and institutions in harm's way in the abandonment of their personal and professional integrity. Such lamentable behavior on the part of those who hold our learning organizations in trust understandably leads civic friends to ask whether colleges and universities are ruled by ideals or self-interest, and whether faculty and administrators have abandoned their servant roles.

In 1995, an Alabama newspaper, the *Mobile Press Register*, engaged in a notable expression of civic journalism and published two Sunday special sections of its paper covering the history and development of Alabama Higher Education—one issue of 16 pages on July 9, 1995, and entitled "Higher Education: How Unruly Aspirations Built a System Alabama Can't Afford," and a November 21, 1995, issue of 20 pages entitled "After Decades of Growth, Now a Search for Quality." Both of these issues included sad stories of integrity issues within Alabama higher education—of shady dealings on facilities, programs, and budgets; of questionable behavior on the part of faculty and administrators. As an example of the difficulty in Alabama, two community college presidents are state legislators. Consider that conflict of interest! Some community colleges have so much financial surplus that they are acting as banks and loaning money at interest to other community colleges. Other two-year institutions have built dormitories and arranged for leased facilities because the state has no regulation regarding capital construction and facilities priorities.

It is appropriate that we should envision our colleges and universities as organizations of nobility and rationality. It is appropriate to see higher education as a manifestation of the highest societal aspirations and political commitments represented in our democratic society. However, colleges and universities are not structural, symbolic, and social configurations free from the imperfections of person and policy. Colleges and universities contain both love and license, passion and prejudice, morality and meanness, sacrifice and selfishness. Some higher education professionals honor the public trust, while others betray the public trust. We believe that there are more stories of nobility and devotion, but just one story of duplicity and selfishness is one too many.

What began in this nation as a relatively modest and small configuration of largely quasi-private institutions, serving relatively restricted and elite purposes and clientele, has evolved into a diverse system having important social, cultural, political, and economic impacts on our nation. American higher education is an investment of spirit, ideas, and resources in which the nation can take high pleasure, and represents major distinctions in philosophy and practice. These learning organizations face important leadership challenges of imagination and integrity as we make the transition to the twenty-first century. To believe, however, that this is the first such moment of challenge in the evolution of American higher education ignores the facts and reveals an inadequate awareness of that heritage. For example, if one looks back to the institutional growth pattern depicted in Table 1.2, one could be led, albeit by mistake, to a linear theory of higher education growth. Westmeyer tells us that of the 800 colleges established between 1776 and 1861, only 180 survived (Westmeyer, 1985, p. 24). Hidden in this fact of history are stories of devotion and disappointment, personal pleasure and pain, ambition and anxiety, and solid achievement and sordid failure. In a 1972 issue of the journal *Daedalus* entitled "The Embattled University," editor Stephen Graubard wrote a quarter century ago that "The propensity to imagine that the future will be like the present, only more so, is as dangerous as the illusion that the past can be recaptured" (Graubard, 1972, p. xiv). Anticipating the dawn of the twenty-first century, who can predict what changes may mark the portraits of American higher education? A moment of danger and risk can be a moment of opportunity and promise.

History takes small note of those navigating the smooth and easy waters of their times but attends more carefully to the journeys of those who meet challenge with creativity and courage. The history of American higher education is the history of achievements forged from the fire and anvil of other breakpoint moments, crafted from the biographies of educators devoted to opportunity and excellence, and from the biographies of imaginative civic and corporate leaders. In chapter ten, we explore more fully the nature of the breakpoint moment in the evolution of American higher education and attend to those leadership values and attitudes that may assist higher education in making the transition and meeting its servant role in society. In the next chapter, we begin our journey of understanding the heritage of higher education by exploring first questions of mission and purpose.

CHAPTER 2

Purpose and Performance

The Evolution of Higher Education Mission and Goals

C onserving the past, criticizing the present, constructing the future—
these are elements of mission and purpose that might be assigned to
higher education in America. Holding hands with the past while
reaching for the future is an organizational mission of no small complexity, an
expectation of purpose guaranteed to produce tension in colleges and universities.

Given the social, political, and moral context of education at every level in
our society, one could reasonably expect diversity of opinion about the basic
mission and purposes of higher education. Robert Hutchins once suggested
that the study of higher education was marked by two unanswerable questions:
What is it for? And how do we know when it has succeeded? (Hutchins, 1968,
p. 185). The difficulty is not that these questions don't have answers, but that
there are many answers, and that higher education is in a constant ferment
over priority and balance issues concerning its purposes. In this chapter, we
will explore the evolution of mission and purpose for higher education,
presenting contemporary and contrasting perspectives on higher education
goals. How a campus operationally expresses its vision and its values will then
be examined. Finally, the changing context for higher education, in which
some scholars and critics lament a lack of balance and a neglect of focus, will
be discussed.

THE EVOLUTION OF HIGHER EDUCATION MISSION

A 1968 publication of the American Council on Education entitled *Whose Goals for American Higher Education?* furnishes an informing yet simple entree to our theme. The organization of the book and opening commentary mark the conventional expression of higher education mission responsibilities: "A college or university has three basic goals: to transmit, to extend, and to apply knowledge. Each of these three missions—teaching, research, and public service—is related to a multitude of programs, intermediate goals, and functions, some of which can be identified with the particular interests of one or the other of the five main constituents of higher education" (Dobbins and Lee, 1968, p. 1).

The five constituents identified in the ACE publication are students, faculty, administrators, trustees, and persons from public life. Thus, the title of the ACE book and the commentary within remind us that mission and goals may be examined from multiple perspectives. Goals may be viewed from both personal and social frames. Is higher education primarily an investment in personal benefit or societal benefit? Mission and goals may be seen from both campus and governmental perspectives—mission and goals as perceived by faculty/academic administrators and as perceived by civic/political leaders, at least in the case of public colleges and universities. For private colleges and universities, it will not be unusual to discover that there are differences in mission and value perspectives between the campuses and supporting bodies, such as religious organizations. Finally, time and context contribute to the shaping of goals. The pressure of enrollments in a time of growing and generous resources may yield access and equity goals of relatively easy consent for academic and civic officials. The pressure of enrollments in a time of seriously constrained or diminishing financial resources may produce a fervent debate on institutional productivity and quality as goals.

In this chapter, we propose an expansion of the three basic and conventional mission expectations of higher education, to transmit, extend, and apply knowledge, adding to those traditionally accepted mission themes as follows:

- Transmission—The Instructional Mission
- Discovery—The Research Mission
- Application—The Public Service Mission
- Conservation—The Library and Museum Mission
- Renewal—The Continuing Education Mission
- Evaluation—The Public Forum Mission

When the first American colleges were formed in the seventeenth century, the basic mission was a teaching in service of preparing ministers. In *The Professor Game*, Richard Mandell writes:

> Though living far from the mother country, the founders of Harvard and the subsequent colonial colleges were not merely creating a bit of English life. As was to be the case with the dutiful founders of hundreds of American colleges, they were preparing for the future. The land before them would need competent rulers and, of course, a learned clergy. . . .The colleges were all essential to reinforce the proper moral precepts in the American elite and to demonstrate the separation of the American upper class from raw nature and barbarism (Mandell, 1977, p. 15).

A more specific flavor of what was intended in the colonial American college may be found in the selected articles of the "Statutes of Harvard" previously presented in chapter one. Reading classical Latin as an admission requirement and reading the Old Testament and the New Testament into the Latin tongue as an exit requirement we may find quaint policy today, but we can hardly quarrel with the clarity of what was expected for both entry and exit at Harvard.

Nor is mission any less clear for the second college established on these shores, the College of William and Mary. The opening passage of the college's 1693 charter may well qualify in the grammar hall of fame as one of the longest sentences on record, but the purpose, curriculum, and governance are easily discerned:

> Forasmuch as our well-beloved and faithful Subjects, constituting the General-Assembly of our Colony of Virginia, have had it in their Minds, and have proposed to themselves, to the End that the Church of Virginia may be furnished with a Seminary of Ministers of the Gospel, and that the Youth may be piously educated in good Letters and manners, and that the Christian Faith may be propagated amongst the Western Indians, to the Glory of Almighty God; to make, found, and establish a certain Place of universal Study, or perpetual College of Divinity, Philosophy, languages, and other good Arts and Sciences, consisting of one President, six Masters or Professors, and an Hundred Scholars, more or less, according to the Ability of the said College, and the Statutes of the same; to be made, increased, diminished, or changed there, by certain Trustees, nominated and elected by the General-Assembly aforesaid . . . (Hofstadter and Smith, 1961, pp. 33–34).

For the first 200 years of American higher education, from the middle of the seventeenth century to the middle of the nineteenth century, the principal focus was on the instructional mission, with a curriculum based in the study of rhetoric, grammar, mathematics, and classical languages. The heritage of that mission lay dominantly with English and European traditions, translated to these shores through the English universities of Oxford and Cambridge.

The establishment of Johns Hopkins University in 1876 and the traffic of American faculty to Germany and back brought the insertion of the research mission to American higher education. Growth of the research mission must be counted as one of the more distinctive developments of the last 100 years in American higher education. A brief look at expenditures devoted to research in higher education gives evidence to the vitality of this expectation. For the larger universities of the land, the accent on research would be considered the sine qua non of the university.

One of the wonders of the modern university is the range of applied and theoretical inquiry hidden behind the porticos of our colleges and universities. At the Stevens Institute of Technology in New Jersey, scientists study the use of gravity force for building more effective and efficient commodes. Not far away in the same state, scientists at Princeton University grapple with more esoteric dimensions of gravity, including the question of whether there is an anti-gravity force, or "fifth force."

Concomitant with the emergence of the research mission came the emergence of the country's state universities and the Morrill Land Grant acts of 1862 and 1892. Following the Civil War, the agricultural and mechanical arts (A&M) and other applied subjects were inserted into the curriculum. The land grant model is frequently illustrated via the agricultural tripartite emphasis on instruction, research, and extension service. In addition to illustrating the land grant model, the development and application of the scientific approach to farming resulted in increased agricultural productivity. The land grant movement also heralded a transformation in access policy from the elite to the laboring man, in the curriculum from the liberal to the practical, and in purpose from knowledge for its own end to knowledge for applied ends. Written in the stone of the University of Minnesota campus is the belief that the university was "founded on the faith that men are ennobled by understanding." The Minnesota idea was to place the talent and energy of the university's faculty in service to the state in a search for solutions to public problems and policy issues. The emerging state university was seen as servant of the state.

Many would argue that while the instructional and research missions are ideas transported from England and Germany respectively, the public service mission of higher education is uniquely American in its origins, intent, and content. Modern state universities operate a range of public services that include not only the application of knowledge for the improvement of agriculture, but also for manufacturing and industry, government and public service, and health care.

While libraries and museums are considered a central part of any college or university resource and facilities, there is often less consideration of the important role they have played in the mission of higher education. For example, one can find records of humankind's nobility and barbarism, evidences of art and culture, stories of policy and political struggles, the outcomes of principles and prejudices, the story of philosophic engagements, the influence of religious yearnings, the debit and credit record of economic systems, to find here records of activities and findings form obscure settings large and small over the world—to enter the doors of a college or university library is a journey always destined to reinforce our sense of wonder. The importance of conserving what we have learned is often overlooked in the privilege of access to our libraries and information systems. We are probably not far from that moment when we will not go to the library but simply purchase a computer disk or other information storage device of the future and take it home for insertion into a personal computer, or we may just dial the phone and have every page of the library available at our intellectual disposal. Such convenience and power, however, may never replace the joy and wonder that comes from browsing the quiet and musty stacks of libraries. Moreover, the importance of the conservation mission will become more apparent if we consider the barbaric state in which we might be left if all our libraries were to collapse and our storage devices were to be wiped clean.

A development of the last half of the twentieth century is the wide range of continuing education programs of modern American colleges and universities. It may be argued that this cluster of activities is in reality a mix of the instructional and public service missions. Perhaps so. It might also be argued that public service is in reality an instructional activity. The expansion of instructional programs to times, places, and learners beyond the more traditional constitutes a notable addition to higher education activity and mission, and one the authors believe warrants separate attention.

On any college or university campus—whether community college or research university—consider the panoply of non-credit offerings, conferences, short courses, workshops, and institutes now routinely available for both personal and professional development, including Introduction to Word Perfect, Conversational French, Changing Leadership Metaphors, and a host of short courses for professionals, such as lawyers and physicians, that bring them up to date. We have used the term "renewal" to describe this mission component to recognize that learners may approach colleges and universities with personal and professional goals during a lifetime of learning.

In the metropolitan area of Phoenix, there are multiple campuses of Maricopa Community College, a two-year public institution, which announced for the fall of 1998 more than 100 non-credit courses. Arizona State University, a public research university, announced for the fall of 1998 more than 200 noncredit courses on topics including antique furniture repair, computers/ cyberspace, private pilot licensure, and horseback riding. This extension of learning services, related not to a credential or a degree but to personal and professional interests, marks a new mission element for higher education and reveals learning as one of those important human drives not to be confined by time, place, or age. These courses are not so much offered only to the traditional age college student, but to students of any age, and are presented not exclusively in the traditional instructional formats, but in a variety of learning options, as to accommodate many different people.

We have proposed one more mission element for American higher education, that of evaluation. Is it not a unique and controversial feature of collegiate organization that we expect our colleges and universities to be critics of the status quo, to continually reexamine the probity and effectiveness of every dimension of our national life?

This expectation takes many forms, from the use of scholar experts to advise local, state, and national government on matters of policy (economic advice on dealing with the depression in the 1930s, for example), to the use of scientists and others to advise and develop policy (e.g., scientific engagement in building the atomic bomb in World War II). Colleges and universities constitute the "public forum," and it might be argued that the "public forum" mission of American colleges and universities represents the most fundamental spirit and purpose of American higher education: the testing of ideas in adversarial and public forum settings and the honoring of paradox and dissent. Today's common sense was yesterday's heresy; and some of the "subversive" ideas that disrupt our prejudices and preconceptions are the pathways to our future.

Whitehead places this collegiate mission of evaluation and public forum in context when he noted that the creation of civilized order is the "victory of persuasion over force" (Whitehead, 1933, p. 25). An instrument of persuasion? This is a cogent way to think about collegiate mission in a democracy, where intellectual analysis and ideological adversity are joined in the constructive criticism fundamental to a search for truth in every field. In the mission of evaluation, higher education is the servant of the truth and of the people and not of power and vested interests.

We are tempted to add a seventh mission . . . one of entertainment. When one thinks of musicals, plays, dance productions, visual arts exhibitions, and other community celebration events taking place at a university, it is difficult not to think of entertainment. And certainly here we may include intercollegiate athletics. When one experiences the spectacle and emotion associated with intercollegiate athletics, especially big-time athletics, clearly there is a large element of entertainment involved. What is intended to entertain, however, may also embrace an educational design as well. There are few cultural moments that do not touch mind, heart, and spirit.

Whether one prefers the traditional tripartite mission of instruction, research, and service, or the more extended elements of our model, it is clear that the mission of American higher education has evolved from the singular teaching mission of the colonial college, to a more complex profile of purpose. While the richness of that mission tapestry is one to be admired, it is also a source of tension and conflict. Some question the venture of higher education into so many arenas, the selection of priorities among these missions, and the capacity of our society to fund this range of missions. We will return to these issues at the close of this chapter. Now that we have taken a more global view of higher education mission, let's explore changing mission accents in the latter part of the twentieth century.

FROM ACCESS TO ACCOUNTABILITY

Mostly white, mostly male, mostly elite—it could be argued that these phrases described much of American higher education through World War II and the 1940s—though clearly advances had been made in expanding the purposes and clientele of American higher education. Following World War II, President Harry Truman established the President's Commission on Higher Education, which issued its first report in 1947. Volume I of this report attended to the question of goals for higher education, and marked changing conditions and expectations for higher education. To summarize the goals presented in Volume I is a difficult task, but these themes are featured in the volume: (1) education for a fuller realization of democracy in every phase of living and for enhanced international understanding; (2) education for enhanced access, with elimination of barriers to opportunity; (3) education for free men, with renewed attention to the importance of general education and the complement of vocational education; (4) education for a range of needs, needs that reach from two-year college programs through graduate and professional schools to adult education needs; and (5) education for the application of creative imagination and trained intelligence to the solution of social problems and to the administration of public affairs (*Higher Education for American Democracy*, 1947, pp. 1–103).

This 1947 report reflects the foundations for increasing access to higher education via a combination of scholarships and enhancement of institutions, including major expansion of two-year colleges.

A decade later two other national reports appeared—one the product of yet another presidential commission on higher education by President Dwight D. Eisenhower, and the other the National Education Association's (NEA) report *Higher Education in a Decade of Decision*. The Eisenhower report focused on the need to deal with a pending shortage of trained teachers, to expand educational opportunity, and to expand educational facilities. These goals anticipated a growing role of the federal government in funding professional development programs for teachers, special programs to fund facilities, and loan/scholarship programs. Enhancing access remained an important national priority. It should be noted that the Eisenhower report emerged at the same time as the Russian launch of the "Sputnik" satellite and the subsequent national preoccupation with strengthening scientific and mathematics education in both schools and colleges. The NEA report articulated five purposes for higher education as follows:

1. to provide opportunity for individual development of able people;
2. to transmit the cultural heritage;
3. to add to existing knowledge through research and creative activity;
4. to help translate learning into equipment for living and for social advance;
5. to serve the public interest directly (NEA, 1957, p. 10).

The societal benefit of higher education and the application of learning for personal and social advance are heralded in this report.

A 1971 report issued by the American Academy of Arts and Sciences entitled *The Assembly on University Goals and Governance* explored several different themes that might be captured under the headings of access, scale, and quality. Most important, however, was the following observation:

> Higher education institutions in America, to their detriment, are imitative. The "front runners" are constantly aped by those with more limited resources. As a result, though there are over 2,500 institutions (authors' note: now over 4,000 in 1999), they converge on a few models. Policies designed to produce greater differentiation, though difficult to fashion, are essential. Colleges and universities should become more discriminating in relating their resources to particular needs, less worried about their standing (often a mythical one) vis-a-vis other institutions and more determined to experiment in every aspect of institutional life (Assembly, 1971, p. 30).

The report notes that there are those who lament the passing of a time when colleges and universities were supposedly "havens of calm inquiry" (p. 43). We will discuss more of these turbulent moments in chapter seven, but those who lived during the wrenching campus events of the 1960s and 1970s and experienced the student and social protest movements of that time will understand the context of this report, and will appreciate the importance of the evaluation and public forum mission previously suggested.

The question of imitation is alive and well after a quarter of a century, and is revealed in this note from the November 1996 issue of *Policy Perspectives*:

> Put simply, there are a lot more institutions that claim a research mission, that call themselves either universities or research colleges, and that make research success a criterion for tenure. What was once the province of the few has become the domain of the many, leaving state legislators and trustees to ask: "When did we agree to pay for all this extra research? Why are state dollars being expended on faculty who avoid our undergraduates?" (November, 1996, p. 5).

A 1973 publication of the Carnegie Commission on Higher Education entitled *The Purposes and the Performance of Higher Education in the United States: Approaching the Year 2000* outlined five themes:

1. educating the individual student and the provision of a constructive environment for developmental growth;
2. advancing human capability in society at large;
3. establishing educational justice for the postsecondary age group;
4. supporting intellectual and artistic creativity;
5. evaluating society for self-renewal through individual thought and persuasion.

While not entirely new, the Carnegie emphasis on educational justice accented the need for the enhancement of postsecondary opportunity for ethnic and age groups previously underrepresented in colleges and universities.

In the introductory remarks to this section, we cited presidential commissions among the entities studying and shaping goals for higher education. Government interest in higher education goals is also represented in the 1991 *National Education Goals Report: Building a Nation of Learners*. This panel gave only marginal attention to higher education, with the most visible higher education-related goal as follows: "The proportion of college graduates who demonstrate an advanced ability to think critically, communicate effectively, and solve problems will increase substantially"(The National Education Goals Report, 1991, p. 5).

In the later half of the twentieth century, states have become more active and assertive in shaping goals for higher education. First, coordinating agencies and statewide governing boards were given statutory responsibilities for managing a rapidly expanding system of higher education designed to enhance access. In addition, executive and legislative branches of government have entered the mission and goals debate. Bogue, Creech, and Folger traced "Shifts in State Policy" in a 1993 publication on the emergence of state-level accountability policy and legislation. They suggested that in the 1960s and

1970s, state policy centered on the planned expansion of higher education and the promotion of equity in access. In the 1980s, the focus shifted to the improvement of quality and an enhanced interest on minority participation and success. The 1990s appear to reflect an interest in assessment of educational performance, the development of accountability and performance indicators, the improvement of both management and educational productivity, and the refocus of campus mission to accommodate cost containment pressures (Bogue, Creech, and Folger, 1993, p. 3).

Other organizations have also taken a proactive role in goal setting, organizations that include regional and professional associations related to higher education. An example of a regional voice is the Southern Regional Education Board, and in 1988 they developed a set of goals for all of education in the region. Among the goals for higher education by the year 2000 were these: (1) Four of every five students entering college will be ready to begin college-level work; (2) The percentage of adults who have attended college or earned two-year, four-year, and graduate degrees will be at the national averages or higher; (3) The quality and effectiveness of all colleges and universities will be regularly assessed, with particular emphasis on the performance of undergraduate students; (4) All institutions that prepare teachers will have effective teacher education programs that place primary emphasis on the knowledge and performance of graduates; and (5) States will maintain or increase the proportion of state tax dollars for schools and colleges while emphasizing funding aimed at raising quality and productivity (*Goals for Education: Challenge 2000*, 1988).

In 1994–95, the Education Commission of the States, a national compact organization interested in education, issued a brochure reflecting its program interests and focus for that year in a publication entitled "Quality Counts: Setting Expectations for Higher Education . . . and Making Them Count." In that publication are these four points of emphasis:

1. A broad constituent-base concept of quality higher education that responds to the needs of students, employers, political leaders, and the public at large, as well as needs of institutions.
2. High expectations for the performance of colleges, universities, and community colleges relative to the needs of the different constituencies.
3. New ways to measure and monitor the results of higher education consistent with this broad concept of quality.
4. A supportive policy environment that encourages higher education to respond to this agenda built around quality.

These reports reveal the changing texture of public conversation on goals for higher education and constitute a partial answer to the two questions

Hutchins posed: What's higher education for and how will we know when it is succeeding? Following World War II and continuing well into the latter half of this century, it's clear that the accent was on enhancement of access and educational justice. The goal was to make college and university opportunity more accessible by reducing and/or removing barriers of place, cost, and discrimination due to age, gender, and ethnicity. This goal remains an active one, and one of conflicting public opinion. The conflict may be seen in current conversation and legal contention on the role of affirmative action in college admissions and in the admission of women to publicly supported and formerly all-male military academies such as The Citadel in South Carolina and the Virginia Military Academy.

The definition, measurement, and nurture of quality in higher education is clearly a point of emerging interest—from the perspective of state, regional, and national organizations. The accountability of higher education is an issue that we will engage in chapter five and again in the closing chapter.

How will we know how a particular campus or system of campuses has made its choices among collegiate purposes and what priorities that campus or system will elect to honor? Let's examine the role of mission statements.

MISSION: THE PRESENTATION AND THE PRIORITIZATION OF PURPOSE

Higher education organizations external to the campus are insistent that effective institutional planning and operation begin with a clearly drawn and distinctive mission statement. Regional accrediting agencies, among the more traditional and respected quality assurance instruments in higher education, and statewide coordinating agencies are two examples of external agencies expecting carefully constructed mission statements. For example, the *Criteria for Accreditation* of the Commission on Colleges of the Southern Association of Colleges and Schools, one of six regional accrediting agencies for colleges and universities, specifies this expectation of mission:

> . . . An institution **must** have a clearly defined purpose or mission statement appropriate to collegiate education as well as to its own specific educational role. This statement describes the institution and its characteristics, and addresses the components of the institution and its operations. The official posture and practice of the institution **must** be consistent with its purpose statement. Appropriate publications **must** accurately cite the current statement of purpose.
>
> The formulation of a statement of purpose represents a major educational decision. It should be developed through the efforts of the institution's faculty, administration and governing board and **must** be

approved by the governing board (*Criteria for Accreditation*, 1994, pp. 8–9).

The accent on the word "must" is a signal that these requirements are not optional but essential in the accreditation of an institution, and thus presumably central to the quality posture of an institution.

Those readers interested in one of the more specific treatments of mission statement purpose, content, and effectiveness are referred to Gardiner's *Planning for Assessment*, 1989. Scholars in higher education are not united in their assessment of the value of mission statements. The following are expository snapshots from six different sources, three affirming the importance of mission statements and three denying that importance:

Affirmation

1. An effective college has a clear and vital mission. Administrators, faculty, and students share a vision of what the institution is seeking to accomplish. (Ernest Boyer, *College: The Undergraduate Experience, in America*, 1987, p. 58).
2. Without an effective mission statement, the institution's activities and practices can take on the role of the mission and drive the institution. (Lion Gardiner, *Planning for Assessment*, 1989, p. 24).
3. If institutions of higher education hope to maintain their relevance to contemporary society, they must strongly affirm their values and ideals openly and clearly. (M. E. Mouritsen, "The University Mission Statement: A Tool for the University Curriculum, Institutional Effectiveness, and Change," 1986, p. 55).

Denial

1. I suggest that the reason so few people have a clear understanding of their institution's vision is because there is really nothing in it worth remembering. (Daniel Seymour, *On Q: Causing Quality in Higher Education*, 1992, p. 62).
2. So the operative thesis of this essay is different from the generative. It is that there are very good reasons not to define institutional missions, especially within state-supported systems of higher education. It is safer to talk about missions than to define them, politically more astute to avoid the confrontations that would be inevitable if mission statements were to be made more precise than they usually are. (Gordon Davies, "The Importance of Being General," 1986, p. 86).
3. We found that when we hid the institution's name, most of the colleges or universities could not be identified from their state-

ments because they all read alike, full of honorable verbiage, signifying nothing. Not surprisingly, few colleges find much use for their mission statements. They are usually not guidelines for serious planning. (Walter Newsom and Ray Hayes, "Are Mission Statements Worthwhile," 1990–91, p. 29).

Apparently, there are multiple realities when it comes to the intent and impact of college mission statements. There are some institutions where the process of mission planning yields an outcome that is inspiring to all those who hold the campus in trust—faculty, staff, students, board members—and also useful for planning and decision in the life of the campus. There are others where the process is routine and restricted—engaged for form and not substance, only to meet some accreditation or state agency requirement.

There are also multiple expectations for mission, especially for public institutions, and some of the tensions in the expectations are captured in the notes and quotes just presented.

Campus officials would rather not be constrained in their aspirations, but civic and political officials may hold a different view, especially in financial hard times. The call for more carefully defined mission statements is more likely to be issued by political officers in tight financial times, when it becomes clear that a state may not be able to afford all that is has been doing in its colleges and universities. Mission statements are thus seen as a device to constrain campus aspirations.

Will campus mission statements then be full of "honorable verbiage" but having little capacity for energizing, guiding, and inspiring a campus; or will mission statements identify and affirm core values that are then operationalized in the community life of the campus? We would like to use this question to entertain a brief discussion on the role of values in mission statements, as we believe this shift is an important contemporary change in the content and function of mission statements.

VISION AND VALUES—NEW APPROACHES TO MISSION

As we noted earlier, writers in both corporate and collegiate sectors have emphasized the importance of "core values" in articulating the mission and purpose of an organization. This may not be a new element in mission statements for private colleges having a religious affiliation, but it would appear to be a new element for public colleges. To ascertain the origins of this emphasis may prove elusive. However, the authors would attribute the concern with core values to the following streams of thought.

There is first a renewed concern with the concept of community in both national and campus life. See, for example, *The Spirit of Community* by Etzioni

(1993) and *Campus Life: In Search of Community* (1990). Americans have understandably and properly invested energy and caring in the affirmation of diversity and dignity on our campuses, as we strive to model the ways in which individual differences can be honored. Some suggest that while we have attended carefully and thoughtfully to the matter of rights, we have neglected the call of responsibility and those values that furnish a uniting force for any organization or society. Sheldon Hackney, former president of the University of Pennsylvania, wrote in the *Teachers College Record* that "Among the core dilemmas we face is the creation of community within both the university and society" (Hackney, 1994, p. 312). The commitment to respect human dignity is a "core value" that furnishes a basis for community.

A second antecedent influence on the identification of "core values" may be found in the current quality assurance movement known variously as Total Quality Management or Continuous Quality Improvement. See, for example, *On Q: Causing Quality in Higher Education* (Seymour, 1992) and *Total Quality in Higher Education* (Lewis and Smith, 1994). The identification of core values is seen as a means of replacing top down and sloganistic approaches to the development of quality with a recognition that what community members have designed and own they will honor and invest with their allegiance.

A third stream of thought centers on the need for colleges and universities to exemplify and model constructive values. A stream of book-length critiques over the past decade has criticized higher education for its ethical emptiness in both its educational and its administrative performance. These are sad and disappointing chronicles of faculty and administrators abandoning their integrity, taking colleges and their clients in harm's way. For an organization whose mission entails the development of leadership for every enterprise in the nation, this neglect of public trust is all the more notable. Other book-length commentaries have directly engaged the subject of values and ethics in higher education, including *Ethics for Higher Education* (May, 1990) and *Moral Values and Higher Education: A Notion at Risk* (Thompson, 1991).

The latter book suggests that "The university has its own customary morality, one which endorses the dualism of fact and value, and assigns to higher education a concern only with the domain of fact. . . . Customary academic morality is quite willing to teach values in the appreciation of arts, literature, and music, or in the pursuit of excellence on the athletic field, but recoils from anything that smacks of teaching an appreciation of the greatness of the human spirit, and the pursuit of excellence in the human heart" (Thompson, 1991, pp.16–17).

Brief statements of core values may prove to be more useful instruments for strengthening the integrity of higher education than more precisely crafted codes of ethics. A recent special Committee on Institutional Integrity of the Commission on Colleges (Southern Association of Colleges and Schools) has recommended the definition of core values for each campus and evaluation of the extent to which the campus is honoring its core values. As of this writing, this report was still under review and the recommendations of this special committee had not been adopted by the Commission on Colleges as a part of its accreditation criteria (Commission on Colleges, 1998). More powerful than any precept or written preachment, however, will be the values manifested in the behavior of faculty and staff on a campus. Values may be more caught than taught, though it may be argued that behavior is but an instrument of teaching.

It may be argued that colleges and universities have a special and important obligation to provoke students to engage and evaluate their moral thinking and values for the simple reason that colleges and universities contribute to the critique of conventional thought and value. Encouraging students to wrestle with value tensions in the dark night of the soul should be complemented with faculty and staff behavior models that reflect nobility of intent and method.

In a 1996 book entitled *No Neutral Ground*, Young suggests seven values that should undergird the values mission: altruism, truth, freedom, equality, individuation, justice, and community (Young, 1996). Young makes an important point in his opening chapter that it is not possible for higher education to take a value-neutral posture: "A person or institution that refuses to transmit one set of values is substituting another in its place. . . . No enterprise can be fully objective or value-neutral, no matter how scientific its nature" (p. 9).

HIGHER EDUCATION MISSION PRIORITIES

In this chapter we have explored the evolution of higher education mission, examined different perspectives on the purposes of higher education, and evaluated the contribution of mission statements to higher education planning and operation.

It is important both academic and civic leaders understand that the mission, purpose, and goals of an educational enterprise in a democratic society will always remain open to debate.

Education at every level in our society is an enterprise with moral complexion and political connection. We stated in the opening of this chapter that colleges and universities stand with one hand holding to the past, carrying in trust the heritage of our society, and one hand reaching for the future, carrying in trust the quality and promise of that future.

In a democratic society, dissent is valued as a public political activity. In an academic culture, dissent is valued as an essential tool for discerning and discovering truth. Therefore it is not surprising to find a lively public conversation underway, at any time in higher education history, concerning both the

content and priority of the various mission elements. In contemporary illustration, journalist and scholar William Henry III suggests in his book *In Defense of
Elitism* (1994) that the greatest American debate since World War II has been
between elitism and egalitarianism. He chastises American universities for
caving "in almost entirely to the rigorous dogma of what might be termed
'special pleading studies.' These purportedly scholarly undertakings are really
intended to redress historic grievances, sometimes by willfully misunderstand-
ing and reinventing the past, as though altering the present and future were
not reform enough. They also seek to instill, and then minister to, a paranoid
sense of victimology among assorted self-proclaimed minorities" (Henry, 1994,
p. 4). Henry's disenchantment with higher education is further proclaimed in
the closing pages of his essays with a proposal to reduce the percentage of high
school graduates going on to college from 60 percent to 33 percent and closing
a number of institutions, mostly community colleges and current or former
state teachers' colleges (p. 165). Henry's comments furnish an arresting
perspective on the question: What's college for? As we earlier remarked, a
philosophy of mission is of no small policy consequence from any perspective,
whether it be social, economic, or political. Indeed a commanding part
of Henry's argument proclaims we are wasting national economic resources on

> . . . overeducating a populace that is neither consistently eager for
> intellectual expansion of horizons nor consistently likely to gain the
> economic and professional status for which the education is under-
> taken. Nor can one justify such expenditures by citing the racial and
> ethnic pressures from those who argue that only a wide-open system of
> higher education will give minorities a sufficient chance. Whatever the
> legacy of discrimination or the inadequacies of big-city schools, a C
> student is a C student and turning colleges into remedial institutions
> for C students (or worse) only debases the value of the degrees the
> schools confer (pp. 164–65).

In addition to individual critical voices such as Henry's, there are also
policy organizations involved. The California Center for Policy Study is an
independent, nonprofit agency established to examine public policy on higher
education in that state. The center has published a range of position papers
ranging from commentary on tuition to mission. In the 1960s and 1970s,
California was widely heralded as a state that had done an effective job of
assigning mission responsibilities to the University of California system, to the
California State System of universities, and to its two-year college sector. The
conflicting pressures of rising enrollment expectations and cost-containment
policies from state government have caused these earlier mission agreements
to become frayed and frazzled. The search for new ways of doing business is
underway in California.

Public concern with mission balance and priority appears to focus less on community colleges and liberal arts colleges than on research, doctoral, and comprehensive universities.

MISSION AND MULTIPLE STAKEHOLDERS—A SUMMARY

Is it unreasonable to expect a growing complexity in mission for colleges and universities in the political, social, economic, and cultural makeup of the nation? Can Americans expect changing mission priorities and themes as a function of the leadership challenges facing a nation at any point in time? As the number of college-educated men and women grows, is it reasonable to expect more assertive criticism of higher education mission?

The evolution of higher education mission and purpose reveals a growing complexity in expectation, from the earlier and singular mission of teaching in the colonial college to the more complex missions of advancing and applying knowledge in research and public service in the modern college and university. While it is possible to circumscribe most higher education activity under this tripartite mission, we have suggested three additional elements of mission: conservation of knowledge as performed by libraries, museums, and information systems; renewal of personal and professional talent, as carried by programs of continuing education; and evaluation/critique of knowledge and policy, as performed by colleges and universities in their "public forum" responsibility.

Giving voice to multiple stakeholders in higher education is another evidence of mission evolution in American higher education. While academic faculty and administrators remain the primary architects of collegiate mission, many other partners have taken a place at the mission forum table—civic, political, and economic leaders; state and federal government; and regional and national educational organizations.

One can also discern a shift in emphasis in higher education goals in the latter half of the twentieth century, from an earlier accent on the enhancement of access and social/economic justice to a contemporary concern with quality, integrity, and accountability. Since education at all levels in the United States is an activity with moral and political context, one should expect continued debate concerning fundamental goals and the balance among those goals. There is certainly a contemporary tension on the question of balance among goals. For example, some leaders, both academic and civic/political, suggest that the research mission has been advanced at the expense of attention to teaching and caring for students, and that there is a need to redress this balance. Additional concern regarding goals is reflected in the current ferment over higher education's role in teaching and testing those values that undergird a democratic society—and in modeling those values within the community of American campuses.

Are America's colleges and universities to serve as:
- Instruments of personal and societal improvement?
- Crucibles of dissent and discovery?
- Means for transmitting knowledge and culture?
- Conservators of heritage and knowledge?
- Engines of economic development?
- Curators of humankind's artistic impulses?
- Forums for constructing and evaluating public policy?
- Enemies of injustice, ignorance, and inertia?
- Guardians of human dignity and civility?

Whether these are purposes to be honored by American higher education, how these purposes are to be expressed and prioritized in the diversity of American colleges and universities and what ends are to be employed in achieving these purposes are certain to remain questions of lively interest and debate. In a democratic society, a continued and even contentious conversation regarding higher education mission and goals is not a sign of pathology but a sign of health and vitality. Dissent over mission may be seen as evidence that higher education is indeed meeting its most fundamental responsibilities for asking what is true and what is good, and for equipping its graduates with both motive and skill to challenge conventional wisdom.

CHAPTER 3

Guardians and Governance

The Culture of Decision and Authority in Academic Life

In the opening volume of *The Story of Civilization*, Will Durant (1954) suggests that to understand civilization, one must explore the political, economic, moral, and mental aspects of human exchange. The first of these aspects, the political, is the story of how cultures govern themselves. To understand colleges and universities, it is also important to explore how they are governed: How decisions are made, how authority is distributed, and how the influence of many different voices is orchestrated. "Who's in charge here?" is a question often posed in organizational life, as one looks for sources of authority and responsibility. For collegiate organizations, the question is simple and straightforward enough, but a crisp and concise answer is more difficult and evasive. The most obvious feature of college governance is the fact that decision processes and authority interactions are neither neat nor always easily discerned and that generalizations from campus to campus and state to state are risky at best. Consider the range of those who might make legitimate claim for involvement in the governance life of American colleges and universities: faculty, administrators, trustees, students, alumni, parents, donors, civic and political officials, and foundations. Understanding who's in charge on any given decision and explaining patterns of authority in the academy are challenges of both discernment and communication.

In chapter two, we suggested that American higher education is expected to serve simultaneously as cultural curator and cultural critic, to serve as cultural anchor and cultural change agent. To this complexity of mission, we add in this chapter a complexity in the orchestration of collegial and bureau-cratic decision processes.

Our plan in this chapter is to look at the patterns of decision and authority "inside" the campus, examine the boundary and bridging role of lay governing boards or boards of trustees, and describe the "outside" role of external agencies, such as statewide boards and government agencies. We will open our exploration of governance by attending first to the complex internal nature of college organizations, with special attention to the principle of collegiality that undergirds decision and authority in collegiate organizations. Second, we will explore the principle of "shared authority" as an important governance principle and then turn to the distinctive principle of lay gover-nance in American higher education. Finally, we hope to identify some of the leadership issues that continue to challenge governance in higher education.

ORCHESTRATING COLLEGIAL AND HIERARCHICAL PROCESSES

Colleges and universities are among the more complex organizational entities. They manifest elements of many conventional organizational principles, but a prominent operating principle in college and university organizations is colle-gial decision making. Part of our engagement in this discussion will be how the more traditional principles of hierarchical organization are married to the collegial principles. But first a brief note about making sense of the complexity of any organization. In their informing and integrative work *Reframing Organi-zations*, Bolman and Deal (1997) suggest that organizational behavior may be understood more easily if we learn to see organizations through four different lenses or frames. The first of these frames, the "Structural Frame," is the more conventionally understood perception of organizations as hierarchical enti-ties, in which there is a pyramidal structure with carefully defined responsibili-ties and roles, formal communication channels, and formal decision authority. This frame depicts the organization from the mechanical and rational perspec-tive of mission and organizational structure.

Universities are certainly structural in their character. While their missions and purposes are unquestionably more diffuse than corporate counterparts, colleges and universities nevertheless have missions, as set forth in chapter two, and there is an obvious organizational structure. For example, the academic life of a college or university begins with the academic department as the most fundamental unit, and a chair/head as the first level administrator. Departments may be clustered into a division, school, or college where a dean is the second level administrator. Primary academic programs within these schools or colleges may be gathered under a vice president for academic affairs (or provost), who may be considered an executive level administrator. The term "provost" often signals that the chief academic officer is also considered an "executive vice president," a second in command. Support programs and services in administration, finance, student affairs, university relations, and development may be directed by other vice presidents (or vice chancellors). These vice presidents (or vice chancellors) then report to the president (or chancellor). The terms president and chancellor are often used to designate the chief executive officer of a campus or a system of campuses. The organizational chart depicting these units and administrative officers is clear and satisfying. However, the structural frame is not the whole truth for either corporate or collegial organizations.

While organizational charts may depict the formal framework for decision making, a "Human Relations" frame reminds us that the men and women of an organization give voice and meaning to its mission. The formal definition of roles and formal position descriptions notwithstanding, these men and women are not like interchangeable parts. They hold membership in a range of both formal and informal groups, within the organization and outside the organization. They have their own aspirations and goals, their joys and their pains. They have their own motives and needs, and they seek meaning and fulfillment within the life of the organization. Organizational charts do not give us access to the reality of human needs and motives, to the psychological drama of human interaction.

And what organization, whether collegiate or corporate, will move in its daily work without conflict over purpose, process, and policy? None! It will prove informing, therefore, to look at organizations through a "Political Frame," as clusters of alliances and influence patterns, networks of both formal and informal relations, depositories of affirmation and threat, and as chronicles of leverage and exchange. Colleges and universities are just as surely "political" in their character as other organizations because in any college or university we will find conflict over its purposes and processes, conflict over resource allocation, and conflict over different levels of personal influence. In other words, the level of one's influence may not correspond to one's formal position or location in the hierarchy. Moreover, the very nature of college and university mission, consisting as it does of contention over ideas, adds another dimension of conflict. It is the constructive management of conflict, the study of influence and alliance, that constitutes the "political" work of any organization, and of colleges and universities.

Finally, colleges and universities may be understood more clearly and completely if we view them through a "Symbolic and Cultural Frame." There is perhaps more celebration and theater in college life than in any organization. Convocations and commencements, athletic contests and award ceremonies, concerts and cultural celebrations, initiations and inaugurations, rites of passage and recognition/reward events are the cultural glue that create a sense of community on a campus. There are ways of doing business, modes of dress and behavior, and a sense of place that constitute the culture of a college or university. In the opening chapter, we tried to paint a portrait of diversity in American higher education. Any college educator who moves from the campus of a major public research university to the campus of an evangelical Christian college or perhaps a two-year rural community college understands immediately the presence and reality of culture. For example, if we want to understand the manifestations of culture, we have only to look at the dress of students and faculty. On a conservative Christian college campus, students will attend chapel worship service every day, but we will not find that requirement on the public research campus. We are unlikely to find 2,000 students and faculty gathered in a large auditorium singing "Amazing Grace" on the public university campus, though we may find small groups of students doing so in various religious houses on the public campus.

To the four frames of Bolman and Deal, we would like to add a fifth frame for college organizations, the collegial frame. If the corporate model of organization may be described as hierarchical, the collegial model might be described as hieratic, a priesthood of the faculty. The collegial model of organizational life places a high degree of emphasis on consensus decision making, professional expertise, and autonomy of the faculty. It accents the unique work and purpose of the academy in searching for truth and developing human potential, both activities in sharp contrast to the somewhat impersonal and production models of most corporate organizations. Just as scientists often have multiple theories to explain a single physical phenomenon (for example, there are at least three theories in the propagation of light), we have several ways of understanding the multiple truths of organizational life.

It may prove helpful to examine the evolution of governance arrangements as a prelude to the discussion about contemporary governance arrangements and newly emerging patterns. In his 1983 book *Academic Strategy* and in a 1989 chapter in *Governing Tomorrow's Campus*, Keller has detailed the shift in collegiate governance. In the early years of American higher education, the authority of trustees dominated. In the 1800s, college and university presidents were thought of as "captains of erudition," and took a strong hand in the educational and philosophical life of their institutions. With the establishment of the American Association of University Professors (AAUP) in 1915, faculty began to assert their responsibilities more strongly, especially in matters related to program and personnel matters. Gilmour (1994) reports that more than 90 percent of institutions have a form of faculty senate or other representative governance body. The faculty or academic senate has traditionally been seen as both a symbolic and substantive expression of the collegium, the collegial form of decision making in higher education. Here, the theory supposes, decisions of policy and program are debated and resolved in discussions among peers, who have both the academic competence and interest to resolve matters on basic academic freedoms—what is to be taught, by whom, and how.

The collegial form of governance also exists at other places and levels in the organization. At the department level, for example, faculty are engaged in discussion and decision over courses and curriculum, program and personnel policy, and student relations. They make the primary judgments on such matters as course content, admissions and graduation, instructional strategies, promotion, and tenure. While faculty judgments may be reviewed and conditioned by collegial reviews at a level above and by administrative oversight, the primary collegial initiative in academic policy matters resides in deliberative bodies of faculty. An administrator may approve or disapprove a course or curriculum but the administrator does not deliver a course or curriculum. Thus, the primary educational standards of a college or university always have their first residence in hearts and mind of the faculty.

What has been characterized as a unique dualism in higher education, the simultaneous existence of collegial bodies such as faculty senates and hierarchical bodies such as presidential cabinets and deans' councils, appears to be transforming on many campuses. This transformation has been detailed in *Strategic Governance* by J. Schuster, et al. (1994). The role and composition of "Strategic Planning Councils," first anticipated by Keller as "Joint Big Decision Committee" (1983), are described in operation on several college and university campuses over the nation.

In the past the deliberations of faculty senates as representative bodies went on with some independence of administrative councils in a form of shared authority. However, in the present these newer strategic councils are composed not only of faculty and administrative members, but in some cases staff and students as well. These strategic planning councils serve, in the words of the authors, ". . . to bring together key constituencies to chart institutional direction and to make decisions, albeit advisory, about how to move their campuses to the future, or so we supposed" (Schuster, et al., 1994, p. 179). We suggest that these newer governance entities are not necessarily replacing senates and administrative councils, but instead are providing a forum that strengthens governance, planning, communication, and leadership development.

Schuster et al. also describe the tension often felt between faculty and administrators in many colleges: "The faculty frequently views the administration as keen to usurp authority and to act autocratically to impose decisions insufficiently respectful of academic prerogative. . . . The administration, in turn, undoubtedly is strongly displeased with perceived foot dragging by faculty, the seemingly interminable process for making decisions, and the faculty's indisputable resistance for making hard choices" (Schuster, et al.,

1994, p. 196). In *College: The Undergraduate Experience*, Boyer reports in a chapter on governance that "Faculty increasingly see presidents as 'managers.' And we found that on many campuses an adversarial relationship has developed, with the allocation of scarce resources often generating tension. Such tensions, often persistent and occasionally destructive, divide the college, weakening faculty loyalty and threatening prospects for a vital community" (1987, p. 238). In their book *Up the University* (1993), Solomon and Solomon suggest that the answer to the descriptive question of who runs the university is "administrators." They suggest that the answer to the normative question of who should run the university is "faculty" (p. 258).

The high degree of specialization within a college or university, the allegiance of faculty members to their disciplines or specialties, and the persistent prejudices between the different partners in academe, often make it difficult to cultivate a sense of community within a college or university. Establishing an agenda of common caring and identifying core values to guide behavior and policy are challenges of community in both corporate and collegiate cultures. How the collegium works turns on the principle of shared authority, to which we now turn.

THE CONCEPT OF SHARED AUTHORITY

In a 1957 court case, *Sweezey v. New Hampshire 354*, U.S. 234, the United States Supreme Court articulated the "four essential freedoms of a university: to determine for itself on academic grounds who may teach, what may be taught, how it shall be taught, and who may be admitted for study." Beyond the content of this decision, one can observe that this decision indicates that one of the voices in collegiate governance is the courts of the land.

A publication of the Carnegie Foundation for the Advancement of Teaching entitled *The Control of the Campus* (1982) details a national study of decision and authority on 39 different categories of decision and 12 different sources of authority, from departmental to state level. The report further examines the interaction of decision type and decision authority by classification of institution. A major contribution of this report was to make plain the concept of shared authority, a concept often cited as a governing principle of higher education and explicated in the American Association of University Professors *Statement on Governance of Colleges and Universities*, which was published in a 1996 issue, volume 52, of the AAUP journal *Academe* (pp. 375–79). This principle was also detailed in a monograph by Keeton entitled *Shared Authority* (1971); a publication by Mason entitled *College and University Government: A Handbook of Principle and Practice* (1972); and a work by Mortimer and McConnell entitled *Sharing Authority Effectively* (1978). Mortimer and McConnell's discussion is particularly informing as it details the differences between the ideal and the reality of shared authority in practice. They explore areas of authority and decision in the areas of program, policy, and personnel within six different decision stages: initiation, consultation, recommendation, review, choice, and veto. Case studies of six different institutions in Pennsylvania suggested that administrator decision roles and authority dominated in most areas of institutional operation—except that of curriculum. The concept of shared authority is one that many in higher education find simultaneously exhilarating and exasperating. The processes of sharing in decision are often fluid rather than formal, encumbered with tedious consultation, and flavored with personality and political spices.

We have indicated that the collegial principle holds the highest authority, as faculty of a college or university have the principal power of decision in the most fundamental academic policy issues of higher education—who gets in (admissions standards), who stays in (retention policy), and who gets out (graduation requirements). They have authority over what is taught (course requirements), how it is taught (instructional strategies), and what standards and processes are used in evaluation (grading, assessment). Faculty also have authority in personnel decisions of appointment, promotion, tenure, and salary. Finally, faculty have major influence in research agendas, although external funding agencies affect this decision as well.

For each of these areas, the decision authority of the faculty may be conditioned and/or confined by one or more other voices in the governance of the campus. For example, while faculties and campus administrators generally initiate and design major academic program and personnel proposals, many of these are subject to review and approval by the campus governing board, and in some cases state coordinating agencies.

In most states with coordinating agencies, new academic degree programs in public campuses must not only be approved by campus or system governing boards but also by the coordinating agency as well, another example of shared authority. Boards and some coordinating agencies also have authority to terminate academic programs. Decisions to terminate degree programs may have their basis in concerns for productivity (low number of graduates) concerns for quality (low evaluations by peer review committees), and concerns for costs (severe reduction in revenues from either fees or state appropriations). In some cases, legislatures have also been known to overrule decisions of coordinating agencies. In Alabama, the decision of a coordinating board to deny a community college a new program in allied health was overruled by the state legislature. In Tennessee, a coordinating board decision against establishing a second medical school was also overruled by the state legislature. And, as we shall see in chapter four, state legislatures will occasionally take a hand in curriculum matters, specifying some policy or course requirement. Thus, political officers will sometimes have a seat at the table of shared authority. Private colleges and universities are, in most states, spared this public political complication. This unencumbered operation constitutes a major strength and contribution of the American system of private colleges and universities. However, the private sector does face other issues. In the case of private colleges having religious affiliation, pressures to maintain orthodox views in the curriculum and in policy may be communicated in both formal and informal ways. For example, on a conservative Christian campus, members and ministers of the religious fellowship may complain about the teaching of a biology teacher on the topic of evolution or complain about a text being used in a course where abortion or homosexuality is discussed. In other cases, when a campus with religious connection creates independence for its governing board by denying the religious denomination or fellowship the privilege of appointing members to the board, the campus may find direct financial support from the denomination withdrawn or denied. Thus, independence may often come with a price. And governance tensions in private colleges may also be subjected to added pressure when liberal and conservative religious groups contend for control of a campus.

Here is an example of how complicated and intriguing the concept of shared authority may become. An assistant professor sought promotion to associate professor and tenured status, but was not recommended by a vote of senior faculty in his department, nor by recommendation of his department chairman. The promotion and tenure committee and the college dean supported this negative recommendation in presenting it to the university's vice president and the president. The assistant professor appealed the decision to a university-wide faculty appeals board, and the negative decision was again sustained. The assistant professor then exercised his right of appellate review to the university's governing board, a right of appeal often found in the bylaws of many governing boards. In this case, the decision was not only academically complicated but became socially intriguing as well. The faculty member held appointment in an esoteric field of study where judgments of his competence were difficult enough. The fact that he was engaged to a socially prominent woman in the community, who was a personal friend to several board members, added a lively social scent and political dimension to this example of shared authority. The chair of the board review committee attempted to have the decision arbitrated by a third party external to the university and the community, but was eventually voted down by other members of the committee; and the decision of the campus not to promote and award tenure was sustained. Even the plain variety of academic decisions can have curious and complicating decision accessories.

Another perspective on the concept of shared authority may be found in the instance where a group of faculty members in a state research university filed a lawsuit against their own campus. The faculty members wanted to prevent the university from possibly taking capital funds dedicated to a new library and using them instead for the construction of a new fieldhouse. The case was settled out of court. Here indeed was an interesting decision in which not only the faculty, the administration, and the board were involved, but the courts played a part as well.

We must not neglect the decision role of students. Students of a comprehensive university petitioned the faculty senate to establish a system whereby students could participate in evaluation of courses and instruction—now an accepted practice for evaluation of instruction on many campuses. The faculty senate politely turned the request aside, whereupon student leadership of the campus decided that the students would design and implement their own system independent of the faculty and would publish the results in open forum. The vice president for academic affairs and concerned senior faculty members fashioned a task force on the issue, composed of widely recognized and respected faculty and students. Working with students, they fashioned a course and instructor evaluation system that enjoyed the endorsement of students, faculty, and administration. For more information regarding this topic, see Cahn's book *Saints and Scamps* (1986) and the September/October 1997 issue of *Change Magazine*. This last example reflects shared authority at its best.

Institutions aspiring to offer degree programs at a level beyond their current authorization—moving to the master's degree from baccalaureate status, for example—must not only have the approval of their governing boards but will find that they must also satisfy review and evaluation by a regional accrediting agency, another example in which authority is shared with an external group of peer reviewers.

It is in the best interest of both faculty and administrators to honor the principle of shared authority if quality and standards are to be maintained. While faculty expertise on the most fundamental academic questions is clearly needed, the occasional narrowness of faculty perspective and the call of self-interest will sometimes influence faculty decision and not serve the cause of quality or integrity. In such rare cases, the intervention of appropriate administrators is warranted.

In those cases where ambition, arrogance, or the absence of leadership intelligence is obvious in administrators, the faculty is justified in turning temporarily aside from program and curricular matters to voice their lack of confidence and to insist upon a change. A collegiate administrator who may temporarily alienate one or more major constituents is at least understandable, if the cause of alienation is honest differences over policy and principle and the administrator is exhibiting courage where he or she should be doing so. Chair or chancellor, director or dean—an administrator who permanently damages his relationships with a major constituency such as faculty, trustees, community, and students because of sustained poor judgment, departure from integrity, absence of social and political intelligence—will have lost the trust of others, and the ability to lead, and will deserve the scrutiny of the faculty.

As a closing comment in this discussion, departures from quality and integrity at the campus level are among the more significant events that invite increased external scrutiny and encourage the shift of decision-making power from the faculty to external agencies. Informing accounts on the partnerships between campus and state and those events that encourage intervention from outside the campus are detailed in Newman's 1987 book *Choosing Quality* and Hines' 1988 monograph *Higher Education and State Governments*.

Our examples thus far have centered on matters academic and leave untouched an equally complex range of decisions related to student life and administrative matters. What policies will govern visitation in residence halls? Who will be the principal investigative office for felony crimes on a campus, campus police or community police? What reimbursement will be authorized for travel? What fee will be charged for campus parking? These and a hundred other decisions that affect the community and student life of a campus are likely to benefit from principal campus discretion and input from campus administrative officers and students. Even here, however, a public campus may be constrained by state policy and regulation on such things as travel and use of public buildings. Some private campuses will be governed in the context of their religious heritage and public campuses will be governed within their role as instruments of government.

This exploratory discussion of decision types and decision stakeholders has pointed to the important role of campus governing boards. The role of the lay governing board in American higher education must be counted as one of the most distinctive principles and features of higher education. Let us turn, then, to the governance role of the board of trustees.

THE LAY GOVERNING BOARD: A DISTINCTIVE HERITAGE

Walter Metzger offers a helpful historical perspective on the evolution of lay governance and cites two principles important to this evolution. The first of these is what Metzger refers to as "laicization," meaning that boards governing colleges were composed not so much of faculty, or "fellows," from the college and ministers but composed more dominantly of lay members from a variety of professions and walks of life. The second is "privatization," which is the "deliverance of the private college from state interference" (Metzger, 1989, p. 13). From the first governing board established for Harvard in 1642 to the board for Dartmouth College in 1769, each of the nine colonial colleges had lay boards selected from among the leading citizens and clergy of the colonies.

In this section, we want to explore the responsibilities, philosophic foundations, composition, and performance of boards of trustees.

Board Responsibilities

In *The Guardians* (1989), Kerr and Gade suggest that the unique system of lay trustees contrasts with other governance forms such as government ministries, faculty and student guilds. They also suggest that this system of lay trustees constitutes one of the features contributing to the strength and international reputation of American higher education. Among the premier responsibilities of the lay governing board, as cited by Kerr and Gade, are the following: (1) selecting, advising, supporting, and evaluating the president; (2) establishing major policies, including approval of the budget and important new programs; (3) reviewing and evaluating the performance of the institution in all its aspects—including academic areas; (4) representing the institution to the surrounding society and in obtaining resources; (5) acting as a "court of last resort" to internal conflicts; (6) being willing and able to fill in gaps in performance by other elements of the institution in emergency situations and then to withdraw when the special circumstances no longer exist; and (7) encouraging adaptation and renewal of the institution to make it more useful and to avoid stagnation and retrogression (Kerr and Gade, 1989, pp. 12–13).

Some have argued that the most important duty a board will ever discharge is to select a campus chief executive officer. It has been suggested, not so seriously, that all board meetings should consist entirely of two motions. The first motion should be to fire the president. If that motion fails, then the second motion should be to adjourn. The idea here is that if the board has done its job well in the appointment of the chief executive officer, then it should have little else to do. That the simplicity of this relationship between boards and their presidents has changed is apparent in recent coverage of these relationships. An article appearing in an issue of the *Chronicle of Higher Education* suggested that many boards of trustees were becoming more conservative and more activist (Healy, August 9, 1996, pp. A19–A20). The article further asserted that the automatic deference once accorded colleges and their presidents by civic and political leaders had begun to erode. Boards are indeed taking activist policy position on such issues as affirmative action, remedial studies, and tenure, and they have moved well beyond the rubber stamp posture in the selection of presidents. This trend toward more assertive postures of external agencies was already in motion a quarter century earlier, as noted in the 1973 Carnegie Commission report *Governance of Higher Education*.

Among more recent publications on roles and responsibilities of governing boards are two handbooks, one for public institutions and one for private, on governing colleges and universities, published by the Association of Governing Boards of Universities and Colleges. The two volumes detail the context and the challenges of board work (Ingram, 1993). From the Association of Governing Boards Handbook just cited and numerous other historic references to the work and responsibilities of governing boards, we may derive the following major board responsibilities:

- Setting mission and purposes
- Appointing the president
- Supporting the president
- Monitoring the president's performance
- Insisting on long range planning
- Reviewing educational and public service programs
- Ensuring adequate resources
- Ensuring good management
- Preserving institutional independence
- Relating campus to community
- Serving as court of appeal
- Assessing board performance
- Fulfilling responsibilities as individual trustee

Purpose, personnel, policy, public relations, performance—this alliterative short list may help to remember some of the premier functions of the board.

In *The Effective Board of Trustees*, Chait, Holland, and Taylor attend to one other strategic responsibility of boards that should be appended to this cluster. They urge the construction of a "governance information system" (1993, p. 106).

Anyone who has observed the complex work of a board and noted the reams of paper and complex data profiles often presented to board members will understand the need for developing and maintaining a critical and crisp set of performance indicators of campus/system performance. A cluster of indicators on campus/system activity and achievement will be essential if board members are to have any strategic sense of the campus/system for which they are responsible.

The Theory of Lay Governance

In a democratic society that looks with suspicion on the monopoly of power and that has constructed its government with a set of checks and balances, we may see lay governance as a way to keep a check on the power of faculty and to keep the heavy hand of government from undue influence on an institution. What some have described as a "gift of history," the essential concept of the lay board is that professional insight should be subject to lay oversight. The essential philosophic theory is that lay boards hold the academy accountable to the public and protect the academy from the caprice and entanglement of political life. Conditioning the occasional intellectual arrogance, political naivete, social insensitivity, and cultural narrowness that may accompany highly trained professionals is achieved by having professionals of the academy stand accountable before a panel of men and women having no direct self-interest in the outcome of policy and decision. It is argued that faculty and administrators who cannot make a reasoned argument before such panels deserve defeat of their plans. Preventing those in civic and public power positions from extinguishing the flame of curiosity and the light of artistic, social, economic, and scientific critique is achieved by having the lay board serve as a buffer between campus and state. "Ye shall know the truth and the truth shall make you free" is a principle that undergirds the operation of colleges and universities in the United States. The unfettered pursuit of truth is seen as a cornerstone of democratic society. American colleges and universities constitute a magnificent investment in the "pursuit of truth" and a precious heritage of this principle.

How do theory and practice coincide? The principles are sound enough. The leadership and imperfections of those who serve on boards can yield both inspiring and disappointing performance profiles. One university was besieged by a governor intent on placing his political stamp on several personnel appointments to the university and on meddling with admissions decisions to several university programs. He was quietly and informally approached by several leading members of the university's board of trustees—trustees of some political, civic, and economic influence—and they were able to persuade the governor of the political and educational liabilities of his actions. They offered the governor a motive compounded of both nobility and self-interest and effectively served both the campus and the governor.

While this illustration of a board at work in the political arena offers a constructive look at shared governance, there are other examples in which boards are willing to pass political positions and pressures from governor to campus, with little or no scrutiny of the merits of the position. Governors have a history of attempting to influence presidential appointments, system structure, and governance arrangements, and indeed the welfare of individual faculty.

One state senator known to the authors is a champion of tenure for a simple and straightforward reason. As a youngster, he saw his college professor father almost lose his position because the governor of the state became seriously disenchanted with the direction of this professor's research. The research centered on the moral and ethical practices of a business field in which the governor had personal financial interests. The governor directed the board and the president of the public institution to fire the professor, but was resisted by both board and president, who made full use of the tenure principle.

Here is another portrait of board performance that would not qualify as either exemplary or effective. In a public meeting, a multicampus governing board approved the appointment of a new campus chancellor for one of its doctoral university campuses. The board took this action on the recommendation of the system president, without ever seeing or interviewing the candidate they approved, and without interviewing any of the other three finalist candidates. While this may be seen as a healthy salute to the "two motion" theory of lay boards earlier described and a vote of confidence in the system president, the board's judgment and integrity were unfortunately marred by what followed later in that same meeting. The board refused to accept the chancellor's recommendation of its research university campus and the system president's appointment of a new football coach, whose selection had also followed a national search. Instead, the board required that the final three candidates for the coaching position be brought before the board for interview. With every major TV station in the state covering the meeting, this board's display of values related to matters athletic and academic hardly furnished an exemplary model of board responsibility, and ultimately earned the scorn of leading civic, economic, and political leaders of the state.

Appointment and Selection of Board Members

How does one get to be a board member? For independent and private colleges, many boards are "self-perpetuating," meaning new members are selected by existing members. Private institutions can thus draw often from a national pool of potential board members, selecting those who have attachment and allegiance to the campus. In some cases, religious bodies hold the right to appoint some members of the board for private institutions having religious affiliation. The complexity of private college trusteeship has been a source of conflict and dissent in a number of private institutions in recent years, as liberal and conservative elements of religious fellowships contend with one another for control of the governance. In some cases, institutions have pulled away from religious fellowships and established self-perpetuating boards. This complex interaction between campuses and their religious sponsors is often a difficult concept to explain to those coming from foreign countries, yet it is a fundamental part of higher education history in the United States. As noted in chapter one, the presence of a significant sector of institutions having religious affiliation and support is a distinctive mark of American higher education. Honoring the "pursuit of truth" principle and honoring the convictions of a religious fellowship are challenges designed to test the most brilliant of mind and noble of heart.

For public campuses, trustees may be elected to office, as is the case in Illinois and South Carolina, or appointed to office—usually by the governor with advice and consent of legislature. Having board members appointed often allows the selection from a broader pool of interest and expertise, and without the appointees being indebted to special interests groups. Elected boards may have more political influence with the legislature and may be able to resist the actions of unfriendly governors. In recent months, the *Chronicle of*

Higher Education has reported different states expressing an interest in moving in opposite directions. Following the dismissal of a university president, the governor of one state expressed the desire of having an appointed board, whereas political leaders in another state expressed the desire of having an elected board—both in contrast to current but different patterns in those two states.

Whether elected or appointed for public institutions, trustees serve limited terms, often designed so that political influence is balanced and a single governor is not able to completely appoint a board. In some cases, authorizing laws will specify regional and even political party representation.

For public institutions, the authors favor the appointment process, given the independence that can be more often found in members selected in that fashion. Appointed board members may not be so much indebted to a particular constituency as they are to the campus they hold in trust and may be encouraged to work more as a team. The quality of board members will be a reflection of the judgment and values of those who appoint. A combination of gubernatorial appointment, subject to the advice and consent of a state legislature, would appear to promote both quality and political influence.

We would now like to examine the profile of board membership. The majority of the 40,000 board members serving public and private colleges across the nation are white males, though the percentage of men has declined from virtually 100 percent in the early part of this century to 73 percent in the early 1990s. The percentage of African-American board members has risen from 3 percent in the early part of the century to 13 percent in the early 1990s (Ingram, 1993, p. 386). An interesting trend is the growth of the number of student members on public governing boards. According to Ingram, up to 40 percent of public boards have student members (Ingram, 1993, p. 385). Faculty members are not often represented on boards, but alumni representatives can often be found as board members. The increased presence of student members, a development of the last 20 to 30 years, raises some interesting questions: What theory supports the presence of student interest and voice in the form of board membership but would deny that interest and voice to faculty, staff, and other campus interests? And does the presence of formal student membership subtract from board independence? It may be that student membership is a political response to the widespread student unrest of the late 1960s and early 1970s on college and university campuses.

Guardians of both heritage and promise, boards of trustees may become even more critical to the effective performance of our colleges and universities, as they engage civic and political expectations for enhanced quality and efficiency, educational and management integrity, and reinforcement of fundamental societal values. Governing boards are boundary agencies, expected to hold the faculty accountable and to also protect the autonomy of the faculty. In fulfilling their role, governing boards, especially public ones, do not work in a power vacuum. Perhaps we should now move outside the campus and attend to players such as statewide coordinating agencies. This will furnish an opportunity to look at the diverse pattern of state structures of governance. The complexity of the shared authority principle will become even more evident as we examine the roles of agencies external to campuses and their boards.

STATEWIDE PATTERNS OF GOVERNANCE: A STUDY IN POLITICAL DIVERSITY

As we open this theme, we begin by noting that private higher education in America is generally exempt from the oversight of state government structures, with one notable exception. Many states have consumer protection laws that require certain minimal standards to be met before an institution of higher education is allowed to operate in a state. These laws are designed to eliminate or minimize "fly-by-night" institutions of dubious reputation and quality, whose principal value and resource is to be found in their letterhead. They "sell" credentials and degrees to either unsuspecting or unprincipled clients. In most cases, private institutions accredited by regional or specialty field accrediting associations (see chapter five) are given exemption and are licensed or certified by the state on the basis of that accreditation. In other cases, evaluation and recommendation by some review agency, usually a coordinating agency, will be required for licensure or incorporation in a state.

Public institutions in the 50 states fall under one of three general governance patterns (McGuiness, Epper, and Arredono, 1994).

Consolidated Governing Board States

Responsibility for governing and coordinating of missions and finance is assigned to one or more statewide governing boards. There may be a single board for all colleges or universities in that state, or a segmental system, in which universities and two-year colleges are governed by different boards. A major and important distinction of the governing board and the coordinating board is that governing boards not only have responsibility for program and financial planning in a state, but they also have responsibility for major personnel appointments and policy, including the appointment of campus chief executives.

Coordinating Board States

Responsibility for master planning and for insuring equity in the allocation of both programs and finance in many states is assigned to coordinating boards.

Berdahl (1973) wrote the initial account of the role and responsibility of these agencies in his book *Statewide Coordination of Higher Education*. In response to the rapid growth in higher education during the 1960s, many states established coordinating boards to bring some sense of order, planning, and equity among competing campuses and systems. Coordinating boards occupy a tensioned posture between campus expectations for advocacy of higher education and political expectations for accountability and efficiency.

Coordinating board members are generally composed of appointed lay citizens, just as members of governing boards. The lay board members then appoint and entrust operational responsibilities of master planning, program review and evaluation, and financial and plant planning to a professional staff. These coordinating boards may be regulatory or advisory, with regulatory boards having statutory authority to approve new academic programs, and in some cases also having the authority to terminate existing academic programs.

Statewide coordinating boards have their authority and responsibility centered primarily in policy and program, not in personnel. This is a useful authority distinction in looking at the roles of governing boards and coordinating boards.

Planning Agency States

A small number of states have little or no formal coordinating authority beyond that of informal and voluntary association of campuses within the state. Among the states falling in this category are Delaware, Michigan, New Hampshire, and Vermont.

GOVERNMENT AND GOVERNANCE

State government is a central player in the life of higher education. Since state appropriations to public institutions constitute a major source of revenue for those institutions, we would expect the state to insist upon an equitable allocation and an effective utilization of state resources in achieving goals important to the citizens of a state. We have already indicated some of the ways in which state government policy influences governance decisions. In chapters five and six, we will attend to specific issues of quality and finance in more detail.

We should not conclude any discussion of governance, however, without also noting the important role of the federal government, which has furnished close to $100 billion annually in support of higher education in recent years. Federal government involvement in American higher education makes itself known primarily in the following ways, each of which influences policy decision and operation of our colleges and universities. The government provides federally funded support and regulation of:

- Research
- Student financial aid
- Programs for developing institutions
- Programs for educational facilities
- Programs for special purposes (math and science education, bilingual education, etc.)

In addition to these funded programs and associate regulation, the federal government has executive orders, regulations, and laws that affect every campus receiving federal funds in the following areas:

- Age, race, and sex discrimination
- Environmental protection
- Occupational health and safety standards
- Americans with Disabilities Act
- Ethical treatment of laboratory animals and human research subjects

This extensive pattern of federal regulation has led some higher education leaders to ask whether independence of higher education might be an important policy issue confronting colleges and universities in the 1990s.

Readers interested in the issue of governmental regulation, from the standpoint of state regulation, are referred to two publications previously cited in this chapter, the monographs by Newman (1987) and Hines (1988).

No discussion of the development of American higher education would be complete without acknowledgment of the powerful effect generated by such federal actions as the Land Grant Acts of 1862 and 1890, which led to the establishment of land grant universities. In this century, the passage of the G.I. Bill, providing college funding for thousands of returning World War II veterans, forever changed the profile of those benefiting from a college education. Later federal actions created not only significant research funding support but notable funding support for scholarships and loans, a matter we will attend to in chapter six.

We should not believe that the federal government has always been a benign or supportive partner. The now infamous House Committee on Un-American Activities, first established in 1938, reached its most intensive peak of activity in the late 1940s and into the 1950s under Senator Joseph McCarthy of Wisconsin. Searching for subversive tendencies among the professorate in the more intense years of the cold war battle between the United States and the Soviet Union, this committee utilized the intimidating tactics of guilt by accusation and guilt by association. Thus, the history of federal government influence on American higher education is one rich in heritage, but not without occasional disappointing moments. The social political struggle between freedom of belief and suppression of belief in society is explored in "Loyalty Investigations," a chapter in Diane Ravitch's *The Troubled Crusade* (pp. 81–113, 1983).

Other agencies of government affecting the governance of colleges and universities are the courts. Though we have touched on the role of courts at various points during this discussion, here may be the place to visit briefly on the involvement of courts as another external agency affecting the governance of colleges and universities.

This is not the place for an extended treatise on college law. We note only that courts at every level have been the arena where a range of personnel, finance, and program issues have been contested. Students have placed lawsuits against institutions on questions of admissions policy and due process. Faculty have lodged lawsuits against institutions on questions of promotion, tenure, and salary. Administrators have initiated lawsuits against campuses/ systems on issues of appointment and termination. Government has launched lawsuits against institutions and states on questions of racial and gender discrimination. Campuses have entered lawsuits against their boards and the state over equity of program and financial treatment. Parents have filed lawsuits against campuses on issues related to security and treatment of their enrolled children. Readers interested in some of the major themes and the flow of judicial theory as it affects colleges and universities are referred to the book *The Law of Higher Education* (Kaplan and Lee, 1995).

FOUNDATIONS AND DONORS

Other actors external to the campus that have a notable effect on the life of a campus are financial donors and foundations. The impact of donors upon institutions can be seen in a recent case in which the name of a public institution, Glassboro State College, was changed to Rowan College in honor of a donor who gave the college $100 million (Mercer, 1995). Many private colleges bear the name imprint of those donors who either provided the funds for creating the institution or furnished a major cash infusion to the institution after it had been established.

Foundations may also be recognized as major supporters of research and policy inquiries in higher education. The Carnegie Foundation for the Advancement of Teaching is a supporter of a series of policy inquiries and a host of other special studies, making them a major influence throughout this book. The PEW Charitable Trust is a supporter of the *Policy Perspectives* series, also cited throughout these chapters. The Kellogg Foundation, Exxon Foundation, Lilly Foundation, MacArthur Foundation, Ford Foundation, Spencer Foundation and a host of other national, regional, and state foundations are also major policy voices in higher education.

GOVERNANCE CHALLENGES

The following are selected leadership challenges that continue to make colle-giate governance a complex matter.

Performance Review

It has been established that faculty are expected to have decision primacy in matters of faculty appointment, promotion, tenure and other forms of recogni-tion. Will a college or university faculty be as diligent and devoted in dealing forthrightly with departures from responsible and effective colleague perfor-mance? There is an unhappy tendency to pass the difficult and thorny "hot potato" decisions to the chair and the dean. This, however, is not responsible behavior and will not enjoy the salute of those who want to honor the principle of shared authority. There can be no shared authority without shared respon-sibility. What does one do with that colleague who is tenured but may only be found in his or her office just a few moments before class and then is ill prepared, according to student reports, and is only marginally involved in the life of the department, college, or institution? What does one do with that colleague whose uncivil behavior in meetings is disruptive and destructive? Will faculty be as assertive and intent in dealing with these performance challenges as they are in fashioning a new course and program proposal or calling to question some action of the dean or chancellor?

Cost Containment Pressures

The pressures to reduce expenditures, reallocate resources, and redefine program priorities are being felt in many colleges and universities at this writing, especially in public institutions. The costs of higher education have risen dramatically and have been rising at a rate significantly higher than the Consumer Price Index. At the same time, support from both federal and state governments has been declining, a matter we engage in chapter six. The pressures to manage resources more effectively, and discontinue or seriously revise programs and services constitute a second major challenge to collegial decision making and to shared authority.

What does one do with a major academic unit whose faculty size is the same as when the enrollment was double its current size, when other academic units have experienced significant enrollment growth but no faculty growth in cost containment times? Will the overstaffed faculty vote itself out of business in a grand display of nobility and collegiality? Will it mandate that some faculty take early retirement?

Will administrative and student services be reduced and who will make those decisions? Will administrators be able to sublimate their welfare and self-interest to discontinue services that can no longer be afforded? Will faculty look over the fence of their academic enclaves at the range and performance of administrative services and will they/should they have a voice in the reduction and/or revision of administrative and student services? Conversely, might financial affairs and student affairs officers have a legitimate right to question expenditures in academic affairs? A July 1995 issue of *Policy Perspectives*, entitled "A Calling to Account," suggests that part of trustee responsibility is "to make certain that the institution does not promise to be 'all things to all people,'" and that trustees should "provide the spur that clarifies institution mission" (p. 8). The challenge of mission refinement and revision constitutes an important and current challenge to governance and teamwork on college campuses.

As the fiscal belt is pulled to a smaller notch, there will be a tendency for self-interests to grow stronger and for community to be weakened. Collegial forms of governance may also be less responsive and responsible, and corporate forms of governance can be more ascendant. A 1996 monograph entitled *Renewing the Academic Presidency*, published by the Association of Governing Boards of Universities and Colleges, argues that the college presidency has become a weakened governance voice and that the authority of presidents must be restored and strengthened. The perspective and theme of this publication reflects the continuing debate over balance of decision authority in collegiate settings. And not unexpectedly we can find a different perspective in an article entitled "Centralizing Governance Isn't Simply Wrong; It's Bad Business, Too" penned by the president of the American Association of University Professors (AAUP) in the February 12, 1999 issue of the *Chronicle of Higher Education* (Richardson, p. B9).

In the view of the authors, the call for more effective resource management will shift a greater burden to college administrators at every level and place before them more intense leadership challenges of compassion and courage as institutions struggle to achieve strategic repositioning.

Public Disclosure and Candor in Decision Making

Clearly, one of the principles that is changing in the life of most contemporary organizations is eliminating the "closet" approach to decision making in favor of the public forum concept. Data on activity, achievement, and finances at the department, division, college, and institutional level are becoming more exposed. The test of public forum is an operational principle that deserves recognition by anyone who plans to hold administrative appointment in colleges and universities. It also deserves recognition by faculty as they make decisions on such things as class size and faculty load and responsibility. Public disclosure tends to furnish more opportunity for conflict, and conflict will continue to prove a test for both collegiality and shared authority.

Academic/Financial Dichotomies

Historically, faculty have tended to emphasize their involvement in academic matters and have not insisted on major engagement in financial matters. A 1968 monograph by Dykes entitled *Faculty Participation in Academic Decision Making* has documented where the bulk of faculty involvement lies. However, this trend is changing. The budget of a department, division, college, or institution is the most fundamental expression of its priorities. And one of the most crucial financial decisions made in an institution concerns personnel positions. When there are retirements, who will make the decisions about whether positions are replaced and where positions will be placed? Since academic programs can be seriously damaged and/or disestablished due to lack of funding, the relationship between academic matters and financial matters is clearly closely related. What information will be brought to focus on these decisions? Here resides one of the major advantages of the joint big decision committee or the strategic planning councils previously described, as they offer some hope of honoring the shared authority and shared responsibility concepts in making difficult strategic decisions.

The Student Voice in Academic Life

The 1966 AAUP *Statement on Government of Colleges and Universities* provides major commentary on the role of the board, president, and faculty. A closing section entitled "On Student Status" points out the impedances to meaningful involvement of students in the governance life of a campus: ". . . inexperience, untested capacity, a transitory status which means that present action does not carry with it subsequent responsibility, and the inescapable fact that the other components of the institution are in a position of judgement over the students" (p. 379).

Ernest Boyer's work *College: The Undergraduate Experience in America*, cited earlier, found that meaningful student involvement in governance was almost nonexistent. Yet the history of American higher education makes it clear that students have been responsible for many policy and program changes in the life of colleges and universities—ranging from the Chautauqua clubs (a series of public lectures) of the 1800s to the range of student activities now found on campus, including intercollegiate athletics. Those faculty and administrators who served during the "time of troubles" of the 1970s would hardly claim that students were uninvolved.

Clearly students are both primary clients and contributors to the quality of their educational life. They are not passive participants in the molding of an educated person. Students furnish the principal voice on what transpires within the confines of classrooms, laboratories, and studios. They offer the principal voice on how a particular academic policy affects their performance and their promise. Students deserve an appropriate voice in the governance of colleges and universities. But what are the appropriate and effective mechanisms for student governance involvement?

Whether or not the current practice of having voting student members on boards of trustees is the best way, it is one way. We have earlier commented on the equity issue of allowing student voices on boards while denying voices to faculty and staff. Students can and should have voice in advisory and advocacy policy committees, along with other campus constituents. This, however, is a matter different from students having a vote on matters affecting their own welfare, which is the case when students hold formal appointment on boards of trustees.

Departments, colleges, and other units are experimenting with student participation in the policy and governance life of those units. Having students present for discussion and debate of academic policy may have a salutary effect on the tone and substance of those discussions. Letting students see the academic process take place can be educational for both faculty and students. It's an appropriate and educational learning exercise where students can experience the responsibility for the consequences of their own decisions.

Political and Policy Pressures

Education in this nation will always reflect the inseparability of political, moral, and educational thought. Current literature makes clear that political officers, in the case of public institutions and often in consort with governing board members, are taking a more activist role in policy formation and evaluation on college and university campuses. The same phenomenon may be seen for private institutions where religious support bodies, again often in consort with board members, are subjecting campuses to forms of policy and personnel micromanagement. This is not a totally new phenomenon in American higher education. What may be new is that many of these policy initiatives represent a more "conservative" tone.

In the best world of collegiate governance, strong boards will select strong presidents who are not just figureheads for board positions, but are scholars who will, as Wildavsky (*Speaking Truth to Power: The Art and Craft of Policy Analysis*, 1979) suggested, speak truth to power. Strong academic leaders will champion what is good and true and will not be puppets of power or popularity. And hopefully faculty will exert their authority and not roll over in the face of political or religious pressures. American higher education is a construction of strong leadership on the part of boards, presidents, and faculty. Shared authority will not work when there is weakness of will, paucity of competence, or absence of courage among any one of the partners.

GOVERNANCE PRINCIPLES

In concluding this chapter, we accent the fundamental philosophical principles that undergird the decision and authority of American colleges and universities. We elect to place these principles in the form of competing concepts that require continuous attention to balance.

Autonomy and Accountability

Fundamentally, the pursuit of truth requires that faculty are free from unwarranted political or governmental intrusion into their inquiries, from meddling that hampers or interferes with following their curiosity. But there can be no such thing as autonomy without accountability. Faculty and administrators are first accountable to their primary clients—their students. Second, they are accountable to one another, as peer professionals. Finally, they are accountable to the boards who hold campus in legal trust and to those who furnish the financial support that makes the pursuit of truth possible. Maintaining this combination of independence and linkage will remain a leadership challenge of the first order.

Rights and Responsibility

Closely allied with the previous concept is the balancing of authority and responsibility. Clearly faculty have primacy of authority on those academic decisions of both program and personnel policy that most directly affect the quality and integrity of an institution. Their professional competence and character will, in effect, define the climate and standards of the institution. However, their values and their will to accept responsibility for the evaluation of performance not only of students and administrators but of themselves will be an essential complement to the maintenance of their proper authority. Likewise administrators and board members must honor the formal authority of their roles by the responsible discharge of duty.

Professional Interests and Public Interests

It may be argued with some force that this particular tension is simply another way to state the autonomy/accountability concept. For educators, we will certainly want a high degree of professional competence and will want to invest that professional with a high degree of trust.

Knowing the dangers of unchecked power and the narrowness and arrogance that can be associated with professional power, we will want to insist that professionals in colleges and universities live at the feet of the people—which is what we should want and promote for other professions in our society as well. A faculty member, student, or college administrator who cannot make a cogent and sensible argument for a program or policy in a public forum deserves, at a minimum, close scrutiny.

Board members and administrators are aware of how political interference can smother the flame of curiosity, so they will buffer faculty from unwarranted meddling and threats to their welfare when unpopular issues are placed on the table for discussion. The power of public forum is a useful instrument, but not an infallible instrument, for enhancing the power of professional judgment and for protecting public interests.

Whatever form governance arrangements may take, they will continue to recognize the tensioned principles just elucidated. Faculty who have the competence to be involved in decision making but who lack responsibility and integrity invite intrusion into their domains of competence. Administrators and board members who fail in their courage and their integrity invite the scorn of those for whom they are stewards and servants. Those who desire autonomy but who are unwilling to accept responsibility invite the cynicism of those who understand that one cannot exist independent of the other.

Diversity and Community

Understandably and appropriately, colleges and universities have been the organization in our national life where the importance of diversity has been centered. Treating each and every person in our society with dignity is essential to a free and democratic society. The debilitating and demeaning effects of systematic and personal prejudice—whether of race, gender, or belief—are enemies of an educated person. Patterson's book *When Learned Men Murder* (1996) keeps us sober minded about whether we may always equate formal educational credentials with humanistic values and the salute of personal dignity. The honoring of diversity with dignity remains an important principle of college life.

As we have already noted in this chapter, our society is more than a collection of individuals and groups pursuing their own self-interest. And our colleges are more than corporate hierarchies and collegial panels. There is community, the core values and commitments that bind us together in shared enterprise, in achievements and endeavors that are more than simply a sum of parts. In addition to Boyer, other scholars writing on the importance of community include Robert Bellah, et al. (*Habits of the Hearts*, 1985), Parker Palmer, (*Change*, 1987), Amitai Etzioni (*The Spirit of Community*, 1993), and Arthur Schlesinger (*The Disuniting of America*, 1992). Defining an agenda of common caring is essential work for an educational community, for without community there will be no caring, and without caring there will be no quality or integrity.

Consensus and Conflict

In this discussion and in others, much is made of the importance of consensus in collegial forms of governance so central to colleges and universities.

The test of "agreement," however, is a test that yields only one half of truth in healthy academic cultures. The test of "adversity," the crucible of contest and conflict, gives us access to the other half of truth in academic life. In an organization that depends upon the public testing of ideas in adversarial forum, composed of men and women who have competing conceptions of reality and how truth is accessed, goverance health and reality must embrace both conflict and consensus.

Leadership in collegiate culture must make provision for differences to be entertained and honored, and we speak here of leadership from both faculty and administrative officers. To make enemies of those with whom we disagree, to attribute mean motives to those who offer contrasting perspective, to accuse those who may oppose us as frail spirits afraid of change and progress— these are not behaviors that construct healthy and effective governance climates on campus.

Diversity of personality and perspective within academic settings must be honored because this diversity contributes a wider range of viewpoints and creative perspective in our search for truth in physical, social, and spiritual realms. We honor community to reveal those value commitments that we hold in common and that are essential to the nurture of quality in any educational setting. There is no way to honor diversity and community without the thoughtful orchestration of consensus and conflict.

Complacency and Courage

In public remarks before policy makers in California, Patrick Callan noted that

> It is much more difficult for those successful institutions that have been acknowledged as such to look beyond their boundaries and identify emerging problems. It is hard for them to see those things in the environment that may suggest that future success will not keep flowing from the same factors that brought success in the past. . . . The most successful corporations in the world—the automobile industry and companies like IBM and General Motors, for example—were unable to recognize those signs in the environment which called for fundamental change. They believed that doing better what they had always done would still allow them to compete. They suffered a great dislocation as a result. Higher education, therefore, must put account-ability issues in the context of recognizing, "Yes, we are successful, but

as individuals and as institution, that very success can get in the way of change (1994, p. 1).

Thus, even as we acknowledge the important principles that undergird collegiate governance and as we celebrate the distinctive strengths of governance in American higher education, the moment calls for a vigilance, an alertness, and exercise of the imagination to enhance our decision and authority patterns to meet the challenges now facing our colleges and universities.

CHAPTER 4

Competence and Conscience

The Challenges of Curriculum and Program Design

I s college-level learning to be undertaken for the simple pleasure of know ing, doing, discerning meaning, creating, or for working and serving? In chapter three on governance, we indicated that one of the freedoms ordinarily reserved to the faculty of American colleges and universities was the freedom to decide on educational purpose, content, and methodology. These are questions and issues of curriculum design. This design work is the central responsibility of the faculty and the heart of the collegiate enterprise. It is also the locus of major debate and dissent within colleges and universities.

This chapter will enable us to (1) trace the evolution of academic creden-tials and programs in American higher education; (2) identify the philosophic questions that undergird issues of educational purpose, content, and method at the college level; and (3) examine selected curricular reform proposals. The curriculum is the place where contesting philosophies of educational purpose and method are engaged and debated. Metaphors of war abound in this debate. We begin with the most fundamental business, the structure of academic degrees.

THE STRUCTURE OF ACADEMIC DEGREES

While it is clear from chapter two on mission that students enroll in colleges and universities for a variety of purposes, and that personal/professional renewal and continuing education are relatively new and vital reasons for enrollment, historically the principal purpose has been to earn a degree and to get a job. An academic degree is a formal certification of knowledge and proficiency, confirmed by a faculty and administration and conferred by the authority of an institution's governing board.

The use of academic degrees is of relatively recent historic origin. The first-known degree was the doctorate awarded at the University of Bologna in the middle of the twelfth century. The bachelor's and master's degrees did not come into use until later. The use of academic degrees spread from the European continent to Britain, where the bachelor's degree was the preeminent degree. Academic degrees in American higher education may be categorized into five levels.

TABLE 4.1	
TYPE OF DEGREE AND YEARS OF STUDY	
Associate's	Two years of study
Bachelor's	Four years of study
Master's	One to two years of study beyond bachelor's
Doctorate	Two years of study beyond master's plus dissertation

Associate's Degree

The associate's degree is the newest to be awarded by American colleges, usually by two-year community and technical colleges. Though the associate's degree was awarded as early as 1875 by a British institution, the degree has its principal American origins in the junior division of the University of Chicago (Eells, 1963), where it was awarded for the two-year program of study in the junior college. The degree was first authorized in 1899 and first awarded in 1900. The associate of arts and the associate of science is awarded to students who complete a two-year curriculum aimed primarily for transfer to a senior college. The associate of applied science is awarded to students who complete a program of study leading to immediate employment, usually in some technical or applied field, including engineering, health, and business. While the University of Chicago appears to have been the first American institution to award the associate's degree, the university discontinued that degree 20 years later, and the degree has eventually become the primary credential of American two-year community and technical colleges.

Bachelor's Degree

From the opening of Harvard in the middle seventeenth century until the Civil War, the American college offered only one degree, the bachelor of arts. The bachelor of science degree was added by Harvard in the middle of the nineteenth century. During the colonial period, the bachelor's degree represented prescribed study in the classics—philosophy, religion, language, mathematics—with the aim of preparing learned clergy and other leaders.

Eventually modern languages, sciences, literature, social studies, and applied arts and sciences were added to the curriculum of the bachelor's degree. The prescribed curriculum gave way to the elective system, and the preparation of clergy was the groundwork for both citizenship and employment.

Clark (1987) indicates that fields of study have come into the college curriculum via four processes: partition, affiliation, dignification, and dispersion. For example, the partition of biology first into botany and zoology and later into other fields such as genetics is one path of curricular development. The movement of such applied fields as law and medicine—once learned through apprenticeship—represents the expansion of curriculum through affiliation. Nursing moved from hospitals, and law enforcement moved from police training centers. The recognition of modern languages and some forms of technology reflect the process of what Clark calls dignification. Finally, there is the dispersion of a single discipline into many other fields, such as the expansion of literature and history. The following chart adapted from Gruber, and also reported in Clark, furnishes an arresting perspective on the growth of academic disciplines:

TABLE 4.2

GROWTH IN NUMBER OF DISCIPLINES

Year	Number of Disciplines	Percentage
Pre 1800	2	1
1800 - 1899	36	9
1900 - 1939	101	28
1940 - 1959	77	21
1960 - 1985	150	41

Source: *Encyclopedia of Associations*, Katherine Gruber, ed. (Detroit, Gale Research Co., 1985).

Clearly, the major explosion of knowledge is a phenomenon primarily of the twentieth century. With this dramatic expansion in knowledge and fields of study, we may understand afresh the issues that surround the question of who is an educated person.

First granted by Harvard in 1642, the bachelor's degree has evolved from an earlier narrow and prescribed curriculum to a degree generally embracing three components. Today's undergraduate student completes a "general education" component designed to develop fundamental intellectual skills, such as communication and critical thinking. This component may also represent other goals: understanding different modes of thought, and ways in which we access truth or acquire cultural, historic, and economic sensitivity. The second component is the "major," in which the student develops in-depth knowledge of a single field of study. Finally, there is an "elective" component that encourages the student to take a selection of other courses that may complement his or her major or that may represent other interests and learning goals of the student. Among the better-known bachelor's degrees beyond the well known bachelor of arts and bachelor of science are the bachelor of science in education, bachelor of business administration, bachelor of science in engineering, and bachelor of music.

Master's Degree

Originating at the University of Paris in the twelfth century, this degree was originally a formal designation of a licensed teacher in the faculty of arts (Spurr, 1970, p. 63). Requirements for the master's degree were specified in the incorporation of Harvard University:

> Every Schollar that giveth up in writing a System, or Synopsis or summe of Logick, Naturall and Morall Phylosophy, Arithmetick, Geometry, and Astronomy; and is ready to defend his Theses or positions: withall skilled in the Originalls as above said: and of godly life and conversation; and so approved by the Overseers and Master of the Colledge, at any publique Act, is fit to be dignified with his 2nd Degree (Statutes of Harvard, 1646).

Originally, the master's degree represented one to three years of study beyond the bachelor's degree, and for many was the terminal degree. For a period of time in the late eighteenth century and early nineteenth century, the master's degree fell into disrepute. Some suggested that the requirements amounted to staying out of jail for three years and paying the requisite five dollar fee. The rehabilitation of the degree took place in the mid and late nineteenth century when completing a formal course of study, passing an examination, and presenting/defending a thesis was constituted. Beyond the master of arts and master of science, a range of master's degrees is now offered under two general categories that include liberal arts master's degrees and professional master's degrees. The latter include such degrees as the master of business administration, master of education, and master of theology. For some fields, the master's degree is considered the terminal degree and requires two to three years of study beyond the bachelor's degree. The master of fine arts (M.F.A.) and master of planning are two such examples. In the latter half of the twentieth century, the thesis requirement has been eliminated for many master's degrees, where the design, development, presentation, and defense of a major paper and/or research project may be no longer required. For some programs, neither a comprehensive examination nor a thesis is required. In some cases, students complete a "problems paper," which explores some theme in detail with an in-depth literature review.

Intermediate Degrees

Several degrees between the master's degree and the doctoral degree have been proposed and tested. Spurr (1970) provides an informing review of these degrees, including the master of philosophy, a degree representing completion of course work toward a doctorate but not requiring the dissertation. The appellation "candidate in philosophy" has also been offered by some institutions to represent significant advanced graduate work without the dissertation. Another intermediate degree offered by many institutions is the specialist in education degree (Ed.S.). This degree represents an additional year to year and a half of graduate study beyond the master's degree for students in the field of education, and usually requires a major paper or thesis. Many school systems offer pay incentives for teachers and administrators who complete graduate work beyond the master's degree.

Doctoral Degrees

Clearly, the most recognized doctoral degree is the doctor of philosophy degree (Ph.D.), which was first offered in this country by Yale University in 1861. Most scholars attribute the development of the Ph.D. in this country, however, to the founding of Johns Hopkins University in 1876. At that time, the degree represented two years of graduate study and the submission of a thesis that might be considered relatively lenient under present-day standards. In the early years of the twentieth century, standards for the degree became more rigorous and fixed, representing three years of study (including at least a year in residence), passing a comprehensive examination, and submitting and defending a dissertation.

Debate continues to swirl about the purpose and content of the Ph.D., and we will discuss this topic further in chapter eight. Is it a research degree, a teaching degree, or a professional degree? At present, much academic disagreement abounds. In some schools, both the Ph.D. and perhaps other professional degrees, such as the doctor of education (Ed.D.) or the doctor of business administration (D.B.A.), are offered with hard-to-detect differences between the two degrees, except for the possibility of language proficiency for the Ph.D. And even the language requirement has been eliminated for many Ph.D. degrees.

Primarily a development of the twentieth century, other doctoral degrees have also emerged to serve different purposes and fields. The doctor of musical arts is a degree designed to represent the highest level of musical performance and composition. As noted, the doctor of business administration and the doctor of education are professional degrees. The quality of the degree is directly dependent upon the standards and expectations of the faculty. While at some institutions the professional degree may permit a more expeditious passage to the degree, in other institutions a professional degree equals or surpasses the Ph.D. in course requirements.

Finally, we have important professional degrees in medicine (M.D.), dentistry (D.D.), religion (D.M.), and law (J.D.). The culminating degree in law has shown interesting development in the twentieth century and illustrates the growth of academic fields of study previously cited by Clark. In its earlier years, law was an apprentice preparation. In the second half of the twentieth century, students could be admitted for the study of law following two years of undergraduate work and earning the bachelor of laws (LL.B.) degree. More recently, however, admission to law school has required the completion of an undergraduate bachelor's degree, and the first degree of law is now the juris doctor degree (J.D.).

Post Doctoral Recognition

Spurr (1970) has identified the extensive practice, especially in the sciences, of post doctoral study in this country, where students undertake more specialized study and/or research following the doctoral degree. At present, there is little formal recognition of such study or creative achievement with yet another degree, though Spurr has suggested the doctor of natural philosophy as such a recognition.

For those interested in more in-depth coverage of academic degree structures and history, the following books by Eells and Spurr will be of interest: *Academic Degree Structures: Innovative Approaches*, by Stephen H. Spurr, 1970; and *Degrees in Higher Education*, by Walter Crosby Eells, 1963.

For a perspective on the number of degrees awarded each year, Table 4.3 presents an approximation for the year 1994–95:

TABLE 4.3	
NUMBER OF DEGREES AWARDED, 1994–95	
Associate's Degrees	539,691
Bachelor's Degrees	1,160,134
Master's Degrees	397,629
Doctoral Degrees	44,446
Professional Degrees (Law, Medicine, etc.)	75,800

Source: Almanac Issue, *Chronicle of Higher Education,* August 28, 1998.

CHALLENGES OF EDUCATIONAL PURPOSE

Questions of curriculum design embrace the identification of educational goals for courses, programs and degrees; the selection of appropriate learning experiences; and the evaluation and certification of what has been learned. Each of these questions calls us to complex philosophic puzzles.

For example, if we engage only the first question of goals and objectives, we are quickly immersed in deep philosophic water. Are the purposes of education related to knowing, doing, feeling, or some combination of these? Shall we be reading Dante's *Inferno* or Ralph Ellison's *The Invisible Man*? Will a biography of Margaret Sanger prove more informing than a biography of Malcolm X? Are there multiple forms of intelligence as suggested by Howard Gardner (1983), Robert Sternberg (1988), and Daniel Goleman (1995)? Should we be shifting our attention from teaching to learning, from the process to the product? In chapter two, we suggested several purposes for collegiate education, and these come to play in curriculum design. Having some appreciation for how we advance on truth, developing advanced intellectual skill in communication and critical thinking, evaluating our value dispositions and understanding how these affect decision, appreciating the cultural heritage of our society, acquiring skill that allows one to do meaningful work, appreciating the role of arts in the enrichment of life—all of these purposes are worthy of an occupation in higher education.

Debate over educational purposes is not a new debate, as any reading of history and philosophy will affirm. Among the ancient Greeks, several schools of thought were predominant. For Plato, the purpose of philosophic study was to produce enlightened rulers and political advisors, a philosophy with elite and applied flavor. Aristotle's goal seems to have centered on methods of reasoning and analysis that enabled one to access and test truth. Antisthenes, Diogenes, and Zeno were authors of stoicism, a system that defies easy summary but that accents happiness and fulfillment derived from a life that is accepting of both pain and pleasure and that is lived with dictates of reason. From Epicurus flowed a fourth school of thought accenting the pursuit of emotional tranquility, self-discipline, and spiritual contemplation. As we shall soon see, elements of these ancient streams of thought have remained interestingly contemporary. A major nineteenth century voice on the purpose of higher education was John Henry Cardinal Newman, whose premier work, *The Idea of a University*, opens with the following statement in the preface: "The view taken of a University in these Discourses is the following: That it is a place of teaching universal knowledge. This implies that its object is, on the one hand, intellectual, not moral; and, on the other, that it is the diffusion and extension of knowledge rather than the advancement. If its object were scientific and philosophical discovery, I do not see why a University should have students; if religious training, I do not see how it can be the seat of literature and science" (Newman, 1982, p. xxxvii). If we follow the vision of Newman, we would not have research in the university, nor perhaps would we concern ourselves with the challenge and nurture of values.

In his essays *The Aims of Education*, Alfred North Whitehead, a scholar bridging the nineteenth and twentieth centuries, defines education as "the acquisition of the art of the utilization of knowledge" (1957, p. 4). In serious departure from Newman, Whitehead avers that "The essence of education is that it be religious. . . . A religious education is an education which inculcates duty and reverence"(p. 14). These are interesting lines from a scholar who was a mathematician, and Whitehead's view stands in bold contrast to the thoughts of Newman, who was a cleric.

In his essay "Universities and Their Function," Whitehead (1957) comments as follows: "The justification for a university is that it preserves the connection between knowledge and the zest for life, by uniting the young and the old in the imaginative consideration of learning. . . . The tragedy of the world is that those who are imaginative have but slight experience, and those who are experienced have feeble imaginations. Fools act on imagination without knowledge; pedants act on knowledge without imagination. The task of a university is to weld together imagination and experience" (p. 93). Bringing together imagination and experience is a worthy guide for the design of any educational experience.

Whitehead's works have a crisp and concise grasp on the purposes of education. Consider, for example, these one-line reflections taken from his essays on *Adventures of Ideas* (1933): "Knowledge is always accompanied with accessories of emotion and purpose (p. 4). . . . The history of ideas is a history of mistakes. . . . The creation of the world—that is to say the world of civilized order—is the victory of persuasion over force" (p. 25). Emotion, mistakes, persuasion—it would be difficult to find lines more intriguing than these to circumscribe the purposes of contemporary higher education.

An interrogatory diversion is in order here concerning Whitehead's note on mistakes. What do we teach college students about the role of mistakes and failures in the advance of truth? Do they learn about the power of mistakes in scientific inquiry when we send them into labs to perform "canned" experiments? Do they learn about the power of persistence and prejudice in these confined learning exercises? Do they learn that failures in intellectual inquiry often harbor the seeds of new thought paradigms? In his book *Medusa and the Snail*, American physician and scholar Lewis Thomas (1974) mused that "If we were not provided with the knack of being wrong, we could never get anything useful done. . . . The capacity to leap across mountains of information to land lightly on the wrong side represents the highest of human endowments" (pp. 37, 39).

John Dewey is certainly a well known and often quoted American philosopher of education. A seminal work is *Democracy and Education* (1916). Dewey emphasized the power of experience and problem solving. The purpose of education, in his view, was to link learning with life, and to place essentials first and refinements second (Dewey, 1916, p. 191). Dewey believed that the compartmentalized and discipline-based college or university worked against both experience-based education and the integration of knowledge. The dichotomies of liberal education and vocational education, of learning by knowing and learning by doing, of intellect and values, ultimately work against the true purposes of education, which seek integration and application. Deciding what is an "essential" and what is a "refinement," however, are not trivial judgments.

Another scholar offering views in contrast to Newman is Thorstein Veblen, who would not exclude research from the purposes of college but would exclude professional and utilitarian education. In *The Higher Learning in America* (1918), Veblen comments as follows: "Vocational training is training for proficiency in some gainful occupation, and it has no connection with the higher learning" (p. 14). Veblen's idea was that practical learning is corrupting to "the higher learning." His view of the "utilitarians" is not kind: "Utilitarians are, without intending it, placed in a false position, which unavoidably leads them to court a specious appearance of scholarship, and so to invest their technological discipline with a degree of pedantry and sophistication; whereby it is hoped to give these schools and their work some scientific and scholarly prestige, and so lift it to that dignity that is presumed to attach to a non-utilitarian pursuit of learning" (p. 23).

If we follow the philosophic disposition of Veblen, we invite literature, science, and philosophy into the house of higher learning, but banish to another house the engagements of engineering, computer science, medicine, law, business, and education.

Abraham Flexner, one of the more influential voices in early twentieth century American higher education, was not far from the views of Veblen when he suggested in his major work *Universities: American, English, and German* (1930) that "A modern university would . . . address itself wholeheartedly and unreservedly to the advancement of knowledge, the study of problems, from whatever source they come, and the training of men"(p. 24). Flexner, however, would not advance the public service mission of higher education, suggesting that it is not the work of the university to do anything about problems being studied.

For Robert Maynard Hutchins, scholar and college president, "The aim of the university is to tame the pretensions and excesses of experts and specialists by drawing them into the academic circle and subjecting them to the criticism of other disciplines" (p. 165). One of Hutchins' major works was entitled, like

Veblen's, *The Higher Learning in America* (1936). His vision of the university was that it would be a place for students to study the great books, the great ideas. His curriculum would be the same for all students and there would be no electives.

While the "great books" theme has faded at the University of Chicago, that philosophical design holds center stage at St. John's College in Baltimore. We might note that the drive from St. John's College to the United States Naval Academy, both schools located in Annapolis, Maryland, is a relatively short one, but the philosophic distance in curriculum purpose and design between the two schools is extensive.

Ernest Boyer was an active and well-respected scholar on the purposes of American higher education toward the end of this century. After observing that students completing the bachelor's degree, and advanced degrees as well, were busy in the pursuit of pay, prestige, and power, he reflected on the purposes of the undergraduate experience:

> In the end, the quality of the undergraduate experience is to be measured by the willingness of graduates to be socially and civically engaged. . . . Is it too much to expect that even in this hard-edged, competitive age, a college graduate will live with integrity, civility— even compassion? Is it appropriate to hope that the lessons learned in a liberal education will reveal themselves in the humaneness of the graduate's relationships with others? (Boyer, 1987, pp. 278–79).

Boyer reinserts questions of community, caring, emotional maturity, and moral competence into those that are posed about the purposes of a college education.

A contemporary scholar with Boyer, Howard Bowen's position affirms Boyer's posture, as Bowen postulated a cluster of both individual and societal developmental goals for higher education in his book *Investment in Learning* (1978). For Bowen, the collegiate experience should be designed to yield cognitive, intellectual, emotional, and moral development; and practical competencies that included interpersonal, citizenship, and economic (work) skills. Societal goals of higher education include the advancement of knowledge, discovery and encouragement of talent, advancement of civic welfare.

Two other scholars prominent in the latter part of the twentieth century furnish perspective on the purposes of a college education and their curricular implications. Developing a tripartite taxonomy of educational objectives, Benjamin Bloom suggested developmental objectives in three domains: cognitive or intellectual, affective or emotional, and psychomotor or physical (Bloom, 1956). In the cognitive domain, for example, Bloom suggested a taxonomy of increasing complexity and sophistication in intellectual function through the following: knowledge, comprehension, application, analysis, synthesis, and evaluation.

How many college professors still think of teaching as telling and learning as the simple acquisition of knowledge . . . and thus structure their courses, tests, and evaluations to examine only this first order intellectual skill?

In an important and widely cited work entitled *Education and Identity*, first issued by Chickering (1969) and published in second edition by Chickering and Reisser (1993), seven developmental vectors were suggested for students in higher education:

1. Developing competence
2. Managing emotions
3. Acquiring autonomy
4. Establishing identity
5. Freeing interpersonal relationships
6. Advancing purpose
7. Forming integrity

This is a legitimate but complex array of developmental purposes for higher education and requires more than simple thinking about whether the student should have six or twelve hours of English and more than one course in mathematics.

How, then, shall faculty think about this philosophic stew and the implications for curriculum design? Shall they think first about the individual student and his/her developmental needs, or shall they think first about the structure of disciplines and fields of study and what they have to contribute to knowledge? Shall they think first about abstractions and theories or about policies and problems, a reflective versus action contention? Shall they think first about autonomy and design for an individual or about conformity, the knowledge and skill that should be common to any degree program. Shall they think first about the need for integration or about the need for specialization? Where indeed in an institution organized around specialized disciplines is integration promoted? Shall they think first about the need to nurture a liberally educated person or shall they think about the need to nurture a vocationally competent person? The continua of philosophical tensions are formidable:

- Culture versus utility
- Depth versus breadth
- Student versus subject
- Election versus prescription
- Mind versus body
- Rationality versus morality
- Theory versus application
- Integration versus specialization

Thus, we have a wide-ranging debate on educational purpose. However, we have not yet ventured into other thorny issues of curriculum design that ask, for example, how shall we recognize the Western and European heritage of American higher education and also appreciate the intellectual contributions of other cultures over the world? And what precisely are the elements of knowledge (scientific, literary, economic, historical, geographical, etc.) that we should master to be, what E. D. Hirsch (1987) calls "culturally literate?" What does it mean to be an educated person in today's world?

In a pluralistic society and in an organization that reveres different modes of thought and ways of accessing truth, is it likely that we could expect academics to fashion a single definition of what it means to be an educated person? It's improbable and perhaps even undesirable.

CHALLENGES OF CONTENT AND METHOD

While we are contending with these questions, a host of contemporary external forces impinge on our curricular deliberations. There are social and economic forces that recognize increasing international independence and the need to understand and appreciate cultures beyond our own. There are the forces of international economic competition and the uneven distribution of scarce economic resources in the world. There are equity struggles of gender and race. There are changes in population composition and age taking place. There are space races and concern for environment that compete for attention.

Rapid emergence of technologies constitutes another force on the curriculum. In a century that has seen the development of atomic and nuclear power, electricity and electronics, air and space travel, computers and the Internet, and the emergence of genetics and genetic engineering, what it means to be an educated person has become an even more complex inquiry than in previous centuries.

Political battles over balanced state and federal budgets have their impact on curricular issues as well. Colleges and universities that grew so dramatically during the years of enrollment, institutional, and financial expansion find curricular decisions more painful and difficult in a time of cost containment and retrenchment—to say nothing of political pressures designed to increase higher education accountability.

When there is plenty of money and courses and programs may be added, the curricular debate is less lively and intense because we do not have to make choices. However, this does not hold true in cost containment times.

Clearly there is ample philosophic tension with the first question of curricular design, educational purpose. The challenges do not become any easier as we explore the many ways of organizing and delivering instruction. Consider the range of options for the orchestration of instruction and learning: lecture, laboratory, gaming and simulation, case study, problem-based learning, tutorial/independent study, seminar, internship/practicum/residency, distance learning, computer-managed instruction, discovery and service learning, technology, and the Internet.

Regarding the Internet, for example, the influence of technology is to be felt in issues of content, delivery, and quality. While we may debate the extent to which television as a technology has influenced major changes in collegiate learning, as it clearly has had some impact. The National Technological University is a consortium of several institutions that more than 20 years ago formed an organization to deliver graduate instruction in engineering via satellite and television. The development of "smart" classrooms in which faculty may, via television, work with students in an on-campus site and other students at "distance learning" sites, and enjoy interaction with both groups of students is not an uncommon technology venture for campuses, some systems, and states.

It is in the field of computer and information technology, however, that lie possible tectonic shifts in the way in which we think about learning at every level. Anyone who has examined the fascination of computer games, explored the power of computer simulations, and experienced the power of computers for enhancing research and communication has a hint of what is possible here.

A view of the world through the World Wide Web is sweeping the country, and no one seems to know what the possibilities—and liabilities—may be for learning and for community. To understand that tomorrow's learners may carry in their palm a device that gives them access not only to great university libraries but to a host of other formal and informal learning resources worldwide urges a profound rethinking of both teaching and learning.

And how will we work with issues of quality in the "virtual university?" Will technology make conventional degree credentials obsolete, yielding to other forms of demonstrating mastery? Will learning really become more collaborative or will learners live more in isolation and solitude? Will morally bent educational entrepreneurs find the World Wide Web a new way to offer empty and shoddy credentials, as suggested in a story appearing in the December 19, 1997, issue of the *Chronicle of Higher Education* (Guernsey, 1997)? And what are the implications for nurturing community and developing essential social skills?

Technology holds promise of a formidable change in the way in which we think about learning and about the nature of colleges and universities. Both the idea of a university and the uses of a university may be changing dramatically in the coming years.

Perhaps as dramatic in its potential for changing our ideas of teaching and learning is the increasing employment of what some call discovery, service, and experiential learning. Tracing imaginative new approaches to experiential learning in settings both national and international, David Lempert (1996) writes in *Escape From the Ivory Tower* that faculty and universities will need to become guides instead of taskmasters (p. 4). Discovery and service learning ventures take students from the confines of classrooms and laboratories into community service settings that include political, environmental, economic, and social challenges. Lempert advocates learning activities that "combine theory with empiricism," an accent on learning by doing, and "combining theory with practice,"—an accent on community service. John Dewey would have liked Lempert's approach to learning.

As with Lempert's book on discovery and experiential learning, entire books have been written on each of the above approaches to instruction and learning. Each of these works builds on some theory of learning, and we have not even touched in this discussion the different theoretical foundations of human learning. Thus, faculty responsibilities for selecting and organizing learning experiences may call on extensive philosophic and theoretical literature. Teaching can be a highly complex art form, a theme to which we will return in chapter eight.

CHALLENGES OF TESTING AND EVALUATION

After the identification of instructional goals and objectives and the selection of appropriate teaching and learning strategies, there remains the obligation of discerning what has been learned. The testing and evaluation of learning is one performance arena where too many college teachers remain amateurs.

A simple demonstration can expose the dangers of being a pedagogical amateur, especially in testing. Consider a 10-question, true-false test and have a class, audience, or other group of participants guess at the 10 true-false questions and write down in advance what they think the answers should be. Then give the participants the correct answers by assigning "T" and "F" in some random order. The mean grade, even in a small group, will almost always be 50 percent and often much higher, with some participants making grades of 80, 90 and 100 even though they have no concept of what the content of the test is about. A student in heavy mental fog with no knowledge whatsoever of the topic under evaluation may make a decent grade on a true-false test just by guessing. How often do we continue to see this approach to evaluation of student learning?

There is serious and substantive literature available on the theory of testing and evaluation. To construct effective objective tests with high reliability and validity is an important skill. Too many professors are unaware that all tests may have error derived from both test conditions and test construction, and this lack of awareness may lead them to believe that a student's score is a true and unvarying expression of ability or achievement. Poor measurement leads to inappropriate and inaccurate decision, and decisions on human talent are important decisions.

Beyond the more conventional paper and pencil assessments are the possibilities of more imaginative and realistic assessments involving performances that reveal mastery of knowledge and skill. Astin's (1993a) and Banta's (1994, 1995)works on the theory and practice of assessment reveal just how rich this literature has grown. Readers interested in good general references on the theory and philosophy of testing and evaluation are referred to a concise work by Ohmer Milton entitled *The Testing and Grading of Students* (1976), and a more recent work by Erwin, *Assessing Student Learning and Development* (1991). There is also emerging literature on computer-adaptive testing that shows how the power of computers allows more efficient diagnostic of learning skills, and which diagnostic may then be combined with computer-managed learning programs.

PROPOSALS FOR CURRICULAR REFORM—THE METAPHORS OF WAR

"But one need look no further than the curricular wars to understand that most students are not looking to broaden their spiritual or intellectual horizons. They see themselves as consumers buying a product, and insist on applying egalitarian rules of the marketplace to what used to be an unchallenged elitism of the intellect" (Henry, 1994, p. 158). Extracted from William Henry's *In Defense of Elitism*, this comment furnishes flavor for curricular debate and reform proposals in higher education. We see the kinds of metaphors used to describe that debate, and most often they are metaphors of war. An example of this is Carnochan's *The Battleground of the Curriculum* (1993).

Before we tour the "battlefield," it may prove useful to encourage a constructive perspective on the conflict and the metaphors. Students enter undergraduate and graduate school expecting, reasonably enough, that some folks are expected to know more than others, and professors should know something that their students don't know. And that something should presumably include knowledge and conviction about curriculum design. If we may return to chapter two on mission and recall the "forum" mission we cited there, the testing and evaluation of ideas in public forum. The "ivory tower," it turns out, is a raucous place—full of dissent and debate, prejudice and politics.

Why should we expect colleges and universities to serve as the "forum" for examining contesting ideas without expecting the curriculum, which delivers those ideas, to also be a place of contest and conflict? There is no need to shield our students from the knowledge that professors have widely different perspectives on curriculum. It might be argued that signs of conflict and contest over the curriculum are signs of health, not pathology.

In *Beyond the Culture Wars*, Gerald Graff (1992) not only gives us another war metaphor but indicates that "The history of modern American education has pitted the liberal pluralist solution (everyone do his or her own thing) against the conservative solution (everyone do the conservative's thing)" (Graff, 1992, p. 10). He further argues ". . . that the best solution to today's conflicts over culture is to teach the conflicts themselves, making them part of our object of study and using them as a new kind of organizing principle to give the curriculum clarity and focus that almost all sides now agree that it lacks" (p. 12).

Accenting the conflict and adding to our war metaphors, Huber (1992) reminds us that "Historical perspective helps our understanding of the curricular wars. Professor-bashing for inculcating subversive doctrines into innocent minds is as old as Socrates, as yesterday as McCarthyism, and as today as beliefs termed 'politically correct'" (p. 41).

In today's argument, those of more traditional persuasion inside and outside the academy argue that there is a canon of great works whose origins are to be found primarily in Western civilization. Residing primarily in the ancient cultures of Greece and Rome and the historic cultures of Europe, Scotland, England, Wales, and Ireland, these works of history and literature furnish the foundation of American culture and constitute the proper and first engagement of the collegiate mind.

In contrast, those of revisionist view hold that this canon is confined by a Eurocentrist bias for the works of mostly white males and is impoverished by its disregard of so great a range of other authors of female gender and diverse ethnicity. This traditional curriculum, whose imminent decline is so greatly lamented by the above conservative scholars, ignores the reality that American culture has been forged from cultural origins of significant diversity.

These contrasting perspectives give us a glimpse as to why war metaphors are used with such frequency in describing curricular debates. More importantly they emphasize the inherent mission duality of modern colleges and universities. These institutions are bastions of free inquiry and aggressive explorers of truth. On the other hand, our colleges and universities are also centers of intellectual authority. Conserving the heritage and challenging the heritage is not a small or simple task.

One of the consequences of increasing diversity of students, faculty, and institutions is a diminishing of unanimity. Historian Lawrence Levine (1996) notes that in earlier, more homogeneous moments in our colleges and universities there was "more, not less, of what today is called political correctness" (p. 28). Readers interested in informing and lively treatments on this theme will find the two works by Henry and Levine previously cited to be provocative intellectual fare.

How can we produce conviction in our students without making them prisoners of a single point of view? How can we alert them to the existence of multiple truths, without leaving them with the idea that there are no anchors? We must place them on the field of debate, in a place rich in potential for learning and in a place with perhaps a bit more intellectual risk. One might ask, however, whether "meaningful" learning, which we earlier celebrated, will be forthcoming without risk.

As a note of historic perspective, the latter part of the nineteenth century featured a "battle" between the proponents and opponents of elective curricula. Opening this debate was Harvard President Charles Eliot, who argued for student choice among a wider range of courses. In rejoinder, Yale University President Noah Porter argued against pandering to popular prejudices and suggested that studies which the student might least desire might also be the studies which the student might most need for correction of ignorance and wayward impulses.

The range of philosophic issues in curriculum design is displayed most sharply in the debate over the content of general education curriculum, the foundation of the American bachelor's degree. Certainly the argument about what knowledge and skill should be mastered by all receiving the bachelor's degree is not a new argument. In illustration, we may begin with the *Yale Report of 1828*, come forward to the Harvard "Redbook" report of 1945, *General Education in a Free Society*, and then consider a host of more contemporary reports in recent years to obtain some sense of the sweep of argument on this theme over time. As an interesting aside, many of the features of the Harvard plan were adopted in institutions across the country though rejected by the Harvard faculty. The 1828 Yale report served to dampen curricular innovation in the early years of the nineteenth century by reaffirming the role and place of classical study. Earlier in that report, we are given to understand the principles undergirding the classical curriculum: "The two great points to be gained in intellectual culture, are the discipline and the furniture of the mind; expanding its powers, and storing it with knowledge" (Yale Report of 1928 in Hofstadter and Smith, 1961, p. 278). The theory of mental discipline suggested that our mental faculties were exercised by a study of the classical languages. Modern languages were rejected as requiring only memorization, as were professional studies. A prescribed curriculum yielded no room for electives or for practical and professional studies. In its definition of both collegiate purpose and curriculum, the Yale Report of 1828 was in sharp contrast to the view expressed by another intellectual leader of that time, Philip Lindsley, president of the University of Nashville. In a more expansive view of higher education purpose, Lindsley commented as follows:

> Wherever there is a privileged order, no matter how constituted—whether like the patrician of ancient, or the ecclesiastic of modern Rome—it will, if not duly checked and counterbalanced, in the long run, become overbearing and tyrannical. I look to the college for a seasonable supply of countervailing agents. I look to a well educated independent yeomanry as the sheet anchor of the Republic. I look forward to the period when it will not be deemed anti-republican for the college graduate to follow the plough; nor a seven days' wonder for the laborer to be intellectual and to comprehend the Constitution of his country (Lindsley in Hofstadter and Smith, 1961, p. 377).

These glimpses into historic perspectives on collegiate purposes and their operational expression in the curriculum clearly reveal that curricular debate is always a timely theme and not restricted to present time and place. The last decade has produced a range of reports on this curricular issue at the undergraduate level. One of the more frequently cited and perhaps most influential of these reports is Boyer and Levine's 1981 monograph *A Quest for Common Learning*. From the research undertaken for this monograph, the authors indicated that in this century alone, more than 50 different purposes for general education could be derived from the literature. Boyer and Levine suggest that most of these could be subsumed under two major themes: the promotion of social integration and the combat of social disintegration. They offer these purposes for the general education curriculum:

- Shared use of symbols (communication)
- Shared membership in groups and institutions
- Shared producing and consuming
- Shared relationship with nature
- Shared sense of time
- Shared values and beliefs

In 1983, Gaff published his book-length work *General Education Today*. Based on important research sponsored by the Association of American Colleges, this volume offered an important update on the debate on purposes, curricular patterns, and evaluation of general education. Gaff suggested that different philosophical schools of thought (idealists, progressivists, essentialists, and pragmatists) are still able to form a consensus on the basic configuration of general education. General education, according to Gaff, has numerous elements: It is rooted in the liberal tradition and involves study of basic liberal arts and sciences. It stresses breadth and provides students with familiarity with various branches of human understanding as well as the methodologies and languages particular to different bodies of knowledge. It strives to foster integration, synthesis, and connectedness of knowledge rather than discrete bits of specialized information. It encourages the understanding and appreciation of one's heritage as well as respect for other people and cultures. General education includes an examination of values, both those relevant to current controversial issues and those implicit in a discipline's methodology. It prizes a common educational experience for at least part of the college years. It requires the mastery of the linguistic, analytic, critical, and computational skills necessary for lifelong learning. Finally, it fosters the development of personal qualities, such as tolerance of ambiguity, empathy for persons with different values, and an expanded view of self (Gaff, 1983, pp. 7–8).

Other apologists and their views of general education include *50 Hours: A Core Curriculum for College Students*, Lynn Cheney (1989); *Strong Foundations: Twelve Principles for Effective General Education Programs*, Association of American Colleges (1994); *The Reforming of General Education*, Daniel Bell (1966); *The Humanities in American Life*, University of California at Los Angeles (1980); *To Reclaim a Legacy: A Report on the Humanities in Higher Education*, William J. Bennett, for the National Endowment for the Humanities, (1984); and *Tourists in Our Own Land: Cultural Literacies and the College Curriculum* Clifford Adelman, for the U.S. Department of Education, (1992).

An informing summary of many contemporary reports in the humanities, social sciences, and sciences may be gleaned from *Integrity in the College Curriculum*, a 1985 publication of the Association of American Colleges.

The philosophic diversity of curricular thought in American higher education may be found in the variety of themes and designs on campus over the nation, including the competency-based curriculum for the baccalaureate at Alverno College in Wisconsin; education in the civic arts at Tusculum College in Tennessee; the great books approach at St. John's College in Maryland; thematic study at Evergreen State College in Washington; experiential education at the University of California at Berkeley; and service and community learning at Virginia Polytechnic University in Blacksburg.

ACCENT ON LEARNING—A CHANGE IN PERSPECTIVE AND PARADIGM

In the minds of many, the assessment movement has encouraged a shift in perspective on the primary questions of curriculum design in higher education from a focus on teaching to an accent on learning. Two of the more informing presentations on this shift in paradigm may be found in articles by Alan Guskin (1994) and Robert Barr/John Tagg (1995). Barr and Tagg comment as follows: "In the Instruction Paradigm, the mission of the college is to provide instruction, to teach. The method and the product are one and the same. The means is the end. In the Learning Paradigm, the mission of the college is to produce learning. The method and the product are separate. The end governs the means" (p. 15).

It is discomforting to suggest a shift in emphasis from teaching to an accent on learning. Barr and Tagg go further in suggesting that fiscal policies should recognize not activity and teaching, as we do now in most funding policy, but recognize instead learning and learning outcomes. We will explore this policy issue further in chapter six. Our discussion in that chapter introduces the concept of performance funding, first adopted in Tennessee in the 1980s. Barr and Tagg would take the performance funding idea and center it more directly on learning outcomes.

THE INTEGRATION OF COMPETENCE AND CONSCIENCE

As we noted earlier, one of the more cogent and influential voices in American higher education in the latter half of the twentieth century was Ernest Boyer, who wrote in *College: The Undergraduate Experience in America* (1987), ". . . the crisis of our time relates not to technical competence, but to a loss of social and historical perspective, to the disastrous divorce of competence from conscience" (p. 111). A century torn by two great wars and a host of lesser conflicts, marked by political barbarities on a scale of cruelty and scope almost impossible to conceive in a civilized time, continually torn by ethnic conflicts over the world is simultaneously a century distinguished by unparalleled and exponential advances in knowledge and understanding in every domain of human thought. Among the important advances include the discovery of nuclear power, genetic codes, computers and air/space travel, and the development of extraordinary advances in medical and health care.

The challenges of curriculum design in American higher education are more than challenges of what should be taught, for what purposes, and how it should be taught. These challenges will, necessarily and appropriately, remain one of continual debate as educators (as well as social, political, and artistic leaders external to the academy) struggle with the deeper philosophic questions of what it means to be an educated person. The possession of certification and of licensed competence may be one evidence of an educated person, but an insufficient evidence. A reverence for human dignity, an appreciation of beauty, a capacity for empathy and compassion, an awareness of responsibility, a sensitivity to the power of paradox, an inclination to persistence and discipline, a yearning for spiritual completion—surely the purposes of education will sing to these questions of meaning as well as develop a skill for living, learning, and the knowledge of heritage.

The effectiveness of curriculum design will be found not only in what knowledge, skills, and values our graduates have acquired, not only in the changes in their aptitudes and abilities, and not just in the glory of our technology, but also in whether our students have acquired a sustained curiosity and a sensitive conscience.

CHAPTER 5

Performance Accountability
The Evidence of Quality

We indicated that one of the main purposes in this work was to render an unfamiliar heritage more familiar. Previous chapters on the diverse mission expectations of American colleges and universities, the many voices laying claim for involvement in their governance, and the continuing debate over what should be studied suggest that the theme of this chapter will be no less complex. One thing is clear: The definition and demonstration of quality at the collegiate level is not a task that can be approached independent of our view of what a college education should mean and what purposes colleges serve.

The definition, development, and demonstration of quality in college and university settings has been a topic of philosophic engagement throughout the history of American higher education. In an 1848 commencement address, Philip Lindsley, then president of the University of Nashville, declared:

> Colleges confer degrees upon unworthy candidates—I admit the fact. . . . But the objection relates chiefly, I suppose, to the first degree—the degree, namely of Bachelor of Arts. Very true: this degree is conferred by all the colleges in the Union every year upon some unqualified—perhaps, in the aggregate, upon many unqualified and very unworthy individuals. This arises from several causes. (1) From the fact, that a portion of the youth who enter our colleges are deficient in intellect. They do not possess the minds capable of high and liberal cultivation. . . . "Though the ass may make a pilgrimage to Mecca, yet an ass he will come back." (2) From idle habits—from lack of industry

and application. No brilliancy of talent will master any science or language without labor. . . . (3) From a defective school education—the want of the requisite qualifications for a college life—or from the extreme youth of the party when admitted (Lindsley, 1848, pp. 377–78).

In a set of essays published in 1930, American scholar Abraham Flexner targeted major public and private universities, including Columbia, Chicago, and Wisconsin, with this tart observation about the rigor and quality of college education: "The sort of easy rubbish which may be counted towards an A. B. degree or the so-called combined degrees passes the limits of credibility" (Flexner, 1930, p. 53).

In the mid twentieth century, Jacques Barzun complained that:

> "Real life," it would seem, has crept in and ousted academic subjects, that is to say, not only those which are best for furnishing the mind and giving order to thought, but those which are alone capable of being taught theoretically. This fundamental distinction, elementary to the trained intellect, is virtually forgotten in the zeal of educators to "offer" as a course whatever is a nameable activity of man. This willingness matches the student's penchant for avoiding hard conceptual work in genuine subjects and for playing at others, which depend on practice for their meaning and whose so-called principles are but platitudes or tautologies (Barzun, 1959, pp. 117–18).

The concern for and debate over the nature and nurture of collegiate quality is thus an historic and contemporary concern. These and other observations on the quality of the collegiate enterprise give voice to a major philosophic tension that has occupied both philosophers and politicians in our nation over its history. How can we honor the egalitarian heritage of our nation, insuring that opportunity is present for each and every talent, while we simultaneously honor the principle of excellence, insuring that each and every talent is working to the far edge of his/her circle of promise and potential?

The purpose of this chapter is to bring historical, technical, and philosophical perspective to these questions. We will begin by exploring the diverse perspectives on the definition of quality, moving then to the evolution of our approaches and to the demonstration of quality, closing with a suggested set of design principles on which the pursuit of quality in college and university settings might be founded.

PERSPECTIVES ON THE MEANING OF QUALITY

A contemporary reflection by Gordon Davies, philosopher and executive director of the Kentucky Council on Higher Education, begins with the idea that we often have facile but shallow conversations about concepts such as quality until we have to define them. This can certainly be said of quality under the familiar phrase "I'll know it when I see it." Davies (1991) offers three definitions of quality: a hegemonic definition, "Whatever is valued (and paid for) in a society"; a market definition, "Whatever the prevailing cultural and economic hegemony defines it to be"; and a subjective definition "Whatever we in higher education think it is" (pp. 37–44).

In counterpoint to Davis, Amy Gutman (1991) argues for rejection of these definitions, suggesting that quality is not merely in the "eyes of the beholder." We should have little difficulty in making distinctions, she avers, between diploma mills and good colleges. Nor is quality to be defined by what people are willing to pay. And there is no single hegemonic standard on which there is a public consensus. She argues for a "principled pluralism in which quality is judged relative to the purposes of higher education" (pp. 45–53).

Can you improve and demonstrate quality if you cannot measure it? And can you measure quality if you cannot define it? And if you cannot define it, does quality really exist? This is where Robert Pirsig (1974) left us in his reflective treatise *Zen and the Art of Motorcycle Maintenance* when he observed that "obviously some things are better than others . . . but what's the betterness? . . . so round and round we go, spinning mental wheels and nowhere finding any place to get traction. What the hell is quality? What is it?" (p. 184). That the Pulitzer Prize-winning book *A Confederacy of Dunces* (Toole, 1982) was turned down by almost every major commercial publishing company in the nation before it was finally released by the Louisiana State University Press says something about the "what's the betterness."

We begin our exploratory journey on the meaning of quality with an initial inquiry into the reflections of those who are observers in corporate sector activity.

Conformance to Specification

As a first example of quality definition, we cite the views of Philip Crosby (1984), a contemporary and widely recognized writer on quality in the corporate sector, who defines quality simply as "conformance to requirements" (p. 60). Under this definition, if a product is built or manufactured so that it conforms to specifications, it is a quality product. Whether anyone will buy the product is another issue.

Mission Achievement and Distinction

Peter Senge, author of *The Fifth Discipline* (1990), makes this observation: "I do not believe great organizations have ever been built trying to emulate another, any more than individual greatness is achieved by trying to copy another 'great person'" (p. 11). Under this assumption, quality derives not from imitating another organization or person but in reaching for and discovering the breadth and depth of one's own promise and talent.

Fitness for Use

In *I Know It When I See It: a Modern Fable About Quality*, Guaspari (1985) suggests that "Customers aren't interested in our specs. They're interested in the answer to one simple question: did the product do what I expected it to do?" (p. 68). This is counterpoint to the conformance-to-specification view. Under this fitness-for-use definition, quality lies in the eye and judgment of the client or customer and in the utility of the product or the service as judged by that client.

Multifactor Perspective

The fitness-for-use theme is also found in the writings of David Garvin (1988). In *Managing for Quality*, however, he suggests that quality is a multifactor concept in which performance, or fitness for use, is one of many dimensions of quality. Others include reliability, durability, serviceability, aesthetics, features, and perceived quality. On the later point, for example, is a Toyota automobile built in the United States perceived to have the same quality as a Toyota automobile built in Japan? And what of a Sony recorder built in this country as compared to one built in Japan?

Continuous Improvement

The man who gave impetus to the rapid enhancement of quality in Japanese industry and an American authority on the management of quality, W. Edwards Deming (1986) indicates that the first obligation of management is to "create constancy of purpose for improvement of product and services" (p. 24). Here we begin to get a feel for the tension evident in discerning the meaning of quality. Striving for and demonstrating continuous improvement may not be the same as meeting some predetermined standard. In the views of some, therefore, one could be improving and still be operating at a mediocre level.

Our understandings of quality in both corporate and collegiate enterprise, but more especially in educational settings, are caught in philosophic tension that flows from two impulses in our democratic society, the egalitarian and the elitist. Our egalitarian motives salute the obligation of providing opportunity to all, and these motives honor the idea that talent may emerge from the most obscure and least-expected places in our society. Taken to its unhappy extreme, however, the egalitarian theme can result in a dull mediocrity where no one bothers to challenge the status quo nor feels any compulsion to rise above the lowest common denominator. This "dumbing down" danger, yielding to the group mean, is depicted in a range of literature, with Ayn Rand's novels *The Fountainhead* (1968) and *Atlas Shrugged* (1957) as examples.

In a chapter entitled "The Museum of Clear Ideas," appearing in his book *In Defense of Elitism*, William Henry III (1994) suggests that American higher education may have pandered to the lowest common educational denominator. The emergence of mass higher education in this nation, whose scope is apparent from data presented in earlier chapters, has produced, in Henry's opinion, no social evolution, "more willfully egalitarian than opening the academy" (p. 150). He does not see this as a happy outcome: "The best reasons for skepticism about mass higher education, however, reach far beyond the decline in meaning of a degree. The opening of the academy's doors has imposed great economic costs on the American people while delivering dubious benefits to many of the individuals being helped" (Henry, 1994, p. 153).

Henry's arguments are vaguely reminiscent of Flexner's concerns cited in opening reflections of this chapter. Henry goes on to assign this disappointing trend in higher education to a transactional vision of college, where students demand courses that affirm their own identities but disdain the thrill of discovery that comes from the challenge of ideas. Henry also believes that the curriculum is determined not so much from what professors love to teach, but more from what students desire to learn (the outcome of viewing students as customers), and he sees a decline in the amount and quality of work expected of students.

Henry is critical that too many students are going to college for the wrong reasons, that they are not developing their capacity for critical thinking or learning how to deal with diversity of opinion and background. He recommends reducing the number of high school graduates going to college from the current 60 percent to 33 percent over five years and eliminating a range of community colleges and former state teacher's colleges, now state universities (p. 165).

There are obvious dangers in the extremes of the elitist motive, where an overemphasis on individual and competitive performance can lead to arrogance and unchecked ambition. In *Excellence*, John Gardner (1984) wrote: "'Everyone for himself and the Devil take the hindmost' is a colorful saying but an unworkable model for social organization. No society has ever fully tested this manner of organizing human relationships—for the very good reason that any society which carried the principle to its logical conclusion would tear itself to pieces" (p. 25).

These two relatively concise collections of essays, the one by Henry and the other by Gardner, will furnish the student of higher education a provocative entree to the philosophical tensions in the definition of educational quality.

THEORIES OF EDUCATIONAL EXCELLENCE

Let us press the theme further. It may be an oversimplification, but one can think about the concept of quality and excellence from three perspectives. One of these assumes that excellence, by definition, is in limited supply, a competitive affair in which a few truly excellent institutions occupy the upper ranges. A second perspective assumes that excellence may be present in each and every institution according to its mission. A third perspective assumes that excellence is to be found not in resources and reputations but in results, in the "value added" by the institution.

The Theory of Limited Supply

There are certain conventional assumptions often widely held by academics and civic friends of higher education. Some believe that quality can only be found in a few colleges with impressive resources and that are high-cost, comprehensive, highly-selective, and nationally-recognized and ranked.

One of the earlier and best-known rankings of college quality was the 1964 study produced by Allan Cartter. Logan Wilson's foreword to Allan Cartter's report contains this arresting opening line: "Excellence, by definition, is a state only the few rather than the many can attain" (Cartter, 1964, p. vii). In the report, Cartter goes on to observe that: "Our present system works fairly well because most students, parents, and prospective employers know that a bachelor's degree from Harvard, Stanford, Swarthmore, or Reed is ordinarily a better indication of ability and accomplishment than a bachelor's degree from Melrose A & M or Siwash College" (p. 3). It is symptomatic of this approach to quality definition that Cartter had no difficulty identifying the top institutions, but had to resort to pseudonyms and poorly disguised racial identification in talking about institutions at the other end of the hierarchy.

Is collegiate quality in finite supply, a commodity of scarce availability? These assumptions can produce a pyramid of prestige in which the larger public and private colleges in our nation reside at the apex of the quality tetrahedron and less prestigious state and private colleges and community colleges occupy the lower levels. One can find this theory at work in the yearly rankings and ratings of "America's Best Colleges" as published by the news weekly *U.S. News and World Report*. These and other rating studies make some acknowledgment of differential mission, however, as they attempt to rank institutions of similar mission: research universities, regional universities, etc. There have been few rating studies, however, of two-year community colleges, colleges that enroll more than 40 percent of freshmen in this nation. And no publication ventures to identify "America's worst colleges."

One example of the unfortunate consequences of the limited-supply assumption has been the documented practice of some private colleges raising fees not because they needed the revenue but because they felt parents of their mostly affluent students would equate price with quality (Marchese, 1990, p. 4). These institutions were building their policy and practice on the assumption that high price equals high quality. The relationship between cost and quality has been put to the test by several studies. In his 1974 book *Quality Education for Less Money*, Richard Meeth noted that "This case study of six small private institutions raises serious doubts about the popular notion that the more money put into colleges and universities, the better the institutions" (p. 96). The relationship between cost and excellence is also put to the test by Pascarella and Terenzini in their work *How College Affects Students* (1991), and also in a more condensed journal version (1992). The relationship between cost and quality brings into play several other philosophical tensions in our understanding of quality. A family that can only afford a Chevrolet automobile may find the quality of a Cadillac automobile irrelevant. Similarly, the quality of Harvard or the University of Michigan may be equally irrelevant to that man or woman whose talent is promising, but whose financial or family circumstance will not permit them to attend those institutions. But to find that the paint is smeared and that the brakes fail on both the Cavalier and the Cadillac would lead one to conclude that issues of workmanship, reliability, and durability are quality issues that can apply to both products. Likewise the standards and performance expectations of a community college close to home and within financial reach are of more than passing interest to that student who might not be able to afford a more distant choice.

The Theory of Quality within Mission

Stripped to the raw essential of expression, the question is whether we desire to conceptualize a system of higher education as one in which there is a quality pecking order—an order of prestige and reputation built on size, selectivity, and program diversity—or whether we desire to conceptualize a system in which we are willing to see quality potential in a variety of campus missions, and insist that the mission delivers its promise.

This theory undergirds the definition of collegiate quality offered by Bogue and Saunders in their book, *The Evidence for Quality*. "Quality is conformance to mission specification and goal achievement—within publicly accepted standards of accountability and integrity" (1992, p. 20). The advantages cited for this definition of quality include the following: (1) It respects and affirms diversity of institutional missions and environmental settings; (2) It requires campuses to operationally define their mission and goals; (3) It focuses debate on purpose so that arguments over quality begin with what the institution intended to achieve; (4) It encourages public disclosure of mission, goals, and performance results; and (5) It contains an ethical test and the assumption that a campus may not make a claim for quality if it cannot demonstrate integrity in program and management. The operative phrase for this vision of quality is diversity with distinction, which carries the idea that each campus should demonstrate quality within its mission.

The Theory of Value Added

In contrast to the views of excellence defined by reputation and resources, Alexander Astin offers what he describes as a "talent development" definition of excellence: "The most excellent institutions are, in this view, those that have the greatest impact—add the most values, as economists would say—on the student's knowledge and personal development and on the faculty member's scholarly and pedagogical ability and productivity (1985, p. 61). There is an appealing simplicity to Astin's definition, as it focuses on the difference an institution makes in a student's knowledge, skill, and attitude.

QUESTIONS OF QUALITY

There are multiple truths in these different definitions of quality. To bring additional clarity to the issue of quality and excellence it may help to pose these questions, questions that can find applicability in both corporate and collegiate sector enterprise.

What Decisions Will Our Information on Quality Affect?

In the corporate sector we make decisions to design, produce, market, and service products. A quality-assurance system for the product might involve voices from each of these activities. In colleges and universities decisions are made to implement, improve, market, revise, and terminate programs. And decisions are made to admit, place, advance, retain, and graduate students. A quality-assurance system would attend to both program and student performance.

What Evidence Will We Employ to Demonstrate Quality?

Customer satisfaction and conformance to specification loom large as evidences of product/service quality in the corporate sector. However, there are other evidences that include reliability, durability, serviceability, and aesthetics. For colleges and universities, we may include the evidence of goal achievement, value added, client satisfaction, peer opinion, and reputation.

If we may employ a quick analogy: When one seeks the help of a physician, he or she will not find a "health" meter in the physician's office. Instead, the physician will obtain a range of medical evidence—blood pressure, blood tests, EKG, X-ray, CAT Scan, and a visual examination—before evaluating this evidence in a holistic fashion. Likewise, the state of quality or excellence in an institution may derive from an evaluation of these multiple evidences.

What Standards Will We Employ to Evaluate the Evidence?

It is perhaps an oversimplification, but in some ways one can examine the meaning of quality in terms of the standards employed to judge performance, whether individual or institutional. Among the standards we employ are:

1. criterion standards—comparing performance to a predetermined criterion level;
2. comparative standards—judging performance against the record of other individuals or institutions;
3. connoiseurship standards—evaluating performance against the opinion of a panel of "connoisseurs" or judges.

Who Will Make the Judgments and Evaluations of Quality?

Earlier we visited the idea that quality is in some ways in the eye of the beholder. Who, therefore, will be employed to make the judgments and evaluations of the evidence—students, faculty, board members, and/or political officers? And who is qualified by knowledge and experience to make those judgments? There are many cooks in the kitchen when it comes to the question of quality in both the corporate and the collegiate sectors.

At What Moment in Time Will We Make Quality Assessments?

In the manufacture of a product, we examine the raw materials and the product along the path of manufacture, make performance tests at the end of the production line, and follow up in seeking evaluations from customers who purchase the product or service. In the collegiate sector, we have quality-assurance obligations for diagnosis upon admission, placement in appropriate instructional settings, monitoring progress in instruction, and insuring mastery of appropriate knowledge and skill prior to credentialing or graduation.

These questions suggest that quality is not to be found in a single data point. There are multiple decisions, evidences, standards, judges, and examination times involved in any system to promote and demonstrate quality. Let us turn now to an examination of the different systems that have evolved to develop and demonstrate quality in collegiate settings.

SYSTEMS FOR QUALITY ASSURANCE

At least four activities may be discerned in contemporary approaches for assuring quality in colleges and universities. Accreditation and program reviews exemplify the more traditional approaches, embracing the principles of peer review and external standard. There is also the assessment and outcomes movement, calling for the development of performance evidence and attention to value-added questions. Total Quality Management (TQM) is yet another movement active in both corporate and collegiate settings, inviting our attention to continuous improvement and customer satisfaction. Finally, we can see that many states, and some institutions, are requiring periodic accountability and performance indicator reporting, seeking to demonstrate higher education's accountability to its many constituencies and marking progress on state-level goals for higher education.

Traditional Peer Review Evaluations

American higher education has fashioned several approaches to quality assurance that include these more traditional instruments:

- Accreditation—The test of mission and goal achievement
- Rankings and Ratings—The test of reputation
- Program Reviews—The test of peer evaluation
- Follow-up Studies—The test of client satisfaction

A more thorough description of the history and philosophic elements for each of these tools and an assessment of their strengths and liabilities may be found in *The Evidence for Quality* (Bogue and Saunders, 1992).

The oldest and best-known seal of collegiate quality, accreditation, is built on the premise and the promise of mission integrity and performance improvement. Campus self-study and introspection followed by a visit and review of an external panel of peers are also centerpieces of accreditation. It is an instrument that is uniquely American and that has had an unquestionable, positive impact on the improvement of higher education. However, accreditation is under frequent assault in contemporary forum for a range of imperfections— described as an episodic exercise in professional back scratching, an exercise built on minimalist standards, whose processes and activities are often hidden from public view. Accreditation is also criticized for failing to prevent problems in both academic and administrative integrity. Another challenge related to accreditation is reconciling the interests of institutional accreditation by the regional agencies who conduct reviews and the interests of disciplinary accrediting associations who conduct program reviews in many different fields. These criticisms notwithstanding, accreditation remains a dominant, important, and constructive form of quality assurance. Its philosophic anchors relate quality to mission and to continuous improvement. What changes may transpire in accreditation are difficult to predict. However, one possibility is that institutional accreditation, currently under the auspices of six regional agencies, might be transformed into national accrediting agencies for different types of institutions—research universities, comprehensive universities, liberal arts colleges, community colleges, etc.

While the review of particular academic programs by external peer reviews occupies a respected position among higher education quality-assurance instruments, especially in the research university, they are occasionally viewed by faculty as empty and futile exercises, serving as busy work and having little relationship to resource allocation. Like accreditation, program reviews generally require self-study and evaluation by an external peer panel. Among the important works describing the philosophic tenets and process of program reviews are those by Barak (1982) and Barak and Breier (1990).

Ranking and rating studies, including the previously mentioned U.S. News and World Report's "America's Best Colleges," and the National Research Council's Committee for the Study of Research-Doctorate Programs in the United States (Goldberger, Maher, and Flattau, 1995), continue to keep the conversation on quality alive. But these same reports are also indicted for offering little help toward improving quality and ignoring one of the largest sectors of higher education, community colleges. College rankings have been referred to as "quantified gossip" and "navel gazing" material for academic journals. While media reports of college rankings feature the "consumer choice" strength of such rankings, the evidence for their use in this way is uncertain. A fall 1995 report in Student Poll suggested that "Rankings such as those in U.S. News and World Report and Money Magazine have little impact on college choice. They are used less frequently by students and have far less influence than most other sources of information and advice" (p. 1).

Readers interested in an extended treatment of ranking and rating studies will find helpful background in The Evidence for Quality (Bogue and Saunders, 1992, pp. 65–93) and in two critical reviews (Webster, 1983, pp. 14–24, and Webster and Skinner, 1996, pp. 25–50). Clearly, rankings and ratings are built on the "limited supply" theory of quality, though most studies of this nature also attempt to recognize institutional mission in comparing institutions of similar structure. Student and alumni satisfaction indices, and other follow-up studies, are a legitimate and essential evidence of quality. They feature a client or "customer" focus and respond to the "fitness-for-use" test cited earlier. However, these satisfaction indices may be inversely related to excellence in educational settings. It is possible for the clients to be happy and satisfied with their educational experiences yet also remain relatively unenlightened by their educational experiences.

The Assessment and Outcomes Movement

The assessment movement in higher education, a development primarily of the last 15 to 20 years, centers on the acquisition of multiple forms of evidence in the evaluation of both student and program performance. Assessment focuses attention on results more than reputation. The nature of personal and organizational performance is too complex to be captured in a single data point. As noted earlier, just as physicians do not have a health meter in their offices, but assess health by examining a cluster of medical evidence, a cluster of performance assessments and evidence to make quality judgments about students, programs, and institutions is also necessary. We can, and should, know as much about our students on exit as we do on entry, including information about the developmental changes in their knowledge, skill, and attitudes. The annual forums on assessment sponsored by the American Association for Higher Education (AAHE) and the emerging presence of directors of assessment on campuses attest to the growing interest in the role of assessment on American college and university campuses. The statement on *Principles of Good Practice for Assessing Student Learning* issued under the auspices of the AAHE Assessment Forum makes clear that what we assess and how we assess flow from our values: "Where questions about educational mission and values are skipped over, assessment threatens to be an exercise in what's easy, rather than a process of improving what we really care about" (AAHE, 1992, p. 2). Here we may also note the involvement of actors beyond the campus, a governance complexity we noted in chapter three. By 1990, two-thirds of the states had policy mandates that required colleges and universities to assess student learning (Ewell, Finney, and Lenth, 1990). In his opening remarks in an Education Commission of the States publication, policy commentator Aims McGuinness suggests that "New concepts concerning the appropriate roles of government-initiated reform appeared to be emerging, contributing to a gradual shift in the landscape of state roles in higher education that include such things as: Broadening the definition of 'accountability' from primarily an emphasis on equitable access and efficient use of resources to an emphasis on performance and results" (McGuinness, 1994, p. 1).

Perhaps the most important and critical challenge remaining is whether assessment activities have been effectively linked to teaching and learning and to the improvement of what happens in our classrooms, laboratories, and studios. The Jossey-Bass publication entitled *Making a Difference* (Banta et al., 1993) offers a range of institutional illustrations that support the constructive impact of the assessment movement. However, there are still some institutions going through the motions of collecting assessment data on students and programs but failing to realize the decision, discovery, and distinction promise of assessment. For those institutions, assessment data serve as ballast and burdens for filling shelves but are not used to inform educational decisions. The discovery or learning potential of assessment activity is often underappreciated. The opportunity to enhance the mission distinction of programs and institutions is also frequently lost in unimaginative routines of assessment. In contrast, institutions such as Alverno College and Northeast Missouri State University (now Truman State University) and others cited in the book by Banta et al., furnish affirming models of how assessment can become an effective instrument for improving decision, facilitating personal and institutional learning, and strengthening mission distinction.

Total Quality Management (TQM)

A more recent system of quality assurance is one originally developed in the corporate sector, especially for the manufacturing industry. Built on the pioneering work of W. Edwards Deming (1986) and several others, TQM places an accent on customer satisfaction, continuous improvement, and systems analysis. An informing and integrating work, one offering a favorable treatment of TQM as applied to higher education, is Daniel Seymour's *On Q: Causing Quality in Higher Education* (1992). Seymour is "convinced that accrediting agencies, program reviews, standing committees, control-minded governing boards, and the occasional well-intentioned task force will not be the instruments for causing quality in higher education" (p. x). He offers TQM as an answer to his question: "Is there a better way to manage higher education?"

Seymour's advocacy of TQM warrants thoughtful review. He suggests that current and conventional quality instruments, such as program reviews and accreditation, make little significant contribution to college quality. He sees these instruments as occasional devices that convey the appearance of quality and that establish a "good enough" mind set. Those who have been on both the giving and receiving end of program and accreditation reviews will know the liabilities of these and other evidences of quality previously cited in these remarks. Both of these instruments are built on the principle of improvement, an ideal central to TQM and a governing ideal that must undergird any effective approach to quality assurance. Is it necessary to depreciate the contributions of quality-assurance instruments already in place in order to appreciate what TQM has to offer? The authors think not. Having accented the principle of continuous improvement, let us examine two additional ideas from TQM. With respect to a second foundation principle of TQM, customer satisfaction, few would argue that we listen enough to our students. There are, however, critical differences between corporate and collegiate settings in the application of this principle, and the concept of student as customer. Any faculty member who has found his or her caring for students in tension with caring for standards knows the limitation of this quality test for colleges and universities. As Seymour suggests, students do indeed vote with their feet, revealing their preference with their presence. It is sad when they occasionally vote for options of questionable merit, with examples to follow in our discussion. When they do, the ideal of quality should not be exchanged for the notion of satisfaction. Advocates of TQM often cite the idea that everyone has a customer, some internal and others external. Thus, TQM training will usually involve the identification of "customers" by those who hold staff and support functions, such as registrar and finance offices. In *Stewardship*, Peter Block (1993) offers this imperative: "Don't call them a customer if they have no choice. . . . Calling people you can demand a response from a 'customer' is manipulation . . . using the language of consideration to soften the coercion in the relationship" (p. 125). Faculty and students have a relationship that is a bit more than seller and buyer.

While some faculty and administrative officers see TQM as appropriate for improvements in the admissions office, business office, facilities maintenance office, campus security office, or other administrative settings, Seymour notes that these are not the only settings where "we degrade, we hassle, and we ignore" (p. 115). Will we be as quick to see opportunities for listening to our clients, continuous improvement, and problem solving in the academic heart of colleges and universities? Here in our classrooms and laboratories, in our studios and seminar rooms, students can be taken in harm's way by low and empty expectations from uncaring teachers, by assessment exercises having little or no application in the improvement of teaching and learning, and by a vision of quality that depends more on faculty publication counts than caring for our students.

Whether the initial euphoria and the subsequent quiet departure of some previously heralded management concepts will, in retrospect, also describe the fate of TQM in colleges and universities remains a test of time. Will TQM make a quick digestive passage, with only moderate long-term impact, or will it constitute a better way to manage higher education? An argument can be made that many of the philosophical principles cited for TQM have been at work in academia for some time. *Change Magazine* editor Ted Marchese said "hello" to TQM in an editorial appearing in the May/June 1993 issue of *Change* and acknowledged in that editorial that one of the more important concepts flowing from TQM philosophy was that "organizations should be driven by the intrinsic motivation in all of us to do our best work" (p. 13). It would be hard to quarrel with that idea, nor is the idea a new one. There have always been elements of that belief behind self-study in accreditation. In a "goodbye, for now" editorial appearing in the May/June 1996 issue of *Change*, Marchese noted the difficulties in translating TQM philosophy into higher education, including most importantly the belief on the part of many in higher education that we don't yet have a quality or productivity problem (p. 4).

As an interesting aside, while collegiate America ventures into TQM, not all is consensus on the application of TQM in corporate sector organizations. In an article appearing in the January 1993 issue of *Management Review* entitled "Ten Reasons Why TQM Doesn't Work," Oren Harari comments that: "TQM is only one of many possible means to obtain quality. In other words, quality is sacred; TQM is not. There's another difference: as we shall see, quality is about unbending focus, passion, iron discipline and a way of life for all hands. TQM is about statistics, jargon, committees and quality departments" (p. 33).

This critique of TQM in the corporate sector may be another instance where we are unhappily inclined to throw out the baby with the bath water. However, it does remind us of an equally unfortunate tendency, prevalent in both the corporate and collegiate world: to seize the latest management fad and associated acronym as the cure for all that ills. Our previous comments suggest that there are useful lessons to be gleaned from TQM philosophy and elements of that philosophy are to be approached with a great deal of care.

We would like to make one other postscript to Harari's notes. While the metaphor of corporate and collegiate leaders orchestrating organizational behavior and serving as organizational maestros can be a confining metaphor, we find it beneficial to retain the image, for it conveys useful truth.

It is possible for an individual musician or an ensemble of any size, including a full orchestra, to play correctly. Meaning the orchestra plays with zero defects and, as the statistical process control folks might say, "in control and capable." But this "correct" performance may not constitute musical quality. In the orchestra hall, customers are patrons, and patrons know that correct music is not necessarily quality music. If the music lacks passion and fire, inventiveness and imagination, "correctness" will not transform a dull and uninspired performance into a quality performance. In the orchestra halls of colleges and universities, our students will also be able to discern when we are correct, and especially when we care.

Accountability and Performance Indicator Reporting

In addition to the more traditional approaches to quality assurance, emergence of the assessment movement, and current applications of TQM in college settings, there is yet a fourth stream of activity discernible. We refer to this fourth stream as accountability and performance indicator reporting. It is clear, for example, that state governments are increasingly interested in the question of quality. A study published by the Southern Regional Education Board (SREB) in 1993 indicated that all but two of the fifteen states in the SREB region had either a legislative mandate or other requirement for an annual comprehensive accountability report imposed upon public colleges and universities in those states (Bogue, Creech, Folger, 1993). The SREB report goes on to indicate that an evaluation of these state accountability policies has yet to occur, and posed the following questions: Have state policies, for example, produced constructive and substantive changes at the campus level, or have campus responses been largely cosmetic and adaptive? Has the implementation of state accountability policies led to increased awareness of, confidence in, and support of higher education? Are political and educational leaders using the extensive accountability reporting? And do states have policies that support improvement in both favorable and unfavorable economic times, and do these policies survive changes in leadership at the executive level? (p. 12).

Accountability reporting and the use of performance indicators has touched most every region of the country. In Wisconsin, the governor created an accountability task force that led to the development of performance measures in seven areas: quality, effectiveness, efficiency, access, diversity, stewardship of assets, and contribution to compelling state needs. Among the indicators reported on a regular basis are:

- Student and alumni satisfaction survey results
- Percentage of all undergraduate courses taught by instructor type
- Sophomore competency test results
- Graduation rate of undergraduates
- Job placement rates, graduate school acceptance rates, and pass rates on licensure exams
- Average credits to B.A.
- Percentage of qualified undergraduate resident students accepted for admission
- Progress toward equal employment goals in hiring, promotion, and tenure
- Faculty retention rates
- Progress in meeting preventive maintenance goals
- Accident and injury statistics
- Employer survey results
- Continuing education enrollments (Gaither, Nedwek, and Neal, 1994, pp. 35–36).

These indicators are not atypical. Indicators frequently found in other state profiles include percentage of eligible programs accredited, degree production, faculty workload statistics, and crime statistics.

What purposes are associated with this relatively new expectation for accountability reporting? A 1994 report released by the Education Commission of the States nicely brackets the three goals of indicator reporting: (1) Demonstrating accountability to public bodies; (2) Establishing trend lines of performance intelligence; and (3) Marking progress on statewide goals for higher education (Ruppert, 1994).

The Joint Commission on Accountability notes in a draft report that "institutions of higher education have an obligation to inform the public about their effectiveness in fulfilling their mission" (Preface, 1994). In a monograph entitled *Measuring Up: The Promises and Pitfalls of Performance Indicators in Higher Education* Gaither et al. states that

> The trend is clear and irreversible: higher education institutions must
> work to develop more adequate ways of judging how well they are

doing the job. Higher education has been reluctant to develop performance indicators because it is felt that the mission of higher education is too diverse to measure, and that short term measurement may not provide adequate measurement of long term student and scholarship success. However, if the members of the academy—faculty, academic leaders, and students—do not participate in the process of developing and improvement use of performance indicators, external organizations will force some form of indicators on them (Gaither, Nedwek, Neal, 1994, pp. x–xi).

The University of Miami has developed an extensive system of "Key Success Indicators," that include an extensive range of information on students, employees, and finance. The institution now has trend lines reaching over several years and a year-to-date report made available to all key administrators (Sapp and Temares, 1992, pp. 24–31). Examples of other institutions and states moving to the use of performance indicators may be found in the proceedings from a pre-conference symposium on performance indicators in higher education edited by Gerald Gaither (1996).

Few would argue that the press for accountability reporting, use of performance indicators, and pressure for quality assurance is without major liabilities. Writing in a special issue of *Change* devoted to the "vexing trend" of accountability reporting, faculty member Roger Peters notes that "Effective assessment requires a diligent search for bad news, which is more useful than good, but accountability encourages the opposite. Campus officials are understandably reluctant to bear bad tidings to those who fund them" (Peters, Nov./Dec. 1994, pp. 18–19). This inclination, of course, is not restricted to collegiate organizations. If one examined the annual report of a business about to enter bankruptcy, it is at least questionable whether one would find a hint of that probability in the annual report. Another criticism is that we tend to construct indicators that reflect the ease of capturing data rather than identifying those that will carry valid evidence of performance. However, one can make an argument that both institutions and states need performance intelligence on activity and achievement, intelligence that allows decision makers to know something about the health of the enterprise, establish a basis for making improvements in both instructional and administrative services, and demonstrate the extent to which it is making progress on selected goals. Writing in *Trusteeship*, Joseph Burke (1994) makes the case that boards of trustees should also insist that campuses in their care present public annual reports of their performance. He describes in this article the development of a performance indicators report developed for the State University of New York system. In this sense, a well-conceived profile of performance indicators allows an institution or a system of campuses to offer an operational expression of its quality and to simultaneously satisfy the call of improvement and accountability.

We should mention that the American Association of Community Colleges has published a monograph entitled *Community Colleges: Core Indicators of Effectiveness* (1994) that outlines a model set of performance indicators for two-year schools, and Gerald Gaither of the Texas A & M University system has a Fund for the Improvement of Postsecondary Education (FIPSE) project underway to do the same for universities. The purpose of FIPSE is to identify a core set of performance indicators for universities.

Governing boards for both public and private institutions are also becoming more interested in the expectation of excellence. One of the six major recommendations to improve quality in a report entitled *Trustees and Troubled Times in Higher Education* (1993), published by the Association of Governing Boards of Universities and Colleges, is "How can this institution set new standards of quality?" (pp. 22–23). This report chides the higher education community for emphasizing a narrow model of quality: "Quality is measured more by the kinds of students excluded and turned down than by the kinds of students included and turned out. . . . Quality, in short, has become something to stoke academic egos instead of students' dreams" (p. 22).

The Malcolm Baldrige Award

While we promised four systems of quality assurance, there is a postscript needed here. Initially created by the Malcolm Baldrige National Quality Improvement Act of 1987, this national award for quality was established to recognize and encourage quality enhancement in the corporate sector of manufacturing, service, and small business. The award was named for Malcolm Baldrige, secretary of commerce from 1981 until his death in 1987. The award is designed to stimulate and enhance performance excellence and to promote sharing of information on successful performance enhancement strategies.

Earlier awards were made to corporate sector businesses, and winners include such companies as Cadillac, Eastman Kodak, Motorola, Texas Instruments, and the Ritz-Carlton Hotel. However, the award has been expanded to include the Educational Division, and in the near future national awards will be made to schools and colleges electing to compete for the award. Among the goals of the award in this division are to help improve school performance via result-oriented performance requirements, facilitate sharing of best practice information among schools of all types, foster partnerships among schools, businesses, and other human service organizations, and serve as a tool for improving school performance (*Malcolm Baldrige National Quality Award Pilot Criteria*, 1995, p. 3).

Writing in an article that appeared in the January/February 1994 issue of *Change* entitled "The Baldrige Cometh," Daniel Seymour suggested that the Baldrige Award can result in serious soul searching in higher education and can lead to much needed reflection and change. In a two-volume work entitled *High Performing Colleges* (1996), Seymour et al. further explicate the theory and concepts underlying the award, evidence of its success in corporate enterprise, criticism associated with the award, and experience of some 20 colleges involved in pilot work with the standards.

As with several previous instruments of quality assurance described in these remarks, the Baldrige will require a serious and introspective internal study and application, and the competing institutions will be evaluated by an external panel on the following criteria:

Baldrige Criteria for Education Division Point Values

1.0   Leadership—90
2.0   Information and analysis—75
3.0   Strategic and operational planning—75
4.0   Human resource development and management—150
5.0   Educational and business process management—150
6.0   School performance results—230
7.0   Students focus and student/stakeholder—230

Some of the philosophic questions already detailed in this chapter may be posed about the Educational Division of the Baldrige Award and its possible impact on higher education. Will the Baldrige Award become something akin to a form of national accreditation? Will winners continue to improve after receiving the award or rest on their laurels? Is the award a recognition of results or a recognition of improvement?

To insure that these systems of quality assurance are integrated, complement one another, and that there is faculty and staff awareness and allegiance to these systems are notable leadership design challenges. We just as surely design climates for learning with our ideals as with our ideas. Thus, another leadership design challenge is to cultivate those values that will honor quality in our daily and personal journeys in colleges and universities. Let us turn to this more personal dimension of quality assurance.

BEYOND SYSTEMS: THE MORAL AND ETHICAL
DIMENSION OF QUALITY

Beyond these systems of quality assurance, it may be suggested that nurturing and assuring quality in colleges and universities is an activity as much moral in its content and tactic as it is technical, as much personal as systemic. Here are examples to illustrate what we mean. This illustration is disguised but not hypothetical. A state university graduate dean is contacted by a state senator, the senator interested in having a student of marginal qualification admitted to graduate school at this state university. Following an unsuccessful try at using persuasion to gain exception to the university's graduate admissions policy, the senator resorted to intimidation and threat tactics. Not a timid academic nor a particularly reticent personality, the graduate dean, a well known and widely respected personality in the region both academically and politically, responded to the threat with one of his own. He suggested to the younger senator in no uncertain tone and with no lack of clarity that if he persisted in his use of threats that he would be faced with formidable and personal opposition in his bid for re-election coming in the fall. And the graduate dean had the authority of competence, character, and alliance to make good his threat.

Did this exchange reflect a quality issue? Certainly! But it had little to do with the traditional approaches of accreditation and program review, little to do with outcome assessments and multiple evidences, little to do with TQM and customer satisfaction, and little to do with accountability and performance indicator reporting to the state. And it is doubtful whether the incident might prove very useful in competing for the forthcoming Baldrige Award. It was about caring and character. It was about a collegiate administrator who knew what was right and was willing to act on what was right.

Thus, it may be argued that the promotion of educational quality has technical and moral dimensions, requiring the conceptual and ethical engagement of collegiate leaders. Beyond our systems for nurturing and assuring quality, there is a personal and ethical dimension.

The illustration of a graduate dean defending the admissions standards of the university reveals that the cause of quality can be advanced or damaged in more personal moments in the lives of both college administrators and faculty, in a thousand "moments of truth" occurring in our colleges and universities every day. Leadership in quality assurance is a responsibility invested not just in those holding formal administrative appointment but also in the mind and heart of each one holding climates of learning in trust—invested in the care of professors, presidents, deans, and directors. Fresh with a new Ph.D., an assistant professor of political science, appointed to a research university, gave his first course examination. While wandering the back of the room, he spotted one of his students glancing at his shirt sleeve with some frequency, a suspicious action considering that this was the end of the spring and short-sleeve shirts were more compatible with the relatively hot and humid weather. The student was a member of the university's baseball team, and was also not known for his spiffy dressing habits. Cotton mesh casual shirts, walking shorts, and sandals were more often seen than his attire for today's test day—white pinpoint oxford shirt, navy blazer, regimental tie, gray slacks, and tassel loafers. Alarm bells began to ring for the new assistant professor, and he racked his brain for memory of some doctoral course or experience that might guide his actions.

Should he call the student out and accuse him of cheating? An option of questionable merit. Might he ask to inspect what appeared to be an informing shirt cuff? Again, a tactic of uncertain but potentially dangerous valence. Should he depend on the observations and witness of students around the offending scholar as a means of fingering the cheater? Would the honor code work? Might he ignore the incident and concentrate instead on the journal article needing his attention so that he could traverse a more certain and speedy path to tenure and associate professor, a safe and easy option?

He decided instead on a test of performance and invited the student over to his office for coffee and conversation after the passage of a couple of days, a salutary and friendly pedagogical gesture. "This analysis on first amendment rights and hate speech codes was interesting," the assistant professor opened. "You didn't really get into the 'fighting words' test suggested by the Supreme Court ruling of *Chaplinsky v. New Hampshire.* Do you see that ruling supporting your analysis?" In a moment, our young assistant professor will discover whether his baccalaureate scholar can do more than catch and throw baseballs. It may be discovered whether this student is willing to honor in the classroom the same test he must live by on the baseball field—the test of performance. And, if he is thoughtful, our young professor will make contributions to both improvement and a standard of excellence in this exchange. If the student has cheated, what actions are suggested? Will our professor flunk the student on this examination or in the course? Or might he, in the spirit of improvement and performance, allow the student to field this play again?

This personal professorial act is one of quality for which we lack a suitable acronym. Such artistic acts of caring for both standard and student, however, may advance the cause of quality. The ideal of quality and the ideal of integrity are linked. College administrators and college faculty have opportunity and responsibility to teach about quality and integrity in collegiate settings. Let's move now to institutional illustrations having a bit more public visibility.

A friend recently sent us a news clipping that appeared in the morning issue of a major West Coast urban newspaper. In this article, only the student's name has been changed:

Why is Sally standing there looking puzzled?

Because she registered at City College by phone—a new system—and then mailed in the fees for two courses, plus $10 for a campus parking sticker.

Simple, wot? Not. Back came a receipt but no parking sticker. However, it did show a $10 overpayment so all is swell? Well: she went out to the school and stood in line for an hour to get the parking sticker. "That'll be $10," said the bureaucrat, at which Sally triumphantly presented the credit slip, to no avail. "You'll have to give me

$10 if you want the sticker now, and then you may apply for a refund, which'll take about eight weeks," he said, not unkindly. Defeated, Sally asked for a refund form. "Here you go," he said, handing her one, "but you won't get any money back. There's a $10 fee for processing a refund" (Caen, 1993, p. 6).

We've seen a number of classified advertisements for the position of director of Total Quality Management in the *Chronicle of Higher Education*. Do they have a director of Total Quality Management at City College? If so, he or she has a good work ahead. Meanwhile, it wouldn't hurt the cause of quality if an alert administrator put a halt to this policy nonsense. Here is another news clip, this one of little bolder presentation and scope. Another article regarding this type of bureaucracy originally appeared in a major city newspaper and later in *USA Today* ("Across the USA," 1994, p. 7A).This front-page article featured a campus that had canceled almost two-thirds of its summer school classes on the second day of classes. Students were given no advance notice nor any reasonable explanation for this action, except the president's state-ment that he had ordered the classes canceled to meet the budget. The story carried a photo of angry students besieging administrative offices. Is this a quality issue? Well, if you are inclined to think about students as customers, this incident surely must be counted a quality issue.

Will an accreditation team arrive and investigate this quality situation? Not likely. Will the assessment plan for this campus address this situation? Improbable. Would we find the director of Total Quality Management in the middle of the fray, tending to the concerns of student customers? We doubt it. And, will the institution's accountability and performance indicators report this incident to the state? Absolutely not.

This number of cancellations might be understandable if classes did not meet minimal enrollment requirements, since many summer schools depend heavily upon fee income. However, many of the canceled classes had full enrollments. How any college president could enter a summer session and not know enough about his or her budget to avoid this kind of behavior is beyond comprehension. Something is missing here. That something is competence and caring. Moral outrage would be an appropriate response to what happened to these students. Apparently, the moral outrage will have to come from outside the college rather than inside, except for those students whose lives and aspirations were affected. As a postscript, the president of this institution resigned soon after this incident. Here is a third media report of collegiate shenanigans and dreary qualitative behavior. This particular story appeared in several city papers, but also found its way to the *Wall Street Journal* (Putka, 1991, p. A1). A professor of engineering apparently engaged in a shady entrepreneurial venture, exchanging his endorsement of shoddy and short work on plagiarized master's and Ph.D. degrees for students who, from the vantage point of their industrial appointments, shuffled lucrative consultant contracts to their major professor. We can only hope that these two students will not work on our bridges, aerospace systems, or nuclear power facilities.

At least responsible administrators and faculty on this campus engaged in a speedy piece of "due process": they arranged a prompt departure for this entrepreneurial but morally bent professor and recalled the faulty degrees from students, who surely must have harbored a flawed notion of educational quality. The reports on this incident do not indicate that the accreditation, assessment, total quality management, and performance indicators systems of the campus were active elements in this quality drama.

The August 16, 1996, issue of the *Chronicle of Higher Education* contained a story of a state university having been investigated by the state's higher education coordinating agency, with the finding that 44 of the 127 degree programs carried in the university's catalog were "unauthorized" (May, p. A9). The trigger for the investigation was a lawsuit entered by one of the university's students who worked four years toward a degree carried in the catalog, a degree which turned out to be one of those "unauthorized" degrees. To invest four years of study, to say nothing of money, toward a published but apparently illegal degree would be more than a notable surprise for any student.

This story actually was an accompanying entry to the lead story in that issue which featured a student of another state university suing his institution for $1 million in punitive damages, claiming that his doctoral degree was relatively empty of substance and standard (*Chronicle of Higher Education*, August 16, 1996, p. A29). Though an institutional review committee found that the student's claims had no standing and the lawsuit is still pending as of this writing, this bizarre academic sparring match can hardly have a pleasant outcome for the field of study, the university, and higher education in general. A student who would go through the charade of earning such an apparently empty degree—only to turn upon those from whom he accepted the credential—might be counted a worthy candidate for further scrutiny. The call of accountability and responsibility, however, clearly rests with the faculty holding this program in trust. Apparently, both student and faculty in this situation have a disappointing notion of what quality means. The alert student of American higher education will, with these stories, begin to understand more about why governance in higher education has become more complex and why public trust has become more troubled.

Consider this final illustration of offense to quality. Here is a campus embarking upon the delivery of a new master's program, an initiative designed to reach a new market of students. Nothing wrong with the initiative. However, here are unhappy conditions of the program following two years of operation and the graduation of the first class. Only a fourth of the graduating class of approximately 20 students met the admissions requirements stated in the college catalog and accreditation candidacy prospectus for this program. While most of the graduating students were employed full time, at least half have enrolled for 12 to 15 hours of graduate work in at least two consecutive semesters. More than two-thirds of the graduates have been given credit for graduate courses that cannot be found in the college's graduate catalog that were not proposed in the original graduate prospectus, have little or no relation to the graduate program mission, and were not authorized for acceptance in the program as originally outlined in the program prospectus. One of the half dozen full-time faculty listed in the college's catalog and personnel records in this field had taught in the graduate program, while the remaining courses had been delivered by adjunct faculty of marginal qualifications. A review of course syllabi files reveals at least one file that contained a syllabus from another university. An easy cross check reveals that the university from whence this syllabus had come is the same university from whence the graduate program administrator had received his doctorate. A good argument can be made that not one but two colleges have something to think about here. For this program and this campus, any reasonable sense of academic standard has fallen before the seductive call of numbers and tuition trend lines. This campus scenario, like the others preceding, is unfortunately real. Here care and competence also seem to be in short supply. A potentially happy ending is that apparently there are some faculty and administrators on this campus who are exhibiting moral outrage over these conditions. How can we measure the damage already done to the ideal of quality and to the competence and character of students who have graduated in this program? These graduates had to know they were being cheated, or they were allowed to nurture a shallow sense of educational standard. Consider the collective impact of these stories and the unfortunate reality of too many others that could be told, disappointing departures from caring and standard. To what extent does the neglect of personal and moral responsibility for quality in higher education contribute to the growing pressures of public accountability, which may, in turn, lead us in a search for systemic solutions? One story in the local newspaper, USA Today, the Wall Street Journal, or the New York Times on the neglect or abandonment of integrity in our colleges and universities may do more damage to the ideal of quality—and to public perception of collegiate quality—than can be redeemed by the adoption of TQM, the development of an assessment plan, recognition of accreditation, or favorable trend lines in our accountability indicators.

THE DESIGN IDEALS

College faculty and administrators can ascertain whether campuses under their care are attending to their quality assurance responsibilities by engaging the following questions: Can the campus offer evidence/indicators of both performance and improvement? Are these evidences of performance being used to make more informed decisions on policy, program, and personnel, and are the decision implications of each approach to quality evident? Is the mission distinction of the campus affirmed and advanced by the evidences of quality and performance indicators selected? Are the various instruments and systems for assuring quality integrated to minimize duplication and to maximize utility, and is there an awareness of and allegiance to the overall approach by faculty and staff? Is there a clear linkage to and impact on teaching and learning for each quality assurance instrument? And finally, is the campus making use of standards that go beyond the confine of its own experience so that there is accountability to an external referent involved?

The concepts of performance evidence, continuous improvement, decision utility, external referenced accountability, and mission distinction are important governing ideals of quality. Designing well-crafted quality-assurance systems that embrace these principles, insuring that these systems are integrated and complementary in function, and taking steps to develop faculty/ staff ownership of and allegiance to these systems are conceptual or "head first" leadership challenges of the first order.

The nurture of quality in our colleges and universities, however, must go beyond these conceptual and technical responsibilities. Accreditation and assessment, TQM and accountability reporting—beyond these systems we need presidents, professors, deans, and directors who have a keen sense of standard and proper behavior, who answer the call to honor and are willing to use moral outrage as an instrument of quality assurance, and who create quality climates via the influence of their ideals as well as their ideas. The more critical design elements of collegiate excellence and quality may be "heart first" actions of caring and courage. Thus, we need to do more than put on the "clothing" and outward appearance of quality via our systems and structures. We need to touch the soul of our colleges and universities. What unites the systemic and the personal dimensions of quality? The uniting element is a habit of mind and heart that creates a community of caring. The visibility accorded to institutions such as Alverno College and Truman State University, both having a substantive and sustained reputation for quality, may derive not so much from the fact that they are models of assessment, having built an intimate link between assessment and learning, but from the many years of devoping a community of caring, one in which the personal and the systemic servants of quality are almost indistinguishable.

In a community of caring, vision and expectation call students and colleagues from the poverty of the commonplace and launch each to the far reach of his or her promise. Courage and compassion create a climate in which a respect for diversity of mission and talent is matched with a scorn for shoddy work, whether individual or institutional. Policy and action translate the call of honor into specific acts essential to the nurture of both students and standards. A community of caring responds not only to the intellectual and institutional call of advancing the truth but to the ethical and personal call of honoring dignity, justice, and responsibility. In a community of caring, quality does not and cannot live apart from integrity.

CHAPTER 6

Forms of Finance

The Uses of Fiscal Policy

Where and how a society spends its money furnishes an operational expression of what that society values, what goals it deems important, and what priority it attaches to the needs of various constituents and services. For individuals and for institutions, budgets are operative expressions of philosophy and priority. This same expression of values can also be applied to a university, looking at where and how money is spent.

For social and economic archeologists of the future, there will be a rich data deposit to mine in the salary profiles of contemporary American society and in the study of how we chose to invest our resources. There will be records of nobility and records of disappointment. For higher education in the United States, the trend lines of financial support will reveal a profile of extraordinary and significant investment over the past century. This investment will speak to the higher motives of Americans. The data will detail, however, important changes in sources and range of support in these final years of the twentieth century.

Who pays for higher education in America, and how do they pay? How do governmental and institutional policies help or hinder students' abilities to attend college (or to attend the college of their choice)? What role does private philanthropy play in the support of American higher education? How

For this chapter, the authors would like to acknowledge the assistance of Maurice Ottinger. He is a Ph.D. candidate in leadership studies in education at the University of Tennessee and is currently serving as a major in the U.S. Army in Washington, D.C.

is fiscal policy used to advance societal and educational goals in our nation? For public institutions, how does government make equitable distribution of funds? These are the questions we hope to engage in this chapter on financial policy in American higher education. Our goals are to furnish the reader with perspective on the financial scope of the enterprise; relative contributions of students, government, and donors; and the impact of public goals and policy, especially the impact of the ebb and flow of government funding. We begin with a profile on the financial scope of the enterprise.

A PROFILE OF REVENUES AND EXPENDITURES

In discussing revenues and expenditures, the questions "Where does the money come from?" and "Where does the money go?" come to mind. Let's explore patterns of income and expenditures from national, state, and institutional perspectives. Table 6.1 furnishes a summary profile and yields immediate intelligence on fiscal patterns in American higher education.

The most obvious finding from Table 6.1 is that American higher education is a large-scale financial enterprise with revenues and expenditures of $189 billion a year—with $119 billion of that in the public sector and $70 billion in the private sector. From whence does the money come? Primarily from student fees in the private sector (42 percent of all income for private colleges) and primarily from state government in the public sector (33.3 percent of all income for public colleges). The federal government plays a significant role in supporting grants and contracts primarily for research in both sectors.

How are these funds expended? They flow first to the primary programs and services of instruction, research, public service, and academic support for those primary services. Second, expenditures are used for institutional support and student services. These functional expenditure categories, or "funds," are subject to definition in college and university accounting. Those interested in further reading on the practices of "fund accounting" for higher education and the question of exactly what activities are included in each of the revenue and expenditure categories in Table 6.1 are referred to publications of the National Association of College and University Business Officers—*College and University Business Administration* (1992) and *The Basic Fund Accounting Training Package* (Greene, 1987).

Table 6.2 identifies another important dimension of higher education funding in the United States. A powerful complement to governmental financial support and student tuition, "voluntary support" for higher education consists of gifts, grants, and donations from such sources as alumni, corporations, and foundations. During 1996–97, for example, voluntary support accounted for a total of almost $16 billion to American higher education.

TABLE 6.1

REVENUES AND EXPENDITURES OF COLLEGES AND UNIVERSITIES, 1994–95

	Public Institutions		Private Institutions	
	Amount	Percent of total	Amount	Percent of total
Revenues				
Tuition and fees	$21,908,104,000	18.4%	$29,598,772,000	42.4%
Federal government				
Appropriations	1,766,412,000	1.5	218,038,000	0.3
Grants and contracts	11,170,894,000	9.4	6,547,698,000	9.3
Research-and-development centers	254,537,000	0.2	3,285,593,000	4.7
State governments				
Appropriations	39,405,865,000	33.0	232,579,000	0.3
Grants and contracts	3,448,815,000	2.9	1,255,793,000	1.8
Local Governments				
Appropriations	4,243,984,000	3.6	3,763,000	---
Grants and contracts	512,900,000	0.5 4.0	405,314,000	0.6
Private gifts, grants, and contracts	4,737,529,000	0.6	6,129,220,000	8.8
Endowment income	693,313,000		3,294,904,000	4.7
Sales and services		3.0		
Educational activities	3,616,034,000	9.5	1,987,217,000	2.8
Auxiliary enterprises	11,373,646,000	10.5	6,962,448,000	10.0
Hospitals	12,527,982,000	3.1	6,572,234,000	9.4
Other	3,652,477,000		3,314,546,000	4.7
Total current-fund revenues	$119,312,493,000	100%	$69,808,077,000	100%
Expenditures				
Instruction	$37,599,194,000	32.6%	$18,120,513,000	26.8%
Research	11,829,665,000	10.2	5,279,876,000	7.8
Public service	5,034,445,000	4.4	1,657,040,000	2.5
Academic support	8,463,236,000	7.3	3,815,455,000	5.7
Student services	5,614,011,000	4.9	3,445,983,000	5.1
Institutional support	9,929,007,000	8.6	6,915,821,000	10.2
Plant operation and maintenance	7,668,919,000	6.6	4,076,986,000	6.0
Scholarships and fellowships	4,622,023,000	4.0	7,623,304,000	11.3
Mandatory transfers	1,373,267,000	1.2	1,049,256,000	1.6
Auxiliary enterprises	11,235,143,000	9.7	5,969,773,000	8.8
Hospitals	11,801,589,000	10.2	6,269,769,000	9.3
Federally financed research-and- development centers	254,424,000	0.2	3,279,859,000	4.9
Total current-fund expenditures	$115,464,975,000	100%	$67,503,635,000	100%

Note: A dash indicates less then 0.1 percent. Because of rounding, details may not add to totals.

Source: Almanac Issue, *Chronicle of Higher Education*, August 28, 1998.

Harvard University was at the top of those institutions receiving voluntary support with gift income of more than $428 million.

These gifts from private sources allow institutions to construct and renovate facilities and to develop significant endowments, with the interest from these endowments used to support such activities as scholarships and endowed chairs and professorships. In the most recent years for which data were available, the size of college and university endowments across the nation ranged from approximately $2 million at the University of Wisconsin at Whitewater to almost $11 billion at Harvard University ("Fact File. . ."

TABLE 6.2

SOURCES OF VOLUNTARY SUPPORT FOR HIGHER EDUCATION, 1996–97

	Amount	Percent
Alumni	$ 4,650,000,000	29%
Other individuals	3,850,000,000	24
Corporations	3,050,000,000	19
Foundations	3,200,000,000	20
Religious organizations	250,000,000	2
Other organizations	1,000,000,000	6
Total	$16,000,000,000	100%

Note: Because of rounding, figures may not add to 100 percent.

Source: Almanac Issue, Chronicle of Higher Education, August 28, 1998.

Chronicle of Higher Education, February 16, 1996; Almanac Issue, Chronicle of Higher Education, August 28, 1998). There are lovely and surprising stories in these endowments, stories that reveal the richness of higher education diversity and the distinctive public/private feature of American higher education. Berea College in Kentucky, with an enrollment of approximately 1,600 students, has an endowment of $522 million, more than many larger state universities such as the University of Illinois and the University of California at Los Angeles.

How do these current patterns of expenditure compare to previous years, and what exactly is the nature of the investment Americans have made in American higher education? To answer that question, let's go back to the middle of the twentieth century and take financial snapshots every 10 years. Table 6.3 gives us a glimpse of how revenue and expenditure patterns have changed over the last 40 to 50 years. There has been a dramatic increase in the

---

TABLE 6.3

HIGHER EDUCATION CURRENT FUND INCOME FOR SELECTED YEARS
(IN MILLIONS OF DOLLARS)

1909–10	$82
1919–20	$200
1929–30	$554
1939–40	$715
1949–50	$2,375
1959–60	$5,786
1959–70	$21,515
1981–82	$72,191
1994–95	$173,000

Source: American Council on Education Fact Book; Almanac Issue, Chronicle of Higher Education, August 28, 1998.

financial investment made in higher education. But there is a clear change in trend, as we shall soon see.

We move now from national patterns of financial support to regional patterns. Every two years, the Southern Regional Education Board (SREB) publishes a set of activity and achievement indicators in the *SREB Fact Book on Higher Education*. In the 1994–95 issue, the following is the lead summary paragraph:

> We are investing less of our public budgets in higher education than we did 10 years ago—even though nearly one million more students are attending college. While our public spending for colleges (adjusted for inflation) has grown 4 percent in the past decade, this growth has not kept pace with growth in other sectors of the public budget. Our public colleges and universities lost a potential investment of $4 billion as states and localities reduced the share of tax dollars going to higher education. At the same time, college enrollments grew by 26 percent (Highlights Inside Back Cover, 1994–95).

Figure 6.1, taken from the SREB book, furnishes informing profiles of what has been happening at both national and state levels on the question of who pays. Clearly, states are paying a smaller share and students are paying a larger share.

The origins of this shift in revenue sources are traced in *The Fiscal Crisis of the States* (Gold, 1995). Steven D. Gold indicates that the factors contributing to the pressures on state revenues include recessionary conditions in many states, the explosion in Medicaid expenses, federal mandates passed to the states, court rulings on such state issues as equity in public school finance and corrections, and in some cases dysfunctional state tax systems. Among his conclusions is the following: "Higher education took the worst beating of any major spending category, with spending virtually unchanged over the three year period. Appropriations in 1992–93 were less than 1 percent higher than in 1989–90" (Gold, 1995, p. 25).

Concern over these changing patterns of revenue is reflected in many sources but is certainly front and center in the February 1998 report *Straight Talk About College Costs and Prices* released by the federally legislated National Commission on the Cost of Higher Education (NCCHE). The Commission expressed concern that the price of college (what students and their families are charged and what they pay) was rising faster than the cost of college (what an institution spends to provide education and related educational services to students).

NCCHE offered five major recommendations in its report calling for institutions to get a tighter control over their costs. Interestingly, one of the five recommendations was directed toward accreditation, which builds

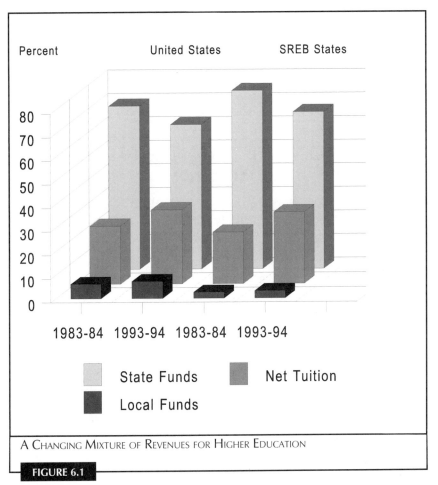

A Changing Mixture of Revenues for Higher Education

FIGURE 6.1

Source: Southern Regional Education Board Fact Book, 1994–95.

the link between quality and funding. While this recommendation centers on the need to reduce the costs associated with regional and specialized accreditation, it also encourages accreditation agencies to "devise standards and review processes that support greater institutional productivity, efficiency, and cost constraint" (p. 32).

We would like to note that these multiple expectations for the role of accreditation reflect again the complex purpose and performance heritage of higher education. Accreditation is known to the public primarily as an instrument of educational quality assurance; but various stakeholders, both academic and civic, expect accreditation to assure other goals such as enhanced diversity in students and staff, efficiency and productivity in fiscal matters, integrity in its educational and management operations, and to keep an eye on big-time athletics.

The central idea, thus far, is that Americans have made a truly splendid investment in higher education, from the standpoint of both governmental support and personal/corporate gifts. There are definite changes in the pattern of that support and serious cost-containment pressures, which we will explore further in the chapter.

FORMULA FUNDING AND THE EQUITABLE ALLOCATION OF STATE FUNDS

Before we move to questions of how societal and governmental goals are advanced via fiscal policy, we pause to consider the manner in which states allocate funds to their public institutions. What criteria are appropriate to make equitable distribution to institutions of widely varying history, mission, enrollment, and location?

At one time, it could be argued for many states that the principal factor affecting the size of an institutional appropriation was the political lobbying power of its president and the size of the previous year's budget. When children of the World War II baby boom began to arrive on campuses in larger numbers in the 1960s many campuses experienced dramatic enrollment growth. This pattern of enrollment growth meant that many states began to feel pressures to expand educational opportunity beyond the traditional state university or universities, which had rarely been located in major population centers of the state. Thus, presidents of newer and growing institutions, such as new community colleges and emerging state universities, began lobbying state legislatures not only for more funds but for a more equitable distribution of those funds.

The response in many states was the creation of an "academic referee" to take some of the pressure from the governor and legislature. In some cases, the referee was a single statewide governing board; but in many states, newer agencies in the form of coordinating commissions and boards were created, as previously detailed in chapter three on governance.

"Formula funding" was the policy instrument constructed by these coordinating agencies for (1) presenting the reasonable needs of higher education; (2) promoting the equitable allocation of those funds; (3) recognizing differences in campus missions; and (4) accomplishing statewide goals. At the risk of oversimplifying the concept, formula funding may be understood as the product of two double-entry matrices as shown in Figure 6.2.

The first matrix is a record of instructional activity, usually in the form of credit hour totals, level of instruction (lower division through doctoral), and by program field (from English to engineering). The second matrix is a record

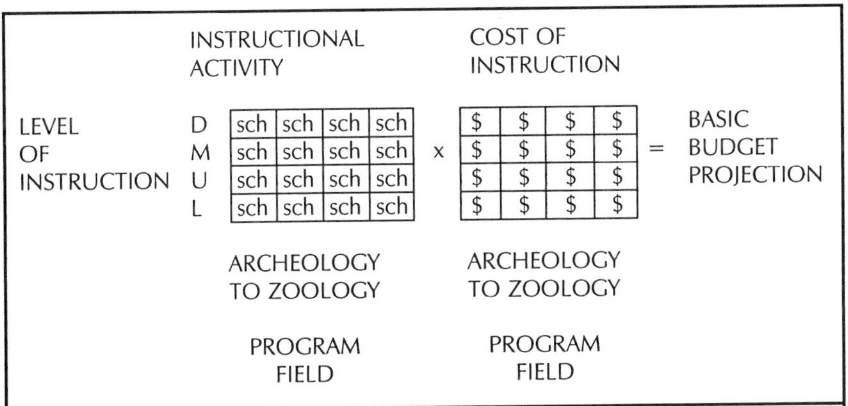

	INSTRUCTIONAL ACTIVITY	COST OF INSTRUCTION	

A BASIC MODEL OF INSTITUTIONAL FORMULA FUNDING

FIGURE 6.2

of how much it costs to deliver a unit of instruction by degree level and program field. The costs for instruction may be derived from actual studies of costs in a state or estimates derived from comparative profiles in other states.

For example, one might expect instructional costs to be lower for undergraduate instruction as compared to doctoral instruction. And one might expect instructional costs to be lower for those disciplines in which expensive capital costs were not required, English versus engineering as an example. Certainly other variables such as library investments for advanced graduate study and the effect of market on faculty salaries also play a role in determining instructional costs.

The basic intent and effect of formula funding was to recognize both mission and enrollment patterns of an institution. Thus, the principle of equity was advanced by means of this policy.

A more advanced expression of formula funding that carries the concepts of mission and enrollment equity another step further is that of "peer funding." It might be reasonably argued that institutions vary in the extent to which market forces affect their ability to recruit and retain faculty and that this affects their costs in a direct way. For example, a research university may be competing more in a national/international market, as compared to a comprehensive university or community college, and these market conditions are reflected in differential salary profiles. Readers interested in such profiles will find the annual October issue of the AAUP journal *Academe* an informing presentation of average faculty salaries by state, institution, and faculty rank. Again, at the risk of oversimplifying the concept, the concept of peer funding may be understood from Figure 6.3. Similar to the basic formula funding just described, an enrollment matrix by level of instruction and academic disci-

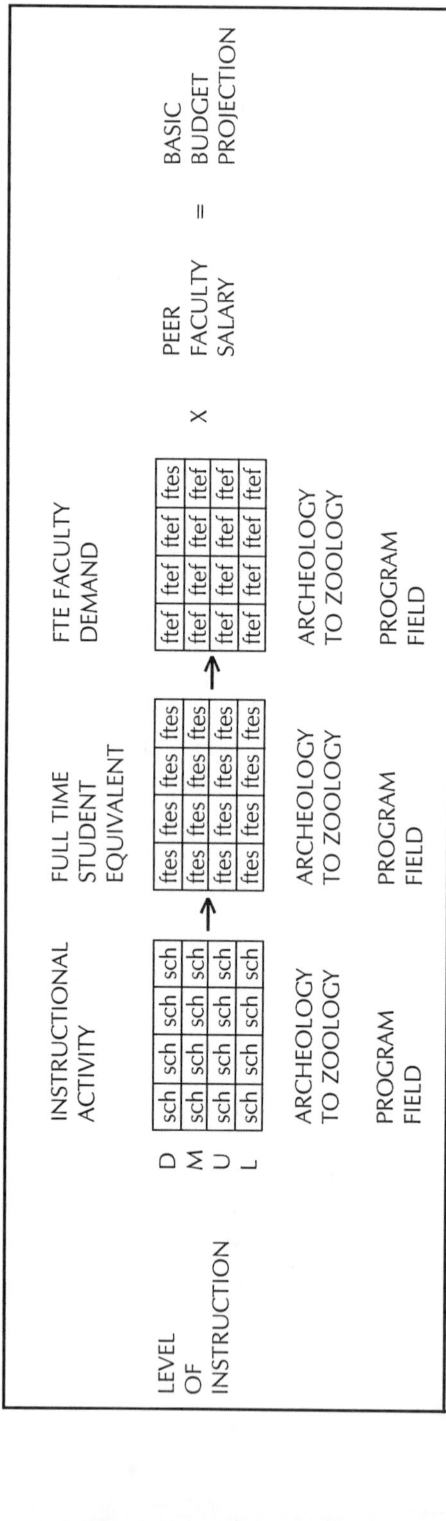

A Basic Model of Peer Institutional Formula Funding

FIGURE 6.3

pline is first developed. Usually the basic data element of this matrix is credit hour activity by level and academic discipline. This matrix is converted to a Full Time Equivalent Student matrix by an agreed-upon equivalence factor. Typically, undergraduate credit hour activity will be divided by 12 or 15 on the assumption that one full time student will take a minimum of four to five three-hour courses. Graduate credit hour activity will be divided by a factor of 9 to 12.

The next step is to translate the Full Time Equivalent Student matrix into a Full Time Equivalent Faculty Demand Matrix. This is accomplished by dividing the full-time student entries, still arranged by level and academic discipline, by a pre-determined faculty/student ratio standard. For example, in a given academic discipline, one full-time faculty may be produced by 25 lower-division students, one full time faculty by 10 master's-level students, and one full-time faculty by 4 doctoral students. The effect is to recognize different instructional loads (by level) and practices.

Finally, the projected Full Time Equivalent faculty need is multiplied by a "peer salary" determined and derived from a study of "peer institutions" previously selected by state policy makers, usually a policy task force of institutional, board, and/or coordinating commission officers. The "peer institutions" for a public research university will be public research universities in other states, while the peers for comprehensive universities located in metropolitan regions and for community colleges will be institutions similar in locale, program profile, and size. Computer identification systems for identifying peer institutions on a range of variables are available for this purpose. The intent and effect of "peer funding" policy as a more sophisticated expression of formula funding is to further recognize mission diversity and enrollment and to further enhance equity of allocation.

The actual operation of state formula funding policies is far more complex than this introductory explanation would suggest. For example, in some states with formula funding policy, the formulas have become almost inoperative when formula projections of higher education need are at some distance from what a state is willing or can afford to allocate to higher education. When actual state appropriations are only 60 percent to 70 percent of need, as projected by the funding formula, the impact of the formula on either requesting or allocating funds may be minimal. Institutions most likely to be disadvantaged under these circumstances are those experiencing dramatic enrollment growth.

Another potential consequence of mismatch between formula projections and state fiscal realities is political ferment and conflict. Governors and state legislatures are understandably not always happy being painted as the actors with black hats, the fiscal villains, when state revenues simply will not allow formula projections to be met in any close proximity. Formulas may come under political scrutiny and higher education officials may come under political pressure on the charge that formulas are not presenting "reasonable" projections of need, where the term reasonable takes on a political connotation.

In one state, for example, to bring a closer approximation between peer institution formula projections and state revenue capacity, the state's coordinating commission was urged to revise peer institution selection from national peers to regional peers. And to be fair, regional costs of living and other variables offered some justification for such a shift in policy.

Other complications of both an educational and political nature may emerge as states grapple with equity and mission issues when some campuses are growing and others are not. If these enrollment changes take place when funds to higher education are remaining level or are being reduced, tensions can become high. The latter condition can bring particularly painful leadership moments to a campus experiencing a decline in state appropriation with rising demands for services. This is precisely the condition described by the earlier comment from the SREB Fact Book.

Readers interested in further exploration of state funding policy and formula funding are referred to earlier works by Gross (1973) and Miller (1964), and more recent works by Folger (1984), Anderson and Myerson (1987), and Waggaman (1991).

Some states have moved beyond basic equity funding to what may be described as performance funding of higher education with attempts to link state dollars not only to enrollment but to achievement. This is one form of using state fiscal policy as an instrument to serve state goals, in this case enhanced quality and accountability.

PERFORMANCE FUNDING AND QUALITY ASSURANCE

In an earlier comment we pointed to the link between quality and funding in citing NCCHE's report on the cost of higher education and its concern with accreditation. One of the higher education policy goals for many states is one of enhancing and demonstrating quality. The funding policy instrument chosen by many states to accent that goal is "performance funding."

"Performance funding" is the term most often used to describe the practice and process by which a portion of the yearly budget amount for each public institution of higher learning is tied directly to the degree to which each institution meets or exceeds certain established criteria. These criteria may include educational performance indicators such as number and percentage of students passing licensure exams, eligible programs holding professional accreditation, level of alumni and enrolled student satisfaction with programs and services, and achievement of minority access goals.

While many states have explored one or more forms of performance funding, the first and longest standing policy in actual operation is Tennessee's performance funding policy originally adopted in pilot form in the 1979–80 year. Full descriptions of the Tennessee policy may be found in the original project report (Bogue and Troutt, 1980) and in a follow-up journal article in the *Harvard Business Review* (Bogue and Brown, 1982, pp. 123–28). Evaluations of the project may be found in journal articles appearing in *Change Magazine* (Ewell, 1985, pp. 32–36) and in *The Journal of Higher Education* (Banta et al., 1996, pp. 23–45).

Essentially, the original 1980 Tennessee policy allowed institutions to earn an additional 2.5 percent on top of their basic formula-projected budget based on their performance on five variables: (1) number of academic programs accredited; (2) performance of students on outcomes in general education; (3) performance of graduates in their major or specialty fields; (4) evaluation of programs and services by alumni, enrolled students, and employers; and (5) peer evaluation of programs.

Adoption and implementation of this policy followed a five-year development effort involving 11 different campus-based pilot projects among Tennessee colleges and universities—three community colleges, five comprehensive universities, one doctoral university, one research university, and the university health center. The project was underwritten by $500,000 in support from the Kellogg Foundation, the Ford Foundation, and the Fund for the Improvement of Postsecondary Education.

The policy, now almost 20 years in operation, allows institutions to earn up to 5.45 percent of their base formula budget on 10 performance variables that include all of the above five in modified form and several others more specifically related to campus mission and goal. For the year 1998–1999, the additional funding was worth more than $6 million to the largest public campus in the state, the University of Tennessee at Knoxville.

During the period of time since the policy was implemented in 1980, more than $260 million may be traced to this performance policy. The extent to which the policy led to substantive academic policy change and improvement at the campus level remains under question, though a number of factors point to favorable educational impact. For example, when the policy was first implemented, only about two-thirds of eligible programs in the state were accredited, and that number is now virtually 100 percent. For another example of the impact of the policy, see the previously cited review by Banta et al. (1996).

Several other states are experimenting with some form of performance funding. Among those are Arkansas, Colorado, Florida, Kentucky, Louisiana, Minnesota, Missouri, Ohio, South Carolina, and Washington. Readers interested in a more detailed account of performance funding policies in these states may find a 1998 monograph *Performance Funding for Public Higher Education: Fad or Trend?* of interest (Burke and Servan, 1998, pp. 25–48). There is a wide range of policy approaches in these states. Minnesota, for example, makes funds available to colleges as they meet various goals such as expanding course offerings through telecommunications, increasing graduation rates, increasing freshman retention rates, and increasing instructional budget vs. administrative budgets. South Carolina is a case of special interest as the policy in that state, imposed by a state law, requires 100 percent of state appropriations to be made on a performance basis. There is a good deal of flux in policy and process as states try different versions of performance funding and the previously mentioned Burke and Servan monograph is informing on these different state policy ventures. As with most policy questions there are contrasting and critical views. For a critical view of the Tennessee Performance Funding policy, see Alexander Astin's commentary in his 1993 book *Assessment for Excellence* (p. 219).

As a closing note, performance funding policies in most of the states previously cited have been imposed on higher education by the action of governors and legislators, the two exceptions being Missouri and Tennessee.

ACCESS TO HIGHER EDUCATION—A PREMIER POLICY COMMITMENT

While a number of societal and state goals have been advanced via the use of fiscal policy at both the state and federal level, none has been more central to American higher education than the goal of enhancing access. One may gain perspective on the relationship between access and fiscal policy when comparing the yearly tuition and fees for a full-time student at the following institutions:

* Navarro College, Corsicana, Texas—$1,000
* The University of Virginia, Charlottesville—$4,500
* Stanford University, Palo Alto, California—$20,000

How much chance and choice do we owe to America's students? Futhermore, how much chance and choice can we afford?

American education has traveled an important philosophical journey from the early years of our nation to the moment when we prepare to enter the twenty-first century. Clearly, one philosophical and financial commitment evident in the nation is the provision of free, public education from kindergarten through the 12th grade, and the expectation that most or all young Americans will graduate from high school. However, most colleges and universities, even state-supported schools funded by tax dollars, still charge student fees and/or tuition for in-state as well as out-of-state students. Therefore, in the strictest financial sense, while we may view K-12 education as a right in American society, higher education remains a privilege.

However, in the twentieth century, Americans have taken several major steps to see to it that those who have the ability and the desire to attend college are able to do so. The first of these steps and commitments has been the establishment in most states of comprehensive community college systems that bring higher education opportunity within financial and commuting range of most state citizens.

A second step has been the dramatic expansion of programs and services available on state university campuses. In 1950, only one state university in Tennessee offered the doctoral degree, the University of Tennessee at Knoxville. Now, six of the state's nine state universities offer one or more doctoral degrees. Thus, access to both basic and more advanced educational services and programs has clearly been enhanced in the state university system. And this also is a trend in every state in the union.

Many states opened new four-year campuses, some with extensive investment in these new campuses. Beginning in 1960, the state of Florida opened five new senior campuses—University of West Florida, University of North Florida, Florida Atlantic University, University of South Florida, and University of Central Florida. In 1992, Florida established yet another senior campus, Florida Gulf Coast University.

Beyond this important investment in campuses and programs designed to serve the goal of enhanced access, both state and federal government have made an even more significant investment in financial aid for students interested in attending college. According to the fall 1998 "Almanac Issue" of the *Chronicle of Higher Education*, total institutional, state, and federal financial aid to students in 1995–96 totaled almost $56 billion, with almost three-fourths of that from federal government sources. Table 6.4 furnishes a detailed profile.

The Higher Education Act of 1965 furnished the first major insertion of federal funds into financial aid programs. Prior to 1972, federal funds were distributed to states who, in turn, dispersed the aid to students. The adoption of the Basic Educational Opportunity Grants (BEOG) marked the transition to direct federal student aid. Other programs include the Supplemental Educational Opportunity Grants (SEOG), College Work Study (CWS), Direct Student Loans (DSL), Guaranteed Student Loans (GSL), and Student Loan Marketing Association (Sallie Mae), all initiated by the Higher Education Act of 1965.

More recent actions of the federal government have shifted federal aid programs more in the direction of student loans than grants. The impact of this shift is the topic of an active public policy debate, and there are some who suggest that the shift to loans may have intensified the cost barrier for many

TABLE 6.4	
STUDENT FINANCIAL AID, 1996–97	
Total spending, by source in millions	
Federal programs	
Generally available aid	
Pell Grants	$ 5,660
Supplemental Educational	
Opportunity Grant	583
State Student Incentive Grants	35
College Work-Study	760
Perkins Loans	943
Ford Direct Student Loan Program	
Subsidized Stafford Student Loans	5,687
Unsubsidized Stafford Student Loans	3,167
Parent Loans for Undergraduate Students	943
Federal Family Education Loan Program	
Subsidized Stafford Student Loans	11,649
Unsubsidized Stafford Student Loans	6,936
Parent Loans for Undergraduate Students	1,734
Subtotal	38,093
Specially directed aid	
Veterans	1,406
Military	463
Other grants	242
Other loans	261
Subtotal	2,372
Total federal aid	40,465
State grant programs	3,190
Institutional and other grants	10,569
Total federal, state, and institutional aid	55,736

Source: Almanac Issue, *Chronicle of Higher Education*, 1998.

prospective students and narrowed career choices because students are not willing to mortgage their future earnings by large loans. The December 1998 issue of the policy bulletin *Postsecondary Opportunity* suggested that the probability of a student earning a baccalaureate degree by age 24 was almost 10 times higher for students from families in the upper quartile of family income as compared to students from families in the lower quartile of family income. This is a troublesome policy trend and one that does not speak well to the policy goal of enhancing collegiate access for all Americans.

A February 1999 policy report bearing a similar message is "The Tuition Puzzle: Putting the Pieces Together," released by the Institute for Higher Education Policy in Washington, D.C. This report concludes that "Overall, average tuition and fees increased almost five fold over the last two decades, or nearly doubled after adjusting for inflation. The significant investment in student financial aid helped to ease, but not erase, the consequences of higher prices" (p. 5). The report further suggested that an incremental enrollment migration had occurred, with middle and higher income students moving toward universities and lower income students remaining concentrated in two-year public colleges.

At least one encouraging note can be found in this trend: Americans have invented colleges to serve those who may not be able to afford more expensive schools or who need to establish their academic confidence. The American two-year community college is an invention of no small moment for our nation, whether viewed in economic or educational perspective.

Some scholars have claimed that rising college costs coupled with increased reliance on student loans has caused the proportion of low-income students attending college to decline (Lee, 1986; Wallace, 1993). This position has been rebutted by Baum and Schwartz (1986), who argue that relatively few high school graduates who desire to attend college are unable to do so for financial reasons. Some claim (Grossman, 1994) that colleges have formed cartels to limit the amount of financial aid a student might receive. Other issues include the practice of "tuition discounting," usually by private schools in which the full "sticker price" is paid by affluent students and scholarships or "discounts" are granted to other students (Sanoff, 1993).

And we should not leave this discussion without noting one other lamentable outcome of federally based scholarship and loan programs. Many students have defaulted on their loan obligations. At one point, the amount in default to the federal government reached the staggering sum of $3.5 billion. While some level of default may be expected, it passes credibility that physicians, lawyers, teachers, engineers, and other college graduates have defaulted on their loans. Proprietary schools and some historically black colleges have been the targets of special concern on the default issue. The concern over default rates has led the federal government to a range of corrective measures, including the review of income tax returns and the recent creation of state agencies called State Postsecondary Review Entities (SPREs), whose purpose was to review any campus, public or private, where the default rate passed an acceptable federal standard. As of this writing, the SPREs appear to have experienced an early mortality, as they were not funded in the most recent federal budget.

Other issues surrounding financial aid policy include an intense debate over the constitutional legality of awarding financial aid to students solely on the basis of race. This issue has experienced a tumultuous history and readers are referred to background pieces by Geyelin (1992) and Baker (1994).

A variety of other policy developments related to financial aid have also emerged over the course of time. In some states, for example, funds have been established for "prepayment" of tuition, thus purchasing a future space at current rates. There appears to be mixed reaction and success of these systems, and it will take years to fully evaluate the impact of such policies. Other institutional and state practices are described in Edward St. John's 1995 monograph entitled *Rethinking Tuition and Student Aid Strategies*.

One other policy development at the state level should be examined before we leave the the issue of using fiscal policy as an instrument to promote access. Some states have developed scholarship programs that guarantee full-tuition scholarships to students who complete high school with specified grade point averages or meet other specific academic standards. In Georgia, the "Hope" scholarships make access to college more of a reality than a dream for many Georgians. These scholarships funded from a state lottery work to keep more talented Georgian students in state.

ATTRACTING AND RETAINING FACULTY AND STAFF

The pay and benefits of instructional and administrative staff are almost always the principal expenditures of any institution. There is a wide variety of opinion and practice concerning how and how well academic faculty and administrators are or should be paid, and what kinds of benefits they receive or should receive. Derek Bok's recent book *The Cost of Talent* (1993) is instructive on this question and suggests that college professors have not been among the more advantaged American professionals in terms of salary growth in recent years. Nevertheless, there remains a concern by many inside and outside higher education regarding the salaries of faculty members, particularly those who are highly paid and/or are in fields that command particularly high salaries, and of chief campus and system executives.

We would like to return to our opening statement that how a society spends its money is an operative expression of what it values. Why our society is willing to pay someone $40 million a year in salary to bounce a basketball while it pays a teacher at any level less than a 1,000th of that sum to furnish the mind, heart, and soul of our students will no doubt furnish thoughtful occupation for philosophers, historians, and social archeologists of the future. And within our colleges and universities we can find equally intriguing profiles as one examines the salary differentials among big-time football coaches, campus presidents, and professors—a topic we explore more specifically in chapter nine on athletics and academics.

FUNDING RESEARCH—INTENT AND IMPROPRIETY

As we noted in the opening section of this chapter, a major source of revenues for many colleges and universities, especially larger ones, is government funding for research. Indeed it may be argued that this federal investment in research has been the principal engine behind major advances in agriculture, science, and engineering in the twentieth century. In addition to providing funds for actual research projects, including salaries for researchers, most government-funded research projects provide additional funds for overhead costs. This is based upon the rationale that the research project should pay its fair-share cost of institutional operations such as office space, maintenance, and utilities. However, the purpose and amounts of such payments have become of significant concern to lawmakers and others because of sometimes extravagant misuses of these funds by certain institutions. Lawmakers and their constituents have also raised concerns about the fair distribution of such research money among various institutions.

Before getting into specific concerns, let's find out just how much money we are talking about and how it is distributed. In 1989, institutions in California, the state receiving the most federal research money, received more than $1.28 billion, while Alabama institutions, towards the low end of the scale, received $115 million (Blumenstyk, 1991, pp. A23, A31). While leading research universities in states like California, New York, Maryland, and Massachusetts get far more money than others; there has been an increase in recent years' funding for institutions in previously overlooked states such as Alabama, Georgia, Oklahoma, South Carolina, and Tennessee. In 1996, the University of California received $105 million in defense department grants and contracts from the federal government (*Almanac Issue* of the *Chronicle of Higher Education*, 1998, p. 38). It is obvious that we are not talking about small change here.

Most of this money is provided either through a merit-review process or as continuing support for ongoing research projects. However, according to one federal report, $270 million was "earmarked" for certain schools in fiscal year 1990, and a total of $900 million was earmarked for about 300 projects over the prior decade (Myers, 1991, p. A27). "Earmarking" here refers to providing funds directly to a specific institution without providing for a competitive or merit-review process to determine which, if any, institution will receive certain research projects. While proponents of this process say that it provides money to schools that have traditionally received less federal research money, the report cited above shows that 40 percent of this money went to only five states and that, at the institutional level, almost 40 percent went to only ten universities.

More recently, *The Christian Science Monitor* ("Don't Put Pork First," 1993) commented on a Congressional Research Service report that showed that 54.4 percent of all earmarked funds went to just 20 institutions, and that 50.5 percent went to just 10 states. In fiscal year 1994, Congress earmarked $651 million for university projects; however, this was actually a decline from a 1993 peak of $763 million which had been increasing steadily each year since the 1990 level of $270 million (Cordes and Ornstein, 1994, pp. A10–21).

Of far more concern to many individuals than the actual amounts of these grants are the instances, both real and perceived, of misuse of such funds by institutions and individuals. A widely publicized instance occurred at Stanford University, where research "overhead" funds were apparently used for such items as yacht trips and furniture for the president's house ("Not Just the Yacht," 1992, p. C6). Following the revelation of these misdeeds during the winter of 1990–91, the IRS launched full-scale investigations targeting Stanford and other universities accused of such misdeeds (Jaschik, 1991b), while the White House Office of Management and Budget proposed limiting overhead reimbursements to 26 percent (Cordes, 1991). Some overhead reimbursements had been as high as 43 to 65 percent. Universities opposed to this move argued that they should still be reimbursed for actual costs incurred, which could sometimes legitimately be higher than the 26 percent maximum.

Although it has been nearly five years since this issue came to the forefront, it still holds considerable interest for lawmakers, particularly Representative George E. Brown, Jr. (D-CA), chair of the House Committee on Science, Space and Technology. Representative Brown called on the White House to issue an executive order directing agencies to ignore any earmarking which appears to have been influenced by lobbyists and continues to comment publicly on his opposition to the influence of lobbyists in the research budgeting process (Wyatt, 1993).

FISCAL POLICY AND OTHER SOCIETAL/POLITICAL GOALS

In addition to the major goals already cited, many states have provided funding for a range of other goals, particularly in the decade of the 1980s. A report of the Forum for College and University Governance entitled *State Incentive Funding: Leveraging Quality* (1990), revealed that states supported a variety of categorical, competitive, and mixed category programs for a total of approximately $1.25 billion in the 1980s. Among the kinds of programs supported by this incentive funding were the following: eminent scholars/ endowed chairs; centers of excellence/program recognition and enhancement; equipment and capital trust funds; grant programs for program/curricular innovation; research and public service enhancements; library enhancement; economic development; and faculty recognition programs.

A more detailed description of these programs may be found in the previously cited resource of the Forum for College and University Governance (1990) and in *The Evidence for Quality* (Bogue and Saunders, 1992).

One of the most frequently adopted options for quality enhancement is one designed to attract and support widely recognized scholars—the eminent scholar/endowed chair option noted above. Typically, the state incentive will match institutional funds attracted for the purpose of endowing a full chair or partially endowed professorship. In Ohio, for example, the state matches institutional funds dollar for dollar, whereas in other states the match may be a 60 to 40 percent match. In some states, such as Louisiana, private institutions may participate in the state incentive program; but in other states, such as Tennessee, private institutions are not permitted to do so.

The major point here is that when state economies and revenue bases are in good shape, states may not only provide good support for the basic operational budgets of campuses, but will also often support enrichment and enhancement programs designed to serve a variety of both educational and economic development goals. These programs are likely to be among the first to be cut and/or reduced, however, when state revenues decline and/or states face more competitive pressures for their revenues, an issue to which we now turn.

COST CONTAINMENT PRESSURES AND THEIR IMPACT

The following headlines from popular and professional press give further evidence of the trend noted in the opening of this chapter on fiscal policy: "Finally, Colleges Start to Cut Their Crazy Costs," Shawn Tully, *Fortune*, May 1, 1995; "A Lot Less Moola on Campus," Christina DelValle, Eric Schine, and Gary McWilliams, *Business Week*, October 5, 1992; "Big Chill on Campus," Richard Ostling, *Time*, February 3, 1992; and "Looming Deficits," Roger Benjamin, *Change Magazine*, March/April 1998. Clearly, there is a new fiscal reality for American higher education. At the beginning of the 1990s, state governments appropriated less money for higher education than they had in the previous year, the first time in 33 years that higher education had experienced a decline in state support (Jaschik, November 6, 1991).

In addition to coverage in the popular press, almost every major policy journal in higher education has featured one or more articles on the new cost containment climate in recent years. The AAUP journal *Academe* devoted its November/December 1993 issue to a case study of shared governance at the University of Maryland at College Park, which lost $45 million in revenue, roughly 20 percent of its state budget. The consultative processes arranged between administrative and faculty leadership on the Maryland campus led to the elimination of seven departments, a college, and twenty-nine degree programs.

The March 1991 issue of *AAHE Bulletin*, a policy publication of the American Association for Higher Education, featured an interview with two New Jersey higher education officials concerning their reaction to cost containment pressures in that state. Deferring maintenance, freezing open positions, reducing scholarships, cutting equipment purchases—these are some of the first strategies that institutions examine when faced with retrenchment and budget cuts. In the interview, Harold Eickhoff, president of Trenton State College, offered this sobering but helpful comment: "The old rules are not very useful. It doesn't work these days to approach the public and say, 'If you fail to fund us at what we believe is an appropriate level, the airplanes will fall out of the skies, the ships will sink at sea.' They won't believe it" ("Coping with the Cutbacks," 1991, p. 6).

The extensive list of states that have experienced dramatic cutbacks in higher education appropriations in the past five years include Maine, Massachusetts, New Jersey, Virginia, Maryland, Michigan, Oregon, and Louisiana.

Change Magazine devoted its entire November/December 1990 issue to the subject of cost containment. The issue contained articles on lessons to be learned from corporate downsizing and health care cost pressures. While the issue is rich with ideas, we focus on two that appear to draw affirmation from the literature.

Zemsky and Massy examine the response of the University of Michigan and conclude that "The most important lesson to be learned from Michigan's public commitment to cost containment may simply be that public colleges and universities cannot be expected to engage in either academic pruning or administrative simplification if they do not first enjoy substantial fiscal and institutional autonomy"(1990, p. 20).

Another policy publication is *Policy Perspectives* of the PEW Higher Education Research Program at the University of Pennsylvania. Several of its issues over the past half decade have engaged directly or indirectly issues of mission and cost. The March 1992 issue featured a dialogue among several prominent policy scholars and practitioners in American higher education and featured this opening note by T. Edward Hollander: "The bottom line is that we in higher education have to learn to do well with less. Unfortunately, we don't have much experience in doing that. In many states, we lack the freedom to do it; and in many institutions, we lack the necessary structure" ("Beginning the Dialogue," 1992, p. 1B).

Whether the "shared authority" relationship between the collegial involvement of the faculty and the hierarchical involvement of administrators will work well under cost containment pressures is a governance question still open for discussion. To what extent will faculty and administrators be able to forego their own self-interest when programs and services have to be reduced and/or eliminated? To what extent will it be possible to maintain a sense of community within an institution when the lifeboat mentality is at work?

Writing in an article entitled "Too Many Administrators," Jay Halfond (1991) reveals that since 1975, EEOC records show that the number of full-time faculty in American colleges and universities rose 6 percent while administrative positions rose 45 percent, faculty salaries after inflation rose 21 percent, while administrative salaries rose 42 percent. Other journals have referred to this trend as "Administrative Bloat" (Bergmann, 1991) and "Bureaucratic Accretion" (Gumport and Pusser, 1995). Such patterns are not likely to go unnoticed by faculty as budget cuts arrive on campuses, and will offer, as we noted in chapter three, governance challenges to both shared authority and community on college campuses.

Associated with more stringent fiscal conditions in higher education is the emergence of what some call "responsibility center budgeting" (Whalen, 1991). In essence, this approach to budgeting calls for organizational units—whether academic or administrative—to align their expenditures more directly with their income. A principal advantage to larger and more complex institutions, responsibility center budgeting places decision making close to policy and program action, and encourages more independence and responsibility in management control. While it may be relatively easy to allocate such income as student fees, the allocation of state appropriations to different academic and administrative service centers is not a small question, nor is the allocation of costs a simple matter.

Some academic units may have more access to enhanced funding than others. For example, professional schools may have access to enhanced sources of income as compared to humanities, arts, and social sciences. The extent to which higher education can and should operate something close to the corporate model of "profit centers" or "every tub on its own bottom" is an issue that will be engaged more fully during coming years. It would be unwise to do what we so often tend to do in higher education, which is to adopt some new management fad as the cure-all for our ills. Nevertheless, it is clear that leaders of both academic programs and administrative services will be expected to draw a closer link between income and expenditures in the future.

Another theme emerging is expressed in the title of the 1997 book by Sheila Slaughter and Larry Leslie, *Academic Capitalism*. The authors argue that "changes in revenue patterns promote academic capitalism because they push faculty and institutions into market and marketlike behaviors to compensate for loss of share from block grants" (p. 111). The pressure to escalate tuition charges and to transform American higher education into more of a market organization are profound policy trends. We will have more to say on this in our final chapter.

At stake here is more than these immediate issues, but also include long-term issues of trust in this nation and its institutions. The pervasive range of layoffs and downsizing occurring in corporate America have left many Americans cynical about the trust relationship between organizations and those who give life and meaning to them. Compassion, candor, courage—these simple values will find more importance in the times ahead as American higher education struggles with decisions of mission, quality, costs, productivity, and priority.

We should not believe that this is the first retrenchment moment, or even the most dramatic moment, in American higher education. Brubacher and Rudy (1976) tell us that almost 500 small colleges opened and closed their doors in this country during the years of the nineteenth century just preceding the Civil War. During the depression years of the 1930s and into the 1940s, state appropriations for higher education were modest indeed, compared to current figures, and most states experienced a decade or more of reduced expenditures for higher education. A historic perspective may not ease the pain of current cost containment challenges, but instead may let us understand that others have traversed similar and more challenging paths before. Cheit was writing on retrenchment in 1971 in *The New Depression in Higher Education*, and Mingle et al. were writing on the same theme in their 1981 book *Challenges of Retrenchment*.

A TRANSITIONAL MOMENT FOR FISCAL POLICY

By any standard, Americans have made a magnificent financial investment in higher education during this century. They have used that investment to advance the goals of enhanced access and quality, and the social and economic health of our nation. The results of that investment are apparent in the number, size, diversity, and achievement of our colleges; in the training, competence, and devotion of those serving in our colleges and universities; and in the recognition accorded American higher education, as other nations send their students to our colleges and universities for developing the leadership promise of their citizens. Americans can take justifiable pleasure in what their personal and political largesse has produced, and American academics can be grateful for that generosity.

If we now face possible constraints in levels of financial support for higher education, historic perspective and sensitivity are appropriate in realizing that this is certainly not the first time such challenges have been confronted. While there is a tendency to face budget and cost containment challenges in linear fashion—what are our priorities and what programs/services might we reduce or eliminate—tight fiscal climates also offer a moment for imagination and creativity. Writing in the spring 1991 issue of *Educational Record*, Peter Smith quotes Mark Twain and then offers his own reflection on higher education's response to cost containment pressures: "Mark Twain once said, 'If you're going to get run out of town, get in front and make it look like a parade.' While this offered a good strategy for survival in nineteenth century America, it may not be much solace for America's colleges and universities in the turbulent 1990s. I think, however, that we can lead the parade. But we must permit and celebrate radical change in the ways we do our business if our leadership is going to be effective" (p. 28).

Continuing to serve the goals of access, quality, and equity, economic development in retrenchment and cost containment climates offers a challenge of mind, heart, and character. American academics will need courage and compassion; daring and discipline; initiative and integrity; persistence and partnership; and radical thought and resilience. These are not bad ideals to model before our students, colleagues, and civic friends.

CHAPTER 7

Student Life and Development
The Mosaic of Student Influence and Involvement

*H*ow College Affects Students is the title of an extensive work detailing the cognitive, attitudinal, socioeconomic, and moral impact of colleges upon students (Pascarella and Terenzini, 1991). This book follows earlier works on the same theme, including Bowen's *Investment in Learning: The Individual and Social Value of American Higher Education* (1978); *Does College Matter?* by Lewis Solomon and Paul Taubman (1973); and *The Impact of College on Students* by Kenneth Feldman and Theodore Newcomb (1973). We can also reverse the question of Pascarella and Terenzini's *How College Affects Students* and ask "How students affect college?" to prompt even further thought on the subject of student life and development in American higher education.

Our aspirations in this chapter are more modest. We first point the reader to some of the important literature on student life and development in American higher education, such as the works cited in the previous paragraph. We also identify how student aspirations, attitudes, and actions have helped shape American colleges and universities. Another goal of the chapter is to reveal how once excluded groups of students now enrich the mosaic of student characteristics in higher education, exploring questions of who attends and why. We touch finally on college impact and influence on students.

For this chapter, the authors would like to acknowledge the assistance of Dr. Jerry Askew. Dr. Askew was formerly dean of students and associate vice chancellor for development and university relations at the University of Tennessee and is now executive director of the East Tennessee Community Foundation.

THE INFLUENCE OF STUDENT ASPIRATION, ATTITUDES, AND ACTIONS

In earlier chapters, we traced how American higher education has changed over the three-and-a-half centuries since Harvard College was chartered. Among the prominent factors influencing the evolution of American higher education are the goals, needs, and expectations brought by increasingly diverse student populations. Students have "voted with their feet" to influence revisions in the curriculum and have gone outside sanctioned boundaries to create a rich and varied developmental agenda beyond the classroom and other more formal academic settings. Students have persuaded colleges and universities to furnish them with meaningful participation in the governance life of the institution, as suggested in chapter three. They have had their constitutional rights as citizens of the United States acknowledged by judicial authority, so that arbitrary and unilateral action may not be taken against them.

Students have always been a powerful force on campuses, and they continue to exert major influence on every major policy domain in colleges and universities. Mirroring the character of the institutions they attend, students are a pluralistic confederacy of competing and cooperating subgroups, individualistic and collective—exemplars of paradox and contradiction, conservators of tradition and champions of change. Students are keen to protect the quality, integrity, and value of their degrees, but are occasionally willing to cheat, settle for mediocre standards, and chart degree paths of low challenge. They will often agitate for meaningful and quality changes in curricula, but sometimes in their hunger for a credential ask only what hurdles must be managed to escape a course or acquire a credential. Most are open to diversity but sometimes self-insulating from those who are different.

During the history of higher education, some college faculty and administrators may have imagined students as malleable raw material waiting to be shaped into a full intellectual and spiritual flower, or worse as empty buckets to be filled. Students, however, have often assumed more active and assertive roles in their college experiences—accepting policy and revolting against policy, yielding to academic authority and stepping outside the established boundaries of behaviors and policy, reflecting apathy and exhibiting aggressiveness on many policy and practice fronts. As we noted in earlier chapters, colleges of the colonial era were committed to a classical liberal arts curriculum linked to the mission of preserving and promoting religious piety. The residential college model of England's Cambridge and Oxford universities, transported by early colonial settlers, was originally intended as a comprehensive intellectual, social, and spiritual experience for students. Students were expected to reside on campus in close association with tutors, the intent being to foster a close-knit community in which students and their teachers lived and studied in common facilities and fellowship.

This residential ideal was sought initially through close control of student time and activities. The minutiae of early college regulations for student life alienated many students, who felt themselves to be virtual prisoners of tutors and student monitors (Brubacher and Rudy, 1976). These circumstances often provided little outlet for creative expression or play, and those charged with the control and operation of the colleges actively suppressed such frivolity in their aims to produce pious and religiously orthodox leaders for a pervasively sectarian society (Church and Sedlack, 1976; Brubacher and Rudy, 1976). This regimen contributed to high rates of dropout, low enroll-ments, and seething resentment that frequently erupted in violent rebellion on the part of some students.

The decline in the colonial effort to emulate the English residential colleges began in the latter half of the eighteenth century and accelerated in the nineteenth century (Brubacher and Rudy, 1976). The relative poverty of institutions, economic diversity of the students, and difficulty of regulating student housing and behavior all contributed to this decline.

The strictly regimented, residential student life in the early colleges was transformed in other ways. Students created outlets for interests and energies that were not provided in the curriculum or programs of the time. By the middle of the eighteenth century, students had formed clubs and societies of various kinds that afforded opportunities to read, debate, associate freely, and live in some comfort away from the constant scrutiny of college officials or informants. Many of these, particularly the literary societies, amassed exten-sive library collections and other resources, supporting the evolution of an independent and powerful student culture. The impact of these developments was far reaching. Rudolph (1990) observed, with little exaggeration, that "through the extracurriculum the student arrived at a position of commanding importance in the American college" (p. 157).

Among the more influential of student initiatives were Greek-letter societ-ies and similar organizations. For example, Phi Beta Kappa, a well-recognized academic honorary society, was founded in 1776. Other societies developed more fully in the first half of the nineteenth century. Many of these groups were secret societies, organized as scholarly societies or as social groups sharing a common residence. Into the mid 1900s, such societies were often the target of criticism, by President Charles Eliot at Harvard and President Woodrow Wilson at Princeton, because their membership tended to include primarily students of affluence and children of powerful alumni. Nevertheless, they remained an active dimension of student life on many campuses. In the latter part of the nineteenth century, similar organizations were founded for female students and followed in many ways the evolution of their earlier male counterparts.

The fraternity and sorority movement served many essential needs for students of the time. They provided for highly personal interaction and comfortable housing at a time when such was often not available through colleges (Brubacher and Rudy, 1976). They came to institutionalize a student way of life that Horowitz (1987) has termed the culture of the "college man" and "college woman." This new ideal, which accented and celebrated life outside the classroom, challenged and accompanied the transformation of the contemplative and religious orientation of the colonial colleges. Increasingly, the conservative climate of the traditional colleges failed to match the interests, aims, and enthusiasms of many students who came to college in the post-colonial era. The college experience came to be seen as both a scholarly and social development opportunity, a chance to become a leader of government, business, or industry.

Strange (1994) describes this transition as follows: In the early American colleges, from colonial period to just prior to the Civil War, the accent was on preparation of the "gentleman scholar," and student development emphasized command of the classics and refinement of civilized graces. The emergence of modern behavioral sciences and the development of psychological measurement and assessment brought knowledge of the many psychological and social factors that contribute to human growth and development, and more specifically development in the collegiate years.

The students of one generation become the college professors and administrators of the next. Eventually, those who furnished leadership for American colleges relinquished attempts to confine the independent student lifestyle and mentality of the mid-nineteenth century, the gentleman scholar concept, and embraced the concept of the well-rounded student. They began to welcome and cultivate student activities as contributors to the overall educational mission of higher education. By the 1920s, college and university administration and faculty actively sought to integrate the curriculum and the co-curriculum (Brubacher and Rudy, 1976; Levine, 1986).

STUDENT DEVELOPMENT AND THE COLLEGE STUDENT PERSONNEL MOVEMENT

The emergence of official interest in supporting and shaping student life outside the classroom became exemplified in the rise of the college student personnel movement in the 1920s (Brubacher and Rudy, 1976). The emergence of this field marked the beginning of a systematic effort to provide a professional framework where all aspects of student life, both the curriculum and the co-curriculum, could be encouraged, coordinated, studied, and better understood. Until 1972, the "Student Personnel Point of View" (1937) informed college and university policy with regard to student life (Brubacher and Rudy, 1976). Following 1972, the primary focus of college student personnel professionals has centered on the psychosocial and cognitive development of students. Several streams of research and literature furnish the foundation for the college student personnel movement in the twentieth century. Strange (1994) attributes the philosophical foundations of the student development perspective to two points of heritage. With John Dewey (1916) as a principal scholarly spokesman, the Progressive Education Movement of the 1920s contributed ". . . an emphasis on student self-direction, the importance of experiential learning techniques, the role of educators as resource guides rather than task masters, the importance of establishing comprehensive evaluative records, and the need for education to work closely with other societal institutions to effect the total development of students" (p. 399). With Patricia Cross (1981) as one of its more prominent voices, the Nontraditional Education Movement of the 1960s ". . . challenged higher education to examine further the nature of student differences and the relationship of those differences to the outcomes of college attendance" (p. 400).

A second stream of literature centers on psychosocial development during college years and on the measurement and assessment of student developmental outcomes. Beginning in the early 1960s with Nevitt Sanford's major works *The American College* (1962) and *Self and Society . . .* (1966), the proposition that student development could be enhanced through campus environments which fostered a balance between challenge and support continued for the next three decades. Scholars developed a series of theoretical frameworks to guide student personnel practitioners in their efforts to promote student growth through experiences not limited to formal educational settings of the classroom, laboratory, and library. Several theorists addressed the psychosocial (Chickering, 1969), intellectual (Perry, 1970; Baxter Magolda, 1992), and moral/ethical (Kohlberg, 1969; Gilligan, 1982) development of individual students. Others focused on personality type and learning styles (Myers, 1980a, 1980b; Kolb, 1976). Still others (Banning and Kaiser, 1974; Barker, 1968) focused on the influence of campus environments on student behavior (Chickering and Reisser, 1993). The combined work of these and other researchers has provided guidance to student personnel practitioners as they attempt to create policies, practices, and environments which result in the growth and development of well-rounded students. A companion literature on the definition and assessment of student learning outcomes has also emerged in the latter half of the twentieth century. It includes the works cited in the opening of this chapter by Bowen (1978) and Pascarella and Terenzini (1991). Other literature on this theme has been cited in chapter five, and includes, among others, the work of Astin (1993a), Banta (1994, 1995), Erwin (1991), and Ewell (1984, November/December 1985, 1988).

Finally, works have emerged that define and distinguish college student personnel professional perspective and philosophy. Included among these would be the previously cited 1937 statement on "The Student Personnel Point of View," and its 1987 revision; journal pieces exemplified by Strange (1994); monographs by Knefelkamp et al. (1978); recent handbooks on student services (Delworth, Hanson, and Associates, 1989; Komives, Woodard, Jr., and Associates, 1996); and books such as *Student Affairs Work, 2001: A Paradigmatic Odyssey* (Kuh, Whitt, Shedd, 1987). In the 1990s, it is taken as a matter of course in American higher education that extensive financial, human, and material resources are marshaled for an extensive array of programs, services, activities, and facilities unified under such titles as "student life," "student affairs," or "student development." The American college or university has come to the present not as a center solely of the cultivation of the abilities and powers of the intellect, but as a powerful socializing force and experience for students.

As a historical note, student activism in higher education is peculiar to neither recent history nor to American history. In early medieval and European universities, particularly those in southern Italy such as Bologna, students exercised no small influence in the life of those early universities. Christopher Lucas (1994) tells us, for example, that students maintained close and often covert supervision over teachers and curriculum:

> Offenses for which a master might be fined or even dismissed included failure to begin a lecture at the appointed hour, not finishing a presentation on schedule, digressing from the announced topic or subject or showing signs of unpreparedness, neglecting to employ the approved disputation method, leaving the most important points of a lecture until its conclusion when students were beginning to wander out, and so forth (p. 47).

While knowledge and perspective on student needs and development have evolved over the years, the voice and influence of students on their collegiate life is not a voice or influence restricted to recent history or American history.

In the way of summary, what might we say about the evolution of student life in the American college and university? Early colleges appeared to operate under a kind of "greenhouse" philosophy, a controlled climate approach. The prevailing belief seemed to be that agrarian and bucolic settings were more conducive to discipline of mind and virtue. Students were kept in residential cloisters that featured a close regimen of mental, physical, and spiritual supervision. "In loco parentis," to stand in place of parents, reflected early college concern for matters of student mentality and morality. We should not believe that elements of this philosophy are entirely absent in some modern American colleges. Nor should we count these features of the early colleges unworthy. An emphasis on character as well as competence, piety as well as erudition, and civic responsibility as well as personal gain is an emphasis worthy of our reexamination today. Over the years, the imagination and initiative of college students led to the development of activities mostly complementary, and a few uncomplementary, to basic academic and curricular experiences. Bridging the late nineteenth century and early twentieth century, enhanced election and choice in degree programs and the addition of newer fields of thought may be traced in part to student influence, as constructive advances in student and college life. In the late twentieth century, students volunteered in service to community and otherwise placed their energy and talent in service in both domestic and international settings, with the Peace Corps begun in the 1960s as one notable example. Over time, these cocurricular inserts into American college life included debate clubs, Greek-letter social organizations such as fraternities and sororities, academic honor societies, and intercollegiate athletics. To the value of learning for its own sake as a purpose of attending college, the value of learning for its own sake was added social prestige and financial advantage. As we have noted, the organized professional concern for "whole person" student development in the twentieth century led to the student personnel movement manifested in most colleges under today's organizational rubric of student affairs and/or student development.

Administrators, faculty, and college student personnel professionals have also contended with ventures less educational on the campus, where more playful behaviors were exhibited. In the closing years of the nineteenth century, the student prank of the time took the form of students bringing alarm clocks to class that would go off at staggered intervals during the lecture. In the 1920s, Flappers danced the Charleston to a jazzy musical beat, while thumbing their collegiate noses at Prohibition. In the 1950s, student energies tackled challenges of how many students might be crammed into a phone booth or Volkswagen beetle car or how many undergarment trophies might be carried back to the men's dormitory following "panty" raids. In the 1960s and early 1970s, "streaking" enlivened campus and community life as naked students, usually male, dashed through and across public places such as basketball courts and grassy malls in front of administration buildings, usually with campus or community police in hot pursuit.

If the 1950s and the early 1960s were considered a little playful and perhaps relatively quiet, student activism and unrest took a more serious turn in the late 1960s and early 1970s. Here our nation navigated through the turbulent waters of the civil rights movement, the cold war with the Soviet Union, and the Vietnam War; and these moments of social unrest brought more radical behaviors to our campuses. Physical confrontations and acts of civil disobedience, both peaceful and more tragic, rocked the tranquility and idyllic settings of our campuses. Classes were disrupted by angry students, student strikes brought campus activity to a halt, buildings and administrative offices were occupied by students and occasionally set afire. Finally on May 4, 1970, four students on the Kent State University campus were killed by national guard troops who had been brought to campus to restore and maintain order following acts of vandalism on campus and in the community.

Diane Ravitch (1983) provides an informing description of this era in her work *The Troubled Crusade*. During the late 1960s and early 1970s, the collapse of civility on many campuses and the politicization of the campus by radical behaviors of both students and faculty drove ideological wedges between groups of faculty and administrators and furnished a fundamental threat to a sense of community. These internal conflicts also offered serious challenge to the concept of academic freedom, an issue to which we will return in chapter eight. The radical behaviors of some students and faculty, actions of some administrators, and values of the counterculture separated some colleges and universities from the civic support of those who saw these behaviors as antithetical to the values of authority, family, patriotism, and morality. Neither sympathetic concession nor hard-nosed authority offered a certain path in restoring order on campuses during this tumultuous period in higher education history.

The closing years of the twentieth century have been relatively quiet on the surface, though student voice and involvement has taken other less radical but not necessarily less effective or activist form. The issues are multiple and include such social concerns as race, gender, sexual orientation, the environment, and abortion. Other issues, such as status and treatment of graduate teaching assistants, may be peculiar to specific campuses. Student life and activity on campuses have both reflected and shaped the social and cultural miles of our times. The enfranchisement of student groups heretofore excluded or marginally engaged by American higher education is one such example of this interaction between college and society.

OPENING DOORS TO THE EXCLUDED

In the beginning, American college students were relatively young, almost entirely white, dominantly male, and culturally European in ancestry. This heritage in student clientele has evolved in dramatic ways. Most of this evolution has occurred in the last half of the twentieth century. The story of increased access and diversity in American college students must be counted as one of the most dramatic changes in the profile of American higher education. Consistent with the legal and philosophical environment of the colonial era and extending well into the nineteenth century, American colleges served young, Caucasian males almost exclusively. Higher education has been, through much of its history, elite in calling and privilege—an exclusive preparatory experience for future leaders of church, state, and society. Over time, enhanced educational opportunities for women, racial and religious minorities, and the poor have been slowly and painstakingly won. Nor should we ignore in this enhanced pattern of college student diversity the older and more mature students. One of the catalysts for change was the voice of students seeking a place in higher education and asking that the college experience be relevant to their needs and aspirations.

Socioeconomically Disadvantaged Students

Changes in the student population of the early colleges are exemplified by the poor, aspiring clergymen who came to the colleges of New England around the turn of the nineteenth century. Their poverty and their needs, and those of the economically disadvantaged students who followed after them, served as the catalysts for the demise of college commitments to strict residential requirements, changed college calendars, altered the basis upon which financial aid was awarded, and even affected the geographic distribution of new colleges (Allmendinger, 1975; Blackburn and Conrad, 1986; Horowitz, 1987; Rudolph, 1990).

The establishment of land grant colleges, founded in large measure to provide practical educational opportunities for the sons and daughters of the agricultural and industrial classes of the middle and late 1800s, was a landmark event in increasing accessibility to those previously excluded. In the years following the passage of the Morrill Act of 1862 (which authorized the establishment of these colleges), 20 colleges of agricultural and mechanical arts were founded and 32 state or territorial universities were established or developed from existing institutions. While the passage of the second Morrill Act in 1890 led to the eventual establishment of 17 more agricultural and mechanical colleges for African Americans (Eddy, 1956, p. 237), some movement on African-American land grant colleges was taking place before 1890, with Alcorn College, for example, being established in 1871.

As we noted in earlier chapters, in the aftermath of World War II, the federal government assumed a major role in increasing access to higher education, first through the G.I. Bill, making it possible for large numbers of veterans to attend colleges and universities nationwide. Later, in response to the Soviet Union's 1957 launching of Sputnik, the federal government initiated a series of grant and loan programs through which awards were made, primarily on the basis of need rather than academic achievement (Bowen, 1978).

Another distinctive American collegiate configuration made no small contribution to enhanced access. Emerging in the late nineteenth century, expanding gradually during the early twentieth century, and then rapidly increasing in numbers in the last half of the twentieth century, the American two-year college has been without question one of the principal instruments for providing access to many Americans with limited economic and financial capacity.

This combination of creating and expanding the mission of state universities, increasing the numbers of both private and public colleges, establishing two-year colleges within physical and financial reach of most Americans, and providing both state and federal programs of financial aid, clearly marks the American commitment to enhanced access to all students, but especially to those of limited financial means.

Women Students

Women in the colonial period were often considered unsuitable for college study and were simply not regarded as serious candidates for admission to college. In the nineteenth century, doubts about the ability of women and the effects of their attendance on the status of colleges and universities remained strong. Institutions for women such as Troy Female Seminary (1821) in the North and Wesleyan Female College (1836) in the South cracked the doors of access open for a small number of women. Students were frequently mocked and disregarded late into the nineteenth century. Levine (1986) has documented the efforts of college administrators to restrict the presence of women and their influence on the institutions of that period. Although women students on many campuses demonstrated academic achievement superior to that of men, they continued to be denied recognition for their achievements by the wider scholarly community and were formally and especially informally denied access to all but a relative handful of disciplines and career choices. While men were regarded as needing a college education for a successful career, women, it was believed, went to college simply because they enjoyed learning. Marriage was regarded as the appropriate life work of a woman (Levine, 1986).

It would be pleasant to note that such attitudes and practices have been completely eliminated from our institutions in the 1990s, but such is not the case. In spite of the force of statutory and case law forbidding discrimination on the basis of gender, women still face barriers to free exercise of choice in academic study or career. As Holland and Eisenhart (1990) have described, women are still bound significantly by cultural definitions of gender roles.

Wresting men, and some women, from their prejudicial views and behaviors toward women's promise has been a difficult journey for our society; and the challenge of understanding, respecting, and developing the talents of women continues. We should not paint these wrenching changes in perspective on male-female roles as a simplistic business of stuffy conservatives finally giving way to righteous liberals in our society. There is serious work to be done in understanding the evolution of role and relationship for both men and women. And that work is being done in large measure, and not surprisingly, in our colleges and universities. Two books that reflect this serious work have been authored by college professors: Carol Gilligan's widely cited *In a Different Voice* (1982) and Robert Bly's bestseller *Iron John* (1990).

This complexity related to changing perceptions of male-female roles and relationship notwithstanding, there is definitive evidence of progress for women in higher education. In the closing years of the twentieth century, women now constitute the majority enrollment in American higher education. The 1996 *Almanac Issue* of the *Chronicle of Higher Education* indicates that 55 percent of enrollments in our colleges and universities are now women (p. 3).

African-American Students

Prior to the Civil War there were few educational opportunities for those who were not Caucasian. By 1860 there had been only 28 African-American graduates of American colleges (Perkins, 1983). Institutions of higher educa-

---

TABLE 7.1

HISTORICALLY BLACK COLLEGES AND FOUNDING DATES

Public	Private
Alabama A & M University (1875)	Allen University (1870)
Alabama State University (1874)	Barber Scotia College (1867)
Albany State Colleges (1903)	Benedict College (1870)
Alcorn State University (1871)	Bennett College (1873)
Arkansas Baptist College (1901)	Bethune Cookman College (1923)
Bishop State Community (1965)	Clafin College (1869)
Bluefield State College (1895)	Clark Atlanta Univ. (1988)
Bowie State University (1865)	Concordia College (1922)
Central State University (1887)	Hampton University (1868)
Cheney University of PA (1837)	Harris Stowe College (1857)
Coahoma Community College (1949)	Howard University (1867)
Coppin State College (1900)	Huston-Tillotson College (1875)
Delaware State University (1891)	Interdeom. Theol. Center (1958)
Florida A&M University (1887)	Jarvis Christian College (1912)
Fort Valley State College (1895)	Johnson C. Smith Univ. (1867)
Grambling State University (1901)	Knoxville College (1875)
Hinds Community College (1917)	Lane College (1882)
J.F. Drake Tech College (1961)	Lemoyne-Owen College (1862)
Jackson State University (1877)	Lewis College of Bus. (1929)
Kentucky State University (1886)	Livingstone College (1879)
Langston University (1897)	Mary Holmes College (1892)
Lawson State Comm. College (1965)	Meharry Medical College (1876)

TABLE 7.1

Historically Black Colleges and Founding Dates *(cont.)*

Public	Private
Lincoln University (MO) (1866)	Miles College (1908)
Lincoln University (PA) (1854)	Morehouse College (1867)
Miss. Valley State Univ. (1946)	Morehouse Sch of Med. (1978)
Morgan State University (1867)	Morris Brown College (1881)
Norfolk State University (1935)	Morris College (1908)
North Carolina Ag & Tech (1891)	Oakwood College (1896)
North Carolina Cen. Univ. (1909)	Paine College (1882)
Prairie View A & M Univ. (1876)	Paul Quinn College (1872)
Savannah State College (1890)	Philander Smith College (1877)
Shelton State Com Coll. (1979)	Rust College (1866)
South Carolina State Univ. (1896)	St. Augustine College (1867)
Southern Univ. A&M College (1880)	St. Paul's College (1888)
Southern Univ.-New Orleans (1959)	Selma University (1878)
Southern Univ.-Shreveport (1964)	Shaw University (1865)
Tennessee State University (1909)	Shorter College (1886)
Texas Southern University (1947)	Southwest. Christ. Col. (1949)
Trenholm State Tech. Col. (1965)	Spelman College (1881)
Univ of Ark.- Pine Bluff (1875)	Stillman College (1876)
Univ. of D.C. (1976)	Talladega College (1867)
Univ. of Md.-Eastern Shore (1886)	Tougaloo College (1869)
Univ. of Tx. - El Paso (1913)	Tuskegee University (1881)
Virginia State Univ. (1882)	Virginia Union Univ. (1865)
West Virginia State College (1891)	Voorhies College (1897)
Winston Salem State Univ. (1892)	Wilberforce Univ. (1856)
Winston Salem Univ. (1892)	Wiley College (1873)
	Xavier University of La. (1925)

Source: Historically Black Colleges and Universities Web site. World Wide Web. http://www.edonline.com/cq/hbcu/

tion devoted to serving African Americans emerged during the reconstruction period following the Civil War. Remarkably, by 1895 more than 1,100 students had graduated from what are now known as Historically Black Colleges (HBCs). As a point of interest, here is a list of those colleges and their founding dates.

Unfortunately, while strides were made during this period, other factors served to restrict opportunity. Racist, yet legal practices combined with unfavorable social and political conditions in restricting opportunities for African Americans to study the traditional liberal arts and related disciplines. The prevailing attitude at the dawn of the twentieth century continued to be that African Americans could not achieve academically. The best they could hope for was incremental improvement in working conditions and opportunities. These attitudes and legal constraints had the effect of continuing educational, political, and economic disenfranchisement (Anderson, 1988).

The prohibition of discrimination on the basis of race contained in the second Morrill Act of 1890 led many southern states to establish separate land grant colleges for African-American students. Racial segregation as a matter of public policy was upheld by the Supreme Court in 1896. This endorsement of segregation in higher education would stand as the law of the land until it was challenged in a number of court cases in the 1930s and finally overturned in the 1950s in the *Brown v. Board of Education* decision (Bowles and DeCosta, 1971). Racial integration of state universities in the southern states did not begin until the 1950s and 1960s. In spite of vehement and sometimes violent resistance to such change, federal law prohibiting discrimination on the basis of race was upheld by the courts, and across the United States overtly discriminatory practices on admissions were ended (Bowles and DeCosta, 1971).

It is questionable whether the pain of legal or systematic prejudice, or its illogic, will ever be fully understood by those never subject to its demeaning and degrading fruits. Unfortunately, African Americans continue to experience difficulties on some campuses. Data on matriculation and graduation in the 1990s suggest that many universities recruit large numbers of minority students who never graduate. Even with special programs and other efforts intended to support them, their retention and graduation rates remain low at many institutions (*Chronicle Almanac*, September 1996). While the reasons for their relative lack of success are most likely varied and complex, some will argue that African-American students fail in large numbers to complete degrees not because of any inherent lack of ability, but perhaps due to attitudes and practices that sometimes blatantly and sometimes subtly act to alienate and marginalize minority students. There are some encouraging but guarded signs of progress. The American Council on Education's *Fifteenth Annual Status Report on Minorities in Higher Education* (1997) indicates that African-American students are making progress in both access and graduation, though they still lag behind white students. Though much progress has been made in a century and a half, much remains to be achieved.

This issue is a social and educational one of majestic complexity where we do the issue a disservice by being too facile in our analysis. It is uncomfortable enough to acknowledge the deliberate sanction of prejudice by law and public policy in the United States. It is also uncomfortable to realize that the translation of promise into performance is also affected by personal factors of motivation, persistence, and aspiration in each one of us, regardless of race. We can also become prisoners of our expectations when no barrier confronts.

The commentary of African-American scholar W.E.B. DuBois tells plainly, however, of the bitter fruits of prejudice when he said that "If you do not lift them up, they will pull you down" (DuBois, 1973, p. 75). Lifting every man and woman's vision of his or her promise and responsibility is an enduring duty of those who serve as educators.

Jewish Students

Although some students of Jewish religious identity attended college in the nineteenth century, they tended to be largely invisible among the overall student body. Jews began attending college in significant numbers around the turn of the century, following years of significant Jewish immigration, especially to the northeastern United States. Eastern European Jewish immigrants emphasized education for their children over a life of labor. They sent their children to public schools and ultimately to nearby urban institutions of higher education. By 1918, Jews composed almost four-fifths of the student body of the City College of New York, almost half of the student body at New York University, one-fifth of Columbia's students, and one-tenth of students at Harvard.

These students often faced profound discrimination. Students protested on some campuses against the admission of Jews. Administrators openly sought ways to restrict the numbers of Jewish students who might attend their institutions. Such practices continued at many institutions until midcentury. Prestigious institutions made it clear that intellectually able but socially undesirable students were not welcome. Social homogeneity continued to be seen as a virtue in maintaining the reputations of the most prestigious institutions (Levine, 1986). Following World War II, discrimination against Jewish students abated significantly.

Religious, ethnic, and class differences were not the only characteristics that made Jewish students unwelcome within the traditional student culture on many campuses. As Horowitz (1987) has documented, the disdain for cultural outsiders was made clear in the derogation of hard-working, academically-oriented students as "grinds"—a form of ostracism experienced more recently by students of Asian descent and by older undergraduates.

Older Students

Undergraduate education has historically been segregated by age. In the nineteenth century, few undergraduates were more than 24 years old. The standardization of American public education and college admissions processes supported the concept of the traditional-aged student. Undergraduates were routinely expected to arrive on campus at age 18 and graduate at age 22. Yet the nontraditional student, for generations defined by age, has become an increasingly traditional figure on college campuses. In the 1990s, students 25 years of age or more have constituted slightly more than 40 percent of the total enrollment in American higher education, and approximately 10 percent of those enrolled are 40 years or older (*Chronicle Almanac*, 1996, p. 17).

Undergraduate students are still segregated by age in important ways. For example, a major portion of those students enrolled in community college programs are not simply older than the traditional college-going age, but live and are employed off campus, are part-time, and are disproportionately female and minority (Vaughn, 1985). The significance of this observation is indicated by noting that in the 1980s community college enrollments came to account for more than half of all first-time freshmen in American colleges and universities (Baker, 1994); and in the 1990s, two-year schools continue to enroll more than a third of all undergraduates. In both two-year and four-year colleges, older students are a minority of those enrolled full time and represent about two-thirds of those enrolled part time (*Almanac Issue*, 1996).

As one can imagine, the arrival of the economically disadvantaged, women, African Americans, Jews, other minorities, and older students has had an enormous impact on the college experience for all students. Over time, other groups have made their collective presence known as well. Students of Hispanic and Asian ancestry, those with physical and learning disabilities, gay/lesbian/bisexual students, and students from other countries each bring their own particular perspectives, needs, and dreams to the academy. The diversity of student populations compels colleges and universities to remain adaptable and dynamic.

It is clear that in the past, this diversity has led to change in both public and private education. The gains made by the various student constituencies on campus have been hard won, and their efforts have in many ways reflected the struggle and growth of the American people. The historical growth in student diversity on American campuses has been not only about opening higher education to many more people. Rather, as colleges and universities have grown, sometimes willingly, often reluctantly, to embrace the mosaic which is the American citizenry, they have also underscored their role as the crucible within which many of America's most important social, economic, political, and philosophical questions are addressed.

WHO SHOULD ATTEND COLLEGE AND WHY?

Consideration of who will attend American colleges and universities must go beyond the historical review of the criteria used to exclude some from such participation. Public and private policy bears testimony to sweeping efforts to eliminate factors such as sex, race, socioeconomic status, or religion as barriers to full participation in higher education. Even complete elimination of the use of such individual characteristics in determining who may attend leaves unanswered the question of whether there are appropriate criteria for determining who should engage in college-level study.

This "should" question may be addressed from both the perspective of students and of institutions. In the colonial era, a fraction of the overall population sought a college education. Well into the mid-nineteenth century, colleges were criticized for being elitist and unresponsive to public needs. Gradually American colleges and universities adjusted curriculum, facilities, policies, and practices regarding student life to address the needs of a much larger and more diverse segment of the populace at large. College and curriculum came ultimately to be shaped more to fit students, in contrast to the earlier belief that students must be shaped in the image of the curriculum (Brubacher, 1977).

As young people and their parents came to the conclusion that higher education was a powerful factor in the distribution and allocation of social and economic status, they sought participation as a way to enhance their economic and social status and mobility. Higher education thus went from being a marginally interesting diversion for the great majority of people to a central event for large segments of the population of late adolescents and young adults.

Reasons why students attend college vary. The annual survey conducted by the American Council on Education and the Higher Education Research Institute at the University of California, Los Angeles, has identified some of those reasons, as shown in Table 7.2.

Yet, even as the social commitment to higher education was growing, enrolled students and potential students began to question their return on investment of time, money, and other resources. Tuition and fees continue to rise faster than the rate of inflation, and the time to complete a degree lengthened. Parents, students, and state legislators are asking colleges and

---

TABLE 7.2

REASONS NOTED AS VERY IMPORTANT TO GO TO COLLEGE

My parents wanted me to go	36.2%
I could not find a job	6.8%
Wanted to get away from home	18.2%
To be able to get a better job	74.6%
To gain a general education	60.7%
To improve my reading and study skills	40.7%
There was nothing better to do	3.4%
To make me a more cultured person	35.7%
To be able to make more money	73.0%
To learn more about things that interest me	74.3%
A mentor or role model encouraged me	14.4%
To prove to others I could succeed	40.7%

Source: Almanac Issue, *Chronicle of Higher Education*, August 28, 1998.

universities to demonstrate that the quality of the student experience is worth the investment. The question of who should attend has, for students in the 1990s, come to include questions of whether the traditional assumption of a connection between college experience and social and economic mobility and success still holds.

While the American two-year college has by design and mission generally been an open-admission institution for students graduating from high school, admissions policies at four-year colleges and universities have varied. Some state universities still attempt to admit any qualified graduate from a state high school, but most have adopted some form of selective admissions policy, since they generally cannot accommodate all those who apply. And this is certainly the case with many private institutions. The central criterion determining who should study at the college level has been an assessment of the student's ability to succeed at an institution. Determination of this ability or readiness for college has relied on a range of criteria. The colonial colleges valued competence in classical languages, particularly Greek and Latin, as a measure of adequate preparation for admission. Over time, additional academic competencies were considered, including mathematics, English composition, and other knowledge and skills deemed essential to preparation for a college education. By the opening of the twentieth century, access to a vast network of public schools and the emergence of mass ability testing made academic screening a relatively standardized process that was refined and further expanded through the course of the twentieth century. The most visible expressions of college admissions testing are the American College Testing Program (ACT) and the Scholastic Aptitude Test of the College Board (SAT). For graduate study, admissions readiness is often measured by the Graduate Record Examination (GRE). A range of other standardized examinations are used for admissions to professional schools such as medicine and law.

However, several issues have also accompanied the emerging use of standardized tests as a means of determining who should attend college. One of these issues is that current tests have tended to operationally define achievement in what many would say is a narrow, limited, and an inadequate view of human potential and promise. In chapter four we mentioned the multifactor view of human intelligence as suggested in the works of Gardner, Sternberg, and Goleman. As a result, students in the twentieth century who were not steeped in the cultural and intellectual traditions valued by institutions of higher education, or who emerged from social or economic circumstances that made it difficult for them to demonstrate achievement or ability in a conventional way, were often denied the opportunity to participate based on standardized methods of assessment of ability.

A second thorny issue is the varying performance profile on standardized tests of different racial and ethnic groups. For example, the range of average scores on the American College Testing examination is shown here in Table 7.3.

What factors might explain the variation in these scores? The unhappy and prejudicial history of African-American education in this nation might be viewed as an explanatory factor, but how do we explain the high scores of Asian students, the newest minority group in this country? What role do families and parental expectations play?

Uneven levels of preparation for college study have been fairly common since the founding of colonial colleges. However, the modern commitment to enhanced access to higher education has raised additional questions about the basis upon which college admission judgments should be made.

These questions come into sharper focus in the community colleges, where policies of open admissions have been championed since the 1960s. Students who, for whatever reason, were not prepared to undertake college-level study have been the intended beneficiaries of programs for remedial and developmental education in community colleges. Institutions of higher education, especially community colleges, have been given major responsibilities for providing education and support to remedy deficiencies in preparation to undertake higher education (Spann and McCrimmon, 1994). The degree to which the opportunity to attend college includes access to education and services that compensate for poverty, irresponsible parents, inadequate schooling, or other factors is a question of less tension in a time of generous resources for higher education than in cost containment climates. Thus, developmental studies programs are coming under increased scrutiny by political decision makers in many states.

Unless our society is prepared to guarantee access to college for every student with a high school diploma, and that seems an unlikely policy given

TABLE 7.3	
AVERAGE ACT SCORES BY RACE AND ETHNIC GROUP, 1998	
American Indian	19.0
Asian	21.8
Black	17.1
Mexican American	18.5
Other Hispanic	19.6
White	21.7
Multi-cultural	21.3
Other	19.6
All	21.0
ACT Scale Scores range from 1 to 36	

Source: American College Testing Program; Almanac Issue, Chronicle of Higher Education, August 28, 1998.

current public debate about readiness for college and the advent of cost containment measures, some basis for determining readiness and for making selective admissions is necessary. Thus, universal access to higher education, in the mode of elementary and secondary education, presumes a level of service and support not currently, and not likely, to be available to college students. The allocation of higher education opportunity, then, will continue to require some means of qualifying students for admission and allowing students to demonstrate appropriate academic readiness and subsequent success.

Seemingly inherent in discussions related to access is the value Americans place on being just. Notions of justice or "fair play" pervade our discourse—whether the topic is Little League baseball or crime and punishment. Therefore, it is not surprising that when issues about college admissions and student support arise, discussions of justice follow closely behind. Many argue that American higher education should define criteria for admission and success on the basis of what is fair. Here we confront a prickly and socially incendiary contemporary issue. To compensate for past prejudice and to enhance diversity of college student bodies, will we establish different admissions standards for different racial and ethnic groups? Some campuses and systems of campuses have clearly established such differential admissions policies. The front page headlines of both professional and public press herald current arguments over the merit of affirmative action programs in college admissions for students and in employment of college faculty and staff. Although there has been at least one federal court action suggesting that affirmative action admissions policies should be discontinued, many would argue that the law is still murky on this subject.

For many, justice is taken to mean that every person should have full opportunity to develop her or his full potential. Astin (1993b), for example, has articulated a vision of the purpose of higher education consistent with this belief, holding that the purpose of undergraduate higher education is no more and no less than the full development of every student's talents. In his 1984 book *Excellence*, American scholar and public servant John Gardner suggested that the identification, selection, and development of talent was at once the most delicate and difficult process undertaken by American schools and colleges. Providing an opportunity for each person in a democratic society to reach the far edge of the circle of his or her promise will remain a leadership challenge for educators at every level, and certainly no less so at the college level.

While a vision of higher education as a vehicle for achieving social justice and for realizing human potential is an attractive one, there remains a tension between the obvious merits of the goals and the reality of finite economic resources. Students have flocked to colleges and universities for acquiring marketable skills and knowledge, as demonstrated in Table 7.2, often neglecting or disparaging studies associated with the development of talent or the "whole person." Interestingly, demands for changes in curriculum, teaching methods, and behavioral expectations have also come from these pragmatic aims. The reality is that institutions must be vigilant in seeking a balance between the popular desires of students and the ideal of developing educated citizens. Though many would assert that the notion of the liberally educated person has been eroded in higher education, the liberal arts still form the center of most undergraduate programs of study. A commitment to broadening students' horizons need not be anachronistic, but rather a rededication to the full purpose and meaning of higher education. If a college education is to be more than career preparation, more than acquisition of a credential, more than status allocation, then careful attention must be paid to the cultivation of cultural, social, economic, political, and ethical awareness—qualities that mark an educated person in a democratic society.

This does not require a renunciation of modern college and university curricula, nor a return to the narrow vision of the Yale Report of 1828. If we are serious about maintaining a partnership with students, there must be continued openness to imaginative new methods of learning and to assessing student learning and growth.

Unfortunately, we tend to frame policy questions on college purpose in dichotomous form. While we have wondered whether the proper work of higher education was to prepare students to make a living or to have a life, the obvious answer is both. Vocational, career, technical, and professional education can be highly liberating as students engage applied issues where the pressure of the application does not allow one the leisure of saying "on the other hand. . . ." General and liberal education is fundamental to effective career preparation because it furnishes mind, heart, and hand with those foundational skills and knowledges that build up over a lifetime. As we noted in chapter four, we should not be anxious over this debate. We should be anxious when arguments about the purposes of higher education, nature of excellence, and avenues of justice can no longer be heard in the halls of our colleges and universities.

Our attention in this section has been centered heavily on issues of admission. But what happens once a student is admitted? Does college make a difference or does it mean, to paraphrase Robert Hutchins, that a student passed an uneventful few years without breaking any local, state, or federal law and that he or she remembered, temporarily at least, a little of what instructors said? There is an extensive scholarship on college impact and outcome, so let us turn to those data.

HOW COLLEGE AFFECTS STUDENTS

In the opening of this chapter, we mentioned several books that had engaged the question of college impact and outcome. These books tend to be rather formidable in size, but the conclusions derived from the extensive research are sometimes thin, and we are left yearning for results more crisp and certain. After a 500-page comprehensive journey through the research literature on college impact, Pascarella and Terenzini borrowed a phrase from an earlier work and offered three general conclusions on college impact: "(1) some do, some don't; (2) the differences aren't very great; and (3) it's more complicated than that" (Pascarella and Terenzini, 1991, p. 556).

The questions are simple enough. In what ways do students change during the college years? Can we attribute these changes to college influence, as compared to maturation, for example? Are changes in students' knowledge, attitudes, and behavior affected by the kind of college they attend? Do changes in the larger context of society also influence changes in students during the college years?

Intellectual and Cognitive Growth

Considerable research shows that college contributes to the development of more complex intellectual and cognitive skill (Astin, 1977, p. 122; Pascarella and Terenzini, 1991, p. 558). Other evidences of this growth is apparent from student performance on licensure examinations in different professional fields of study: nursing, engineering, architecture, teaching. While it is possible that a student might engage in a program of independent study of sufficient merit to produce successful performance on the many professional licensure examinations, a four-year college program is more likely to do so. Indeed, performance on licensure examinations is one of the indicators now used to demonstrate accountability and is often one of the indicators mandated by state level policy. See chapter five for previous discussion on performance indicators.

The growth in knowledge and skill also involves the more fundamental intellectual functions such as oral and written communication skill, abstract reasoning, and critical thinking. Regarding the development of college admissions tests, we may point to the development of a number of standardized outcome or exit examinations now available. These include, among others, the College Outcomes Measures Program (COMP) of the American College Testing Service, the College Base Examination, and the Academic Profile published by the Educational Testing Service. Most of these examinations have been developed in the last 15 to 20 years.

Beyond these national examinations, some colleges now specify "competencies" required for the bachelor's degree and have established assessment instruments and processes for ascertaining whether students have mastered these competencies. For a more extended discussion of how assessment programs have developed see *The Evidence for Quality* (Bogue and Saunders, 1992), *Making a Difference . . .* (Banta et al., 1993).

There are variations in patterns of student growth and development, and Astin has pointed to some of those (Astin, 1977, 1994). See also Kuh's 1994 monograph *Student Learning Outside the Classroom*. In general, persistence and successful academic performance in college is positively associated with residential life, involvement in campus life, and smaller campus size.

Value and Attitudes

There are advances in aesthetic and cultural interests and in the importance students attach to liberal learning and exposure to new ideas. In general there is a liberalizing trend in student value and attitude (Pascarella and Terenzini, 1991, pp. 559–61. There is evidence of enhanced sense of competence and self-worth (Astin, 1977, pp. 31–71).

An inclination to question values and attitudes, a readiness to explore previously held prejudices, an ability to see the power of paradox rather than simple black and white in issues, an openness to the power of intrinsic motivation in work and other settings, a reluctance to accept authority without questioning both its legitimacy and competence, the use of reasoning to evaluate moral issues are also discernible changes in student behavior associated with college attendance (Feldman and Newcomb, 1973, p. 326). And would we not be concerned if evidence of this kind were not forthcoming?

Socioeconomic Outcomes

Certainly the performance and attitudes of individual students is a central variable in their success following college. In general, however, the evidence is that college promotes the probability of higher incomes over time and entry to relatively high status and high-paying positions (Pascarella and Terenzini, 1991, p. 575; Astin, 1977, pp. 134–63). Earlier, we commented that the social and economic context also affects students. Waves of liberal and conservative views ebb and flow through our society as we tend to the competing calls of opportunity and responsibility, social justice and personal responsibility, respecting diversity and nurturing community, balancing individual and society needs. As we noted in chapter two on mission and chapter four on curriculum, colleges are forums where ideologies are contested. Hopefully we will furnish our students access to the argument rather than serve them dull and digested intellectual dishes that prevent them from knowing and appreciating the process of how we advance on truth.

FROM INMATE TO CLIENT AND PARTNER—A SUMMARY

Students in the colonial era were heavily dependent on the tutelage and patronage of college. Due to the fact that students were often academically, spiritually, and physically confined, the term "inmate" is not an altogether inaccurate descriptor of their status. Higher education was a privilege that only a few could enjoy. As American higher education evolved, study at a college or university remained primarily a privilege, but a privilege that was becoming increasingly more available. In the post World War II era, higher education opportunities were opened to a vastly larger and older segment of the American population by the rapid and extensive expansion of public universities and community colleges and by the creation of need-based financial aid systems at both state and federal levels.

In the history of American higher education, it is clear that the role of students in the development of programs and services has been significant, not only because students are a primary "client and customer" of colleges and universities, but because they are partners in a dynamic interaction of intellectual, social, and personal forces that drive colleges and universities to constantly reconsider, however reluctantly, their mission, methods, and outcomes.

In the late twentieth century, there is much discussion, debate, and dissent about the best method to meet the challenges and needs of a nation of such great cultural diversity. There are some who wring their hands in fear of this new age, as there no doubt were 200 years ago at the prospect of admitting impoverished and rough-mannered young men, or 100 years ago at the prospect of admitting ambitious young women and African Americans. Nevertheless, if higher education is to prosper into the next century, faculty and administrators will have to face critical questions: How will colleges and universities continue to meet increasing demands for programs, services, and facilities given static or shrinking financial resources? How can colleges and universities become more efficient and effective and make use of technology without de-humanizing the educational process? Are the theoretical underpinnings upon which student affairs administrators have built their programs sufficient to meet the needs of increasingly diverse student bodies? Perhaps most importantly, how can colleges and universities maintain a sense of community among their various constituencies in a time when it seems that society as a whole is becoming increasingly fractious?

Students will be, and should be, at the table for engaging these questions. Their participation in the engagement of these issues and questions should be, as noted in chapter four, an involvement central to their education.

Diversity has never hurt our colleges and universities, but it has commonly been resisted. If there is a lesson in studying the role of students in our higher education heritage, it might be that diversity, in both demographic background and educational need, has been an engine driving colleges and universities to greater heights of service, opening new frontiers for research and scholarship, and presenting new opportunities and demands for teaching. The size and scope of American higher education today rests on a foundation of increasing inclusion. Though not all of the developments of the past two centuries show a steady march toward progress, we can and should embrace the challenges and opportunities of diversity that are in many ways uniquely American.

CHAPTER 8

Faculty Role and Responsibility
The Perceptions of Professorial Performance

What comes first to memory when one reflects on the legacy of his or her college career? Unadorned red brick, beige stucco, or ivy covered stone—perhaps mental snapshots of buildings emerge. Maybe a smile will accompany pleasant recollections of friendships formed and fellowships enjoyed during those years. It is unlikely that student memories will include remembrance of such statistical matters as faculty-student ratios, expenditures per student, and the number of volumes in the library. For most, it is highly probable that those remembrances will include some professor who lifted their vision from the poverty of the commonplace, who saw some promise in their talent that they themselves could not discern, who challenged their mind and heart, who opened new vistas of imagination for their curiosity, who launched them on a path of learning and service.

It was certainly this exemplary model of the college professor that Gilbert Highet had in mind when he wrote *The Immortal Profession* (1976), a series of essays celebrating the call to teaching and the pursuit of learning. Here is a story of the men and women whose work it is to help furnish the minds and souls of those who will give leadership in every sector of our national life. There will be few among us who cannot remember with affection and appreciation a professor who led us to discover promise and meaning in our life.

Unfortunately, there are less flattering contemporary views of faculty performance. The titles of these more critical works telegraph both theme and tone. For example, *Profscam*, by Charles Sykes, opens a "bill of indictment" with this evaluation of college faculty: "They are overpaid, grotesquely under worked, and the architects of academia's vast empires of waste" (Sykes, 1988, p. 5). Sykes goes further to describe the contemporary professor as ". . . mobile, self-interested, and without loyalty to institutions or the values of liberal education. The rogue professors of today are not merely obscurantists. They are politicians and entrepreneurs who fiercely protect their turf and shrewdly hustle research cash while they peddle their talents to rival universities, businesses, foundations, or government" (p. 7). *How Professors Play the Cat Guarding the Cream* by Richard Huber (1992) also does not present a flattering portrait of professorial life and responsibility, nor does *Imposters in the Temple* by Martin Anderson (1992).

As a matter of historic perspective, college and university professors have always been the objects of both love and libel. Writing in *American Higher Education: A History*, Christopher Lucas (1994), for example, indicates that Martin Luther referred to universities of his time as "asses' stalls, dens of murderers, temples of Moloch, synagogues of corruption, and nests of gloomy ignorance" (p. 85).

There are multiple truths here. There is first a commanding reality of goodness and nobility among those who hold our colleges and universities in trust. Stories of nobility and caring, however, do not always make good material for best-selling books and sensational news weeklies. It is easier to catalog our criticisms than it is to catalog pleasant memories of those faculty who nurtured competence and conscience in our lives and caused us to search for meaning and purpose in the application of that competence. Good news is not news. Just one departure from nobility of purpose or method is grist for journalistic grinding mills.

In this chapter we examine the evolution of faculty role and responsibility, and explore major issues confronting the contemporary college professor. Our aspiration is to bring some understanding of the role and recognition of faculty and to examine the tensions of expectation and context that faculty face.

THE EVOLUTION OF FACULTY ROLE AND QUALIFICATION

What are the role and responsibility expectations of the contemporary professor in American higher education? These role expectations may be summarized under teaching, research, public and professional service, and institutional governance and operation. There are important variances in these expectations as a function of institutional type and mission, and there are also tensions between public and professional expectations of faculty role and responsibility.

The primary role of the professor in early American colleges was as teacher authority, parental substitute, and spiritual exemplar. A large portion of the faculty in antebellum American colleges was composed of clergymen, consistent with the conception of liberal education as a means of cultivating religious piety and moral rectitude. As for scholarship, some of the more influential college presidents of the first half of the nineteenth century, such as Mark Hopkins of Williams College and Eliphalet Nott of Union College, openly disdained scholarship as a central faculty concern. True to their times, they were much more concerned with higher education as a means of building religious faith (Rudolph, 1990). Though faculty members of colonial times were not necessarily expected to be scholars or researchers, some were. Here we take the term "scholar" to describe one involved in inquiry/research and in the dissemination of scholarship outcomes in public forum, usually in the form of invited professional presentation, publication in journals, or display of scholarship outcomes in other ways that allow for peer review and evaluation. In his essay, "The American Scholar," Ralph Waldo Emerson (1929) referred to the scholar as *Man Thinking* (p. 26). The role of the "speculative" man, the man thinking, had to emerge in a nation built on the fruits of the practical man, the man laboring.

The foundations of American scholarship were established in the eighteenth century at Harvard, where the results of scientific research were published in American and English journals; and by 1818 the *American Journal of Science and Arts* was founded as a learned journal by Yale's Benjamin Silliman (Brubacher and Rudy, 1976). The rise of the modern university in the last quarter of the nineteenth century ushered in further changes in the role of the faculty and an emphasis on scholarship. The two world wars of the first half of the twentieth century, separated by the Great Depression, Korean War, cold war era, space race, and the Vietnam War all brought additional calls on faculty expertise in both basic and applied research. The scholarship capacities of American colleges and universities emerged as engines of scientific, cultural, and economic development. Thus, faculty entered into new roles in the pursuit of scientific and technical invention and in the application of these findings to our society. The balance of attention among the three basic roles of faculty in teaching, research, and service produced a major tension in the closing of this century.

As a second question on faculty, what may we observe on the question of faculty qualification and credentials? Through the first two-thirds of the nineteenth century, relatively few college professors held degrees beyond the baccalaureate. The master's degree in the early colleges was usually earned more as a matter of continuing on a year or so beyond the bachelor's degree, and was not well defined or structured until graduate education was developed in the latter half of the nineteenth century. The emphasis on research and scholarship in the modern university contributed greatly to the emergence of the Ph.D. as the badge of merit and accomplishment desired most by the leading colleges and universities of the United States.

In spite of the new research emphasis of American universities emerging in the 1870s and 1880s, the Ph.D. was a prestigious but still relatively rare credential prior to 1890. For example, in 1884 Harvard had only 19 faculty members holding Ph.D.s out of a total faculty of 189. Similarly, the University of Michigan, with a total faculty of 88, included only 6 Ph.D.s among them. The importance of the Ph.D. as the *sine qua non* of the faculty gained momentum through the course of the twentieth century as graduate schools turned out more and more doctorates in the growth era following World War II. However, as late as 1948, less than 40 percent of all college and university faculty members held a doctorate. This proportion increased to just over 60 percent by the late 1970s. In the mid 1990s, even small four-year institutions reported 75 percent or more of their faculty holding the doctorate, and major research universities reported 95 percent or more of their faculty members holding the Ph.D. or equivalent for their fields.

Throughout the history of American higher education, expectations for faculty role and responsibility moved from the singular expectation of teacher and moral exemplar to the more complex expectation of faculty as researcher, teacher, and public servant—the discoverer, the disseminator, the public service expert. As noted in chapter two, the development of extension services and major research centers accompanied and aided this expansion of faculty responsibilities. The extent to which there is harmony of expectation between faculty and those who supply support for colleges and universities and the extent to which these complex roles are well balanced remains a contested issue as we approach the twenty-first century. A reasonable way to explore that issue is to inquire into the status of teaching.

THE STATUS OF TEACHING

Historically, the Ph.D., and most other doctoral degrees, had never been a degree primarily aimed at preparing people to teach, and until more recently had almost nothing to contribute formally in the way of instructional methods, preparation, or curricular insight. The Ph.D. has been primarily a research-oriented degree. The difficulty is that many Ph.D. faculty find themselves in faculty assignments in which research and scholarship are expected, but a primary duty is also teaching—a complex art form for which some new Ph.D.s are not well prepared. Teaching is a journey of the heart, a work completely positive and constructive in outcome when rightly done, a work seriously damaging to mind and spirit when done without care or competence. To take a student in harm's way because we do not know or do not care is a reprehensible professorial act. Just one mind, heart, or spirit injured by igno-rance or duplicity is one too many. In a 1997 *Change* article on "The Heart of a Teacher," Parker Palmer notes that "As I teach, I project the condition of my soul onto my students, my subject, and our way of being together" (p. 15). He accents the art form of teaching and the importance of professor identity and integrity as follows: "Reduce teaching to intellect and it becomes a cold abstraction; reduce it to emotion and it becomes narcissistic; reduce it to the spiritual and it loses its anchor to the world" (pp. 15–16).

Is the teacher a disseminator of knowledge or a facilitator of learning? Is the teacher a teller of truth or a coach? Writing in A Journey of the Heart, one of the authors suggested that "Teachers save us from the poverty of the common-place. The purpose of teaching is to promote and facilitate learning. The acts of teaching are these: To inform and inspire, To discipline and discomfort, To evaluate and encourage" (Bogue, 1991, p. 7).

In his thoughtful complement to academic freedom, Donald Kennedy writes in Academic Duty (1997) that "If we ask . . . about the influence of teachers rather than about what they do, we realize that in many ways they are functioning as moral teachers, making a difference in the way students choose to conduct their lives" (p. 60). Thus, we can open an important philosophic work if we pose questions only about the role of the teacher.

Beyond these questions and visions on the role of teaching, there is a serious and substantive content that undergirds the art of teaching. A professor unfamiliar with Bloom's A Taxonomy of Educational Objectives (1956) may continue to live on an elementary and primitive level of instructional expecta-tion. A professor unfamiliar with the literature of Kolb (1976) and Gilligan (1982) on learning styles and ways of knowing may miss an opportunity to link more effectively with the learning readiness of his or her students. A professor unfamiliar with the work of Howard Gardner (Frames of Mind, 1983), Robert Sternberg (The Triarchic Mind, 1988), or Daniel Goleman (Emotional Intelli-gence, 1995) may miss the idea that there are many ways to be smart and that learning research is causing us to reframe our notions of intelligence. A professor who is unaware that student scores on a test may reflect error components related to test construction and test context may be making critical human decisions on an inadequate data base. And we have not touched on other questions of teaching art that may include different ap-proaches to motivation, instructional sequence, and integration of technol-ogy.

Over time there have been various efforts to better prepare those earning doctorates to teach. Plans for distinctions between doctor of philosophy degrees, with a research orientation, and doctor of arts (D.A.) degrees, with a teaching orientation, have risen and fallen during the course of the latter half of the twentieth century. In the 1990s, a renewed accent on teaching by national organizations, publications, and networks has supported efforts by some universities to better prepare doctoral students as teachers. And the establishment of centers for instructional development in many colleges and universities is another evidence of concern for improving teaching. Although teaching responsibilities are highly valued by stakeholders within and without the university, there remains the question of the extent to which those earning the doctorate are systematically prepared to teach, and are appropriately recognized and rewarded for this role.

The only comfort we may take from a college teacher who is a poor exemplar is that we may also learn from our bad teachers. In *Sand and Foam*, Gibran (1973) observes that "I have learned silence from the talkative, toleration from the intolerant, and kindness from the unkind; yet strange, I am ungrateful to these teachers" (p. 58). Better, however, to learn from those teachers whose mind, heart, and soul sing to their work, who know the joy of touching lives and influencing the future for good, whose curiosity about the art form of teaching and learning sets a happy model for their students.

Much is made of the "teaching vs. research" dilemma. Critics claim that professors spend the majority of their time engaged in noninstructional activities, when public perceptions and expectations of higher education are centered first and foremost on the teaching responsibilities of faculty. Yet the majority of faculty members who took part in a 1989–1990 study conducted by the Higher Education Research Institute (HERI) at UCLA reported teaching as the activity consuming more of their work time than any other single professional responsibility. The researchers found that about one-third of college and university faculty members reported that they spent 16 hours or less per week on teaching, while about one-fifth reported spending 34 hours or more per week teaching. The other approximately one-half reported spending 18 to 32 hours per week on teaching. Data on other student-centered activities, advising, or counseling show almost three-fifths of respondents indicating that they spent 4 or fewer hours per week advising or counseling students, with another 30 percent reporting between 4 and 9 hours—a total of just under 90 percent reporting less than 9 hours per week (*The Chronicle of Higher Education Almanac*, September, 1995, p. 22).

The picture of faculty activity and expectations is complicated by the diversity of American higher education. Much discussion of faculty role takes place as if higher education were a monolithic enterprise; but, as we have already shown, there is substantial variation in faculty role as a function of institutional types and mission. The relative emphasis on teaching responsibilities of the faculty in various types of institutions is instructive. In research universities, teaching duties are often assigned at the rate of 6 hours of "contact time" per week, compared to typical teaching loads of 12 to 15 hours per week at liberal arts and community colleges (Clark, 1987). These numbers are somewhat misleading, however, in that the roles and responsibilities of faculty in these different types of institutions vary so greatly. As an aside, some writers have noted the inclination in colleges and universities to refer to the "teaching load" of faculty, but they do not refer to a research or public service "load." An implication that can be read into this terminology is that teaching is a burden to be borne but research and service are not.

There are important additional responsibilities to be recognized within these role variances. For example, faculty in a research or doctoral university are expected not only to remain current with the professional literature in their field and actively contribute to it, but also have responsibilities for advising graduate students and directing their dissertation research, the latter activities being highly labor intensive. The advanced undergraduate and graduate courses taught by faculty may require a level of review and updating beyond that of introductory courses. The other side of this coin is that in the community colleges especially there have been heavy burdens of remedial and developmental education for students who are not well-prepared for post-secondary education. The policy accent on increasing access, to which we referred in chapter six, has brought to colleges and universities many students having important deficiencies in their readiness skills; and this in turn has called for a large segment of the faculty on some campuses to dedicate their time to instruction at remedial or secondary-school levels.

These tensions in role and reward in the life of faculty have been the subject of research in several major studies of faculty life in the latter part of the twentieth century. In a widely known and referenced work, Caplow and McGee (1958) summarize their findings of The Academic Marketplace as follows: "It is only a slight exaggeration to say that academic success is likely to come to the man who has learned to neglect his assigned duties in order to have more time and energy to pursue his private professional interests" (p. 221). Caplow and McGee's view on the role and expectations of faculty is an earlier version of the view later offered by Huber (1992), that ". . . university teaching is the only profession in which you can become a success without satisfying the client" (p. 11).

The contemporary pressure for a more effective balance between faculty responsibilities in teaching and research may be felt most keenly in research universities and in those comprehensive universities who are "on the make." The latter are trying to look like research universities. Perhaps this is because, as we noted in chapter five, American higher education tends to be imitative, because we have limited models of excellence and because academic prestige in American society inclines to bigness and comprehensiveness. Put in simple terms, the national reputation of major institutions is garnered through the research reputation of their faculties. And this narrow model of educational excellence is unfortunately the one most recognized by academics and civic friends alike. It is difficult for some Americans to recognize diversity with distinction. We often use the term "flagship" to refer to the largest institution in a state or system. Perhaps this term should be returned to the Navy and left there, as it encourages a pyramidal view of excellence. Small American liberal arts colleges, public and private, and two-year colleges are important jewels in the crown of American higher education. These are complements to our large doctoral and research universities. It is more than difficult for an institution to resist the drift toward that magic word "university," as the number of public and private schools taking on that name in the last 40 to 50 years will attest. And it is equally difficult to resist a singular model of faculty role and recognition.

For research and comprehensive universities, one suggestion to help in achieving a more effective balance is for universities to arrange a "fifth rank," a distinguished teaching professor (Boyer, 1987, p. 127). Most American colleges and universities appoint and promote their professors on a four-rank system of instructor, assistant professor, associate professor, and professor. Beyond these four ranks, however, many universities already recognize distinguished appointment beyond full professor via endowed chairs, endowed professorships, or other similar appointments. While most such appointments usually accent the research record of a faculty member, there is no reason why these appointments cannot also recognize teaching expectation and performance. At the moment, distinguished research scholars are more mobile and better compensated because of market effect and because there is at least some consent on the measurement and recognition of research scholarship. Teaching effectiveness, for the moment, is primarily a matter of local recognition, and is certainly known to students and to colleagues. There is no barrier for universities in establishing clusters of distinguished teaching professor appointments, appointments that in title and compensation would send the message that teaching is valued at the university level. Indeed, some universities have begun to do just that.

In the role and work of the faculty, therefore, we may note the following: (1) There is an important variance in the investment of time among the major role expectations of teaching, research, public and professional service, and institutional governance as a function of institutional type and mission; and (2) there is an important tension between the expectation for how faculty will primarily invest their time and talent and the manner in which they are rewarded and recognized. Teaching is the central and fundamental work of every campus, else one could argue that students were at best incidental or at worst a nuisance in the life of our colleges and universities. Yet reward and recognition of faculty often center on research, publication, and grant acquisition, focusing less on the work of teaching.

Thus we have a paradox. Most faculty teach, and for the majority, teaching is their dominant responsibility. For many, teaching and associated activity is their only responsibility. Yet teaching is not the faculty responsibility most recognized or rewarded by many in the profession nor by many of our leading institutions.

Our discussion on the status of teaching has opened questions on the nature and definition of what constitutes "scholarship" and "scholarly work." Let us move, then, to the debate on what "scholarship" means in academic discourse and what it might mean.

THE DEFINITION OF SCHOLARSHIP

Boyer (1990) sought to transcend the dichotomy of teaching versus research and to open our understanding of scholarship by suggesting that the scholarly work of the faculty revolves around four core elements: advancing knowledge, integrating knowledge, transforming knowledge, and applying knowledge. Even the most traditional view of research and scholarly activity accents the idea that faculty members will engage in lifelong learning and active involvement in the life of the mind and its products.

The traditional view holds that teaching is intimately connected with research and scholarship, and that part of the role of the faculty was service to the greater community—most clearly exemplified in the creation of the land grant universities and the community college systems (Bok, 1993). The assertion that research, scholarship, teaching, and practice should be intimately related is certainly not a new idea in applied fields like business, education, medicine, social work, engineering, or environmental studies.

The consideration of teaching as a "scholarly" activity turns heavily on teaching being subject to peer review and evaluation. Contemporary scholars such as Eble (1972) argue that teaching should be a "public" activity, open to the scrutiny of peers. Physicians will perform their surgery before the evaluative eye of colleagues. Attorneys will argue their cases in the public forum of the courtroom. Visual and performing artists yield their work to public review in galleries and concert halls. Writers place their work in the hands of reviewing editors and critical readers. There are important challenges in the evaluation of any art form, and we made reference to some of this in chapter five on the question of judging quality. In *The Courage to Teach* Palmer suggests that "Unlike many professions, teaching is always done at the dangerous intersection of personal and public life. . . . A good teacher must stand where personal and public meet, dealing with the thundering flow of traffic at an intersection where 'weaving a web of connectedness' feels more like crossing a freeway on foot. As we try to connect ourselves and our subjects with our students, we make ourselves, as well as our subjects, vulnerable to indifference, judgment, ridicule" (1998, p. 17).

These challenges notwithstanding, will college teachers hide in their classrooms, studios, and laboratories, shielding their work from public review? There is an encouraging change emerging. One approach to place teaching activity in a public forum is the use of teaching portfolios, in which faculty may offer multiple evidences of teaching scholarship (Seldin, 1997). Both the act of teaching and the products of teaching may then be open to peer evaluation. Emerging pedagogical applications of technology may also assist in bringing teaching more into public forum and therefore open to peer review. A follow-up to Boyer's work is a 1997 monograph entitled *Scholarship Assessed* (Glassick, Huber, Maeroff). That work suggests the application of six standards for evaluating any work of scholarship: (1) clear goals; (2) adequate preparation; (3) appropriate methods; (4) significant results; (5) effective presentation; and (6) reflective critique. Even though this monograph, and the previously cited monograph on Scholarship Reconsidered by Boyer, argue persuasively for a more encompassing view on the nature of scholarship, the question of whether faculty and academic administrators will find the argument persuasive remains.

Another aspect of the issue related to definition of what constitutes "scholarship" in a college or university is the ability to differentiate both the definition and relative importance of scholarship in different disciplines or fields of study. The more traditional definition, the definition of discovery, may fit well into the science disciplines of universities. An academic department in a professional college of business, nursing, or education, however, may well want to accent the integration and application elements of Boyer's view of scholarship. The extent to which the modern college and university will welcome and recognize such differentiation in the work of the faculty is a current leadership challenge.

The status of teaching and the definition of scholarship are issues of continuing debate, and those who live within a college or university are not expected to be uncomfortable with the debate. Our colleges and universities are marked and sustained by perpetual argument, and tensioned dialogue that engages the intellectual life of every member of the community. There are other lively arguments concerning American colleges and universities, two of which center on the nature of academic freedom and the role of tenure.

THE CONCEPT OF ACADEMIC FREEDOM

Perhaps the single most powerful and critical foundation principle undergirding the American college and university is the commitment to unfettered investigation of questions and problems without restrictions based on political ideology, religious doctrine, or popular opinion—the concept of academic freedom. "Ye shall know the truth and the truth shall make you free" is a biblical admonition central to the health of a democratic society. The journey of defining, understanding, and preserving academic freedom has been a difficult journey, one that deserves our attention. As we earlier remarked, the emergence of the modern college and university was accompanied by an evolution, in our view, of faculty role and responsibility. How does an institution honor social heritage while challenging that heritage? How does a college or university inculcate its students with orthodox and accepted doctrines—whether doctrines of economics, science, religion, etc.—and simultaneously cause its students to think critically of these doctrines? Building on the German concept of *lehrfreiheit*, or freedom of teaching and research within the university, on which claims to academic freedom were based, American scholars have also been influenced by American traditions of political freedom and the philosophical tenets of pragmatism. Pragmatism, espoused in the late nineteenth century and early twentieth century by such leading intellectual figures as John Dewey, William James, and Charles Peirce, called for the testing of truth by its practical consequences in the world of experience. From this perspective, professors could hardly be true to what they believed their proper role and duty in society if they were restricted to a relative freedom within the walls of the academy and the bounds of prevailing opinion.

Highly publicized attempts in the late nineteenth century and early twentieth century to dismiss faculty members because of unpopular or controversial research findings, opinions, or ideas accented the seriousness of this struggle over the heart of the modern university. Two examples include the dismissals of Richard Ely, economist at the University of Wisconsin, for advocating the use of strikes and boycotts, and Edward Bemis, an economist at the University of Chicago, for comments against railroads.

One of the more celebrated cases in the early twentieth century was the dismissal of Professor Edward A. Ross, a Stanford University sociologist. Following a speech given by Ross opposing Asian immigration and the use of unskilled Asian labor in building railroads, Jane Stanford, wife of Stanford University founder and benefactor Leland Stanford, directed President David Starr Jordan to fire Ross, and Jordan did so (Lucas, 1994, p. 195). Would the American university then become an object of popular political, social, and economic pressures . . . or a marketplace of ideas, a center for free expression and exchange of information and perspectives? Though the issues were never that simple or clear-cut, the changing status of the faculty was still to be defined in the modern university. Within the larger and more bureaucratic institutions of the modern era, the faculty was not initially central to the administration and governance of the university, and if they could be dismissed for arriving at unpopular conclusions resulting from their research, they seemed to have little sovereignty over the realm of their specialized knowledge. The relatively autocratic behavior of some presidents, such as Jordan at Stanford, was testimony to the absence of partnership and shared authority principles previously detailed in chapter three.

Such circumstances raised profound questions about the role of the faculty in defining the nature and destiny of the American college and university. The guild culture of the great European universities had not yet found hospitable conditions for growth in America. The eighteenth century College of William and Mary professor denied by the Virginia courts in his claim that he could hold independent tenure in his faculty chair had much in common with the faculty at Columbia a century later, where President Nicholas M. Butler pointed out that the university charter "provided specifically that officers of instruction should serve at the pleasure of the trustees" (Brubacher and Rudy, 1976, p. 371).

The position of the faculty in seeking to gain clarification of their status as members of the university community and to assert the primacy of principles of academic freedom found its most influential articulation in the statements that grew out of the first meeting of the American Association of University Professors (AAUP) in 1915. The AAUP sought to clarify the concepts and purposes of academic freedom and faculty tenure as well as define the role of the professor in American higher education and society. These ideas, although central to the traditional conception of the role of the faculty, are still instructive in thinking through the role of faculty in the modern university.

How do we know what we know? The initial AAUP statement saw epistemological questions as central to the work of the faculty. Framers of the statement argued that the core responsibility of the academic profession was to deal with sources of knowledge and ways of accessing and defining truth. From this basis, they advanced the corollary point that in order to undertake this core function, professors had to be free to pose questions, investigate them, and draw conclusions without undue influence from factors irrelevant to the accuracy of their data or the thoroughness and appropriateness of their analysis.

While the AAUP authors acknowledged that there was no obligation for anyone to accept the conclusions reached, professors should in turn be entirely free from the obligation to adhere to popular opinion, or to the opinions of institutional financial supporters, administrators, or civic and corporate leaders. The AAUP held that the duty of the professor was to society as a whole, not to a specific board or group of individuals. Thus, the principle and practice of tenure was to be aimed at ensuring the independence and autonomy of the faculty. The AAUP founders further emphasized the importance of peer review of faculty in any decisions on termination of an academic appointment. Peer review was asserted as more appropriate to the academic profession than the court of public opinion or a lay board as a basis for judging the competence of a faculty member.

The AAUP authors held that restrictions of academic freedom would impair the role of the university in enhancing the range of public thinking on a wide variety of issues. They argued that while new ideas were often not popular, the university was a place where new ideas might be put forward and critically reviewed and analyzed.

Today's common sense may have been yesterday's heresy and the path to new modes of thought is often wrenching and painful. A work describing the difficult challenge of making pathways from old models of thought to new is Thomas Kuhn's *The Structure of Scientific Revolutions* (1962). In a cogent and concise statement issued in 1972, former Yale University President Kingman Brewster indicated that "If scholarship is to question assumptions and to take the risk of testing new hypotheses, then it cannot be held to a time table which demands proof of pay-out to satisfy some review committee (Brewster, p. 382).

Finally, a key point made by the early AAUP was that just as investigation and teaching had to be free, free dissemination of the findings of investigation was equally essential. The authors tempered this assertion, however, with cautions that professors' views should be presented responsibly, after careful review, and "with courtesy and dignity of expression." Professors were expected to share their research and judgments with their students, but were always expected to encourage their students to think critically and form their own opinions, based on their own best independent thinking and judgment.

Thus, if one looks carefully at the concept of academic freedom, one finds it coupled with the expectation of academic responsibility and the obligation of placing research findings and professional conviction in public forum, where they may be examined, debated and otherwise tested for validity in method and substance. This is a part of the "academic duty" of faculty, as earlier referenced in Donald Kennedy's book by that same title.

When a faculty member holds up a mirror to society, however, a mirror that causes that society to look at unsavory or unethical policy or practice in our civic, economic, or political life, it is not so hard to understand that the pain of that forced examination may bring a desire to dispatch the messenger. The civic mind knows that colleges and universities have been established in our midst to seek truth wherever that may lead. The civic mind knows the importance of unfettered inquiry to a democratic society. The call of self-interest, however, may not welcome the disturbance occasioned by the search for truth. As Saul Alinsky wrote in *Rules for Radicals*, "one's concern with the ethics of means and ends varies inversely with one's personal interest in the issue" (Alinsky, 1971, p. 26). Faculty members prospecting for truth in another's backyard are welcome—but perhaps not so welcome if the dirt is being shoveled into our own.

Four additional complications related to academic freedom warrant our attention before we close this discussion. The first is that the right of professors to exercise their academic freedoms may become entangled with their citizen "free speech" rights under the protection of the First Amendment. In *The Law of Higher Education*, Kaplan comments as follows:

> The concept of academic freedom eludes precise definition. It is a concept that draws from both the world of education and the world of

law. Courts have increasingly used academic freedom as the catch-all term to describe the legal rights and responsibilities of the teaching profession. This judicial conception of academic freedom is essentially an attempt to reconcile constitutional principles with the prevailing views of academic freedom's social and intellectual role in American life (Kaplan, 1985, p. 180).

In general, the freedom of faculty to research and inquire, profess and to publish on themes both popular and unpopular, and exercise their best professional judgment on matters academic has generally been supported by the courts. Courts, on the other hand, have not been reluctant to decide against faculty on issues such as unwarranted use of profane speech and unrelated materials and illustrations.

A second complicating factor related to academic freedom concerns the limits of artistic expression in painting, sculpture, photography, and music, and the clash of principles between what faculty believe should be allowable and what supporting friends—whether civic or religious—believe should be allowable. On this point, the doctrine and teachings of a religiously affiliated college and the concept of academic freedom also may clash. Might we expect, for example, discussions on abortion to unfold with the same degree of openness and protection on a public research university campus as compared to an evangelically related Christian college? Clearly not. Readers interested in a brief and contemporary summary of this issue are referred to a monograph by Poch (1993).

Third, it must be recognized that faculty themselves may become enemies of academic freedom. While this is an uncomfortable note to sound, it is a necessary one. Kingman Brewster indicated that "In strong universities, assuring freedom from intellectual conformity coerced within the institution is even more of a concern than in the protection of freedom from external interference" (Brewster, 1972, p. 382). Thus, intellectual narrowness and rigidity, unwillingness to admit error, personal jealousy, academic prejudice, political differences, and personal animosities may create internal climates confining and even demeaning to academic freedom. While much of the earlier literature on academic freedom deals with the threat and dangers of external interference, there is an emerging literature on "political correctness" detailing how accepted beliefs and assumptions within the academy and faculty tend to dampen ideological debate, shape faculty behavior, and affect reward and recognition of faculty. In a chapter entitled "The Assault on Faculty Speech" appearing in their 1998 work *The Shadow University*, Kors and Silvergate furnish a number of troublesome examples in which the academic freedom of faculty has been confined by policy and actors within the academy. Other works that engage this topic include books *Beyond the Culture Wars* (Graff, 1992), *Debating P.C.* (Berman, 1992), and journal pieces by Gross (1992),

Parr (1990–91), Shurden (1990), and Trachtenberg, (1992–93). Scholar Seymour Martin Lipset contributes an important perspective by reminding us that "correct" behaviors and intellectual perspectives have historically been a part of American intellectual life—whether in the form of doctrinal expectations of early-American, religiously affiliated colleges or in the ethnic, social, gender, and religious criteria applied in some earlier admissions and faculty hiring decisions. Lipset concludes that "Repression from the Left, though it draws its legitimacy from populist values, must suffer the same fate as repression from the Right" (Lipset, 1992, p. 11). Thus, when ideological and methodological conviction become so fixated that they are transformed into a narrow and unbending prejudice, the destructive internal effects on academic freedom and faculty welfare can be significant.

Moreover, repression of academic freedom may be found in the occasional mean spirited behaviors of some faculty and in the ill-mannered and ill-informed behaviors of others. Brilliance of mind in some faculty may be accompanied by surprising displays of emotional and interpersonal intelligence that can only be described as infantile. Some college and university faculty who are quick to champion their right to place policy and practice in our society under critical scrutiny can be the same faculty who are impatient with and intolerant of colleagues who question their theories and methods. Faculty who yearn for truth and academic freedom yearn in vain if they lack the will and the ability to treat dissenting colleagues with dignity. Civility among the faculty is not a small condition for the nurture of academic freedom.

Threats from both the political right and the political left can endanger academic freedom. In their eagerness to root out communistic sympathizers in American colleges and universities, right-wing officials at both state and federal levels brought to American colleges and universities in the late 1940s and the 1950s the repression of guilt by association and loyalty oaths. From the bitter experience of these years, we learned that it is impossible to exemplify and teach intellectual freedom by denying that freedom to those who have views different from the majority. Scholar Alexander Meiklejohn stated the case for democracy plainly:

> . . . whenever, in the field of ideas, the advocates of freedom and the advocates of suppression meet in fair and unabridged discussion, freedom will win. If that were not true, if the intellectual program of democracy could not its own in fair debate, then that program itself would require of us its own abandonment (1949, p. 10).

In the 1960s and the 1970s, amidst the social and political turmoil associated with the civil rights movement and the Vietnam War, threats to academic freedom came not so much from the right as from the left—from the actions of radical students, professors, and pressure groups. Radical students invaded classrooms to suppress faculty teaching and invaded offices of both professors and administrators, destroying both property and the scholarly work and manuscripts of faculty. They burned buildings and brought disorder to campus.

"On strike, shut it down!" "Power to the people!" and "Up against the wall, motherfucker!" were loud and profane slogans new to the contemplative climates and the delicate consensus balance of college campuses. Radical students and professors inciting students to engage in illegal actions brought to some campuses a collapse of civility and brought also the presence of police force and national guard troops to restore order, often with sad and tragic consequence that included injury and death to some students, events well chronicled from the University of California of Berkeley to Kent State University.

In *The Troubled Crusade*, scholar Diane Ravitch (1983) furnishes an informing account of these years in American higher education and concludes her treatment with this note: "When political interference comes from right-wing elected officials, university trustees, and pressure groups, then faculty members and administrators join to defend academic freedom. When the challenge comes from radical students, teachers, and pressure groups, as it did in the 1960s, the university is internally divided, which puts academic freedom at risk from those who most need its protection" (p. 227).

The principle and benefits of academic freedom have been fashioned on the hard anvils of debate and disorder in our society, where painful lessons have been derived from both philosophy, experience, and investments of both thought and action. Thus, of concepts and principles fundamental to academic life in American colleges and universities, probably the two best known but often misunderstood by civic and political friends of higher education (and sometimes by academics themselves) are academic freedom and tenure. The history and complication of academic freedom we have engaged. Let us now probe the role and future of tenure.

THE FUTURE OF TENURE

The concept of tenure emerged in this century as an instrument to guarantee the independence of faculty in their search for truth, to assure them of due process, to offer a degree of employment security as a partial compensation for the relatively low salaries associated with work of the mind, and to protect them from the caprice of the politically and financially motivated, mostly external to the campus and the narrowness and meanness of colleagues who hold different views. However, tenure has come to be viewed as an instrument that shields the uncaring, incompetent, slothful, and duplicitous from corrective action. Whether other faculty employment options might offer promise of fulfilling the constructive motives of tenure without the perceived negative outcomes is the center of current public and professional debate. The journey of discovery may not be taken if American academics are not willing to engage in the dialogue. From the principles initially advanced by the AAUP in its Statement on Academic Freedom and Tenure in 1915 and reissued in 1940, faculty and administrators came to general agreement on policies for establishing and administering programs for faculty tenure. By the end of the 1960s, virtually every institution, public and private, had established tenure as part of faculty life. Interestingly, by the time tenure became a routine part of faculty life it also came under renewed attack as an anachronistic means of protecting a pampered "old boys club" that made for inflexible personnel circumstances in changing social and economic times and that insulated the faculty from criticism (Brubacher and Rudy, 1976).

Though still widely accepted as a norm of faculty life and success, tenure has continued to draw severe criticism in the 1990s. By the end of 1995, several institutions had abandoned tenure completely, some on the initiative of governing boards and some on the initiative of faculty themselves (Magner, March 1995; Trower, 1996). In 1995, the American Association for Higher Education (AAHE) began a two-year study to explore the merits of tenure and alternatives to conventional tenure processes (Magner, March 1995; Rice, 1996).

Among the issues under consideration by the AAHE forum were the definition of financial exigency, means for ensuring academic freedom separate from tenure, and the economic value of tenure to faculty members. Each of these issues addresses specific arguments long made by the AAUP and others related to tenure. First, except for cause, tenured faculty members may only be dismissed in cases of financial exigency, a condition the courts have interpreted as extreme financial distress. Second, tenure is essential to assuring the freedom of the faculty to pursue research and draw conclusions without regard to popular opinion or pressure unrelated to the scholarly merit of the work. Third, tenure is a means by which to enhance the appeal of the academic profession to people of high ability, the "best and the brightest" of each generation that undertakes advanced study.

Thus, tenure has come to be seen as the major instrument for protecting the vital and fragile independence of the faculty (Bowen and Schuster, 1986). There is a historic basis to this view. The generations of professors who labored with modest financial remuneration, who served at the pleasure (and not infrequently the whim) of presidents, boards of trustees, and political officers (and even donors' spouses) in previous years, who were overwhelmed with work and care, paved the way for the flourishing of a powerful faculty culture in the twentieth century. Tenure and the intellectual independence of the faculty have, in the twentieth century, been instrumental in the cultivation of the largest, most diverse, most influential and productive system of higher education the world has ever seen. Those who have an acquaintance with the political and educational realities of other countries will appreciate even more America's investment in and guarantees of the pursuit of truth.

It seems not a little ironic, then, that an arm of the National Science Foundation in 1992 described the current system of tenure, promotion, and reward as "our greatest barrier to a better future" (Rice, p. 31). The prevailing lore of higher education in the 1990s is fueled by an ample supply of anecdotal evidence that conventional notions of faculty achievement and tenure derail the careers of budding young teachers and unconventional scholars while protecting professorial "deadwood," a favorite term of tenure opponents (Parini, 1995). As Rudolph (1990) pointed out, this view is not uniquely contemporary, but has retained its vitality over many decades. The life of the teacher/scholar is one of the most difficult and demanding when rightly done and one of the easiest to neglect by the unscrupulous and uncaring. Certainly the work and performance of faculty can be affected by policy context, such as tenure. However, the difference in performance is also a matter of individual faculty motivation and devotion, the courage and care of faculty colleagues, and the courage and care of academic administrators. Both moral outrage and effective policy can be useful instruments of faculty performance accountability.

In the 1990s, one way in which some institutions and systems of higher education have sought to address the issue of faculty "deadwood" is through the use of post-tenure evaluation (Magner, July 1995; Rice, 1996). Such practices have varied from universal reviews of all faculty members to reviews restricted to those who receive consistently poor merit reviews (Magner, July, 1995). Licata (1998) offers a useful summary of the principles undergirding post-tenure review and some of the challenges encountered in implementation. This review should be continuous in the professional life of the faculty member. Expectations for professional activity should be clear and measurable. The friction has occurred historically on what is measurable: the ambiguity of professional expectations;and the collective will of the faculty to take on difficult and disappointing performance of colleagues. The former has often degenerated into procedures for counting refereed articles, while the other has been a hodge-podge of formal and informal statements and practices that vary between and within institutions. The last may take the form of "pass the buck" behavior, usually to the department chair or "head-in-the-sand" behavior in which stewardship violations are simply ignored.

In the previous discussion, reference was made to "deadwood" on the faculty. Lucas (1996) suggests that tenure also protects the "rotten wood" that might be found on the faculty—"the aggressively disgruntled, the chronically disaffected, the angry malcontents who, in reckless disregard for the ordinary canons of decorum and collegiality that make organizational life possible, pursue their own narcissistic ends regardless of cost to others" (p. 182.) Such faculty, Lucas rightly asserts, can exert "a malign influence disproportionate to their numbers" (p. 183).

A second option now being explored and implemented on some campuses is that of fixed-term renewable contracts. Sykes (1988) states that "The replacement of lifetime tenure with fixed-term renewable contracts would, at one stroke, restore accountability, while potentially freeing the vast untapped energies of the academy that have been locked in the petrified grip of a tenured professoriate" (p. 258). Other internal critics of tenure suggesting renewable contracts include Solomon and Solomon, who pose and answer an important question:

> Won't a contract system encourage "sucking up" to authorities and a return to more traditional, less risky teaching? Assistant professors are already forced to prostitute themselves for six or seven years, and most of them have trouble getting rid of the habit once they get tenure. Won't it intensify already bitter academic politics? With more or less equal vulnerability, academic politics might even become more civilized, with more emphasis on rights and responsibilities and less nonsense about matters of mere status and privilege (Solomon and Solomon, 1993, p. 250).

There are those within and without the academy who suggest that any institution of merit will protect the academic freedom rights of all of its professors, whether they are tenured or not. Under this condition, the argument that tenure is an instrument for preserving academic freedom becomes specious. Well-crafted grievance policies and processes are offered as one option to tenure. Others argue that it is the collective authority of the tenured that guarantees that the rights of the untenured will indeed be protected. Assaults on tenure, under this view, hold promise of shifting the foundation pillars of the academy. Richard Chait, a frequent writer on questions of tenure, has urged that faculty not engage in defensive and "circle-the-wagons" behavior when tenure comes under public scrutiny nor that they see the issue only in terms of how to preserve tenure. He suggests instead that academics honor the principle of open debate as they would in other matters of university life and ask whether tenure, as it is currently conceived and employed, allows colleges and universities to achieve their educational goals (Chait, 1997). Chait urges choice, not conformity, as an idea to guide the debate and discussion:

> If we fail to do this, a riskier fate may await us: public referenda, legislative incursions, and trustee initiatives that preempt further discussion. Even more dangerous, the academy's aversion to a robust,

open-minded exploration of employment arrangements would signal to society at large that the bastion of academic freedom rests on a very insecure foundation (Chait, 1997, p. B5).

It is an uncomfortable intellectual posture to place under public scrutiny what one takes to be an important philosophical foundation on the argument that this same philosophical principle is what calls for the public scrutiny. Thus, faculty are placed in an unhappy position if they argue for academic freedom and tenure but propose that ideas affecting their welfare are to be excluded from debate.

These arguments over principles fundamental to the life and welfare of the faculty are made more interesting and more lively by the growing diversity of faculty voice. The movement of these new voices into the policy life of our campuses is the subject of our next and final discussion.

THE GROWING DIVERSITY OF FACULTY

In understanding the American faculty, one must attend issues of diversity in terms of institutional types and the demographics of the population. The early colleges had, for the most part, clear missions and expectations. They served a small and well-defined segment of the general population. And their faculty were almost without exception Caucasian men. The expansion of American higher education to embrace students from a more diverse range of backgrounds, as detailed in chapter seven, is being accompanied by the gradual diversification of the faculty as well. The early universities tended to exclude women and minorities as candidates for faculty appointment, partly because job searches were conducted primarily through networks of personal contacts. The idea of advertising openings was considered somehow inappropriate and there seems to have been little recognition that such a lack of openness was unfair (Wilson, 1979). While African-American academics found positions in the African-American colleges that sprung up in the South after the Civil War, and in the 1890s at the land-grant colleges of the South, there were few opportunities for them in majority Caucasian institutions (Wilson, 1979).

There was an initial surge in the numbers of women faculty members in the 1870s, as a generation of pioneering women academics opened doors long closed to them. However. the twentieth century witnessed both the general decline in the numbers of women completing degrees at midcentury, and a decline in the proportion of women in academic positions between 1940 and 1960 (Wilson, 1979).

Efforts to end and reverse discriminatory practices and patterns in faculty hiring were aided by a 1965 executive order banning discrimination on the basis of race, religion, color, or national origin. This was followed by an executive order in 1968 expanding this ban to include discrimination on the basis of sex. Although these orders affected only institutions holding contracts with the federal government, for all practical purposes, almost all colleges and universities were affected.

Through the 1970s, a plethora of lawsuits, administrative rules, and statutes addressed the challenge of achieving greater representation and balance in the demographic spectrum of the faculty. Though there were many well-intentioned efforts to find a balance between the need for genuine integration and affirmative action to increase the racial and gender balance of the faculty, there was also concern that demographic characteristics were overshadowing issues of merit in hiring as well as promotion and tenure decisions (Wilson, 1979). This tension in public policy continues to this day.

Data for the faculty in American colleges and universities from fall 1992 show that among full-time faculty members with teaching responsibilities, just under one-third were women, and of those women, 86 percent were Caucasian. Of the two-thirds who were men, 87 percent were Caucasian, and Caucasian men comprised almost three-fifths of the entire professorate. Comparatively, just under 5 percent of all full-time faculty members were African American, although almost one-third of all service and maintenance employees of American colleges and universities were African American. Further, a greater proportion of minority and women faculty members were at lower academic ranks than Caucasian males, who made up just over three-fourths of all full professors (*Chronicle*, Sept. 1, 1995).

A significant difficulty for institutions in trying to enhance the diversity of their faculties is reflected in the proportion of those seeking advanced degrees who are women or minorities. Figures for 1992–93 show a 21 percent increase in the number of doctorates earned compared to the five previous years. Almost two-thirds (62 percent) were granted to men and 38 percent to women. However, the field of education alone accounted for more than a quarter of all doctorates earned by women. Almost two-thirds of doctorates earned by women were earned in five fields of study: biological sciences, education, health professions, psychology, and the social sciences (including history) (*Chronicle Almanac*, September 1995). In technical and scientific fields, men continued to earn doctorates in numbers far beyond those earned by women. Women earned fewer than 10 percent of engineering doctorates and 22 percent of doctorates in the physical sciences (*Chronicle Almanac*, September 1995).

Even more troubling is the fact that in 1992–93, less than 1.5 percent of new doctorates were conferred on African Americans. In fact, for the same period, more than 63 percent of doctorates were conferred on Caucasians, and slightly more than 27 percent on foreign students. The fact that less than 10 percent of earned doctorates were earned by Native Americans, Asian Americans, African Americans, and Hispanics does not bode well for future efforts to enhance the racial and ethnic diversity of the faculty (*Chronicle*, September, 1995).

Recent data present a more encouraging picture of the composition of the faculty (Magner, February 1996), indicating that more than a third of all faculty members are in the first seven years of their careers. Still, the composition of this new faculty population is predominantly Caucasian and tenure rates show men gaining tenure at far higher rates than women. The largest gains for any single racial or ethnic group are for those of Asian heritage. The largest gains for any demographic component of the faculty population were among those who are not U.S.-born citizens. Further, the new faculty tend to be less likely than their older counterparts to hold tenure-track positions or to teach in the core arts and science fields of the modern university.

While a range of state, regional, and national programs have emerged in recent years to enhance the number and proportion of underrepresented populations moving into academic life, the data reveal some successes, an encouraging trend for women, and also some disappointments, a not-so-encouraging record for African Americans.

Clearly there is ample leadership challenge remaining in enhancing the diversity of the American professoriate. A moment of some opportunity is now presenting itself as American higher education moves into the twenty-first century. A large number of faculty appointed during the rapid-expansion years of the 1960s and early 1970s are already taking retirement and others will follow over the next five to ten years. Finding replacements for these faculty should offer additional opportunity for initial appointment and for promotion of new and younger faculty from all sectors of our population.

We have not in this discussion treated another expression of increasing diversity in American college and university faculty. This manifestation of faculty diversity does not take ethnic or gender form. There is a growing use of adjunct and part-time faculty in American higher education, from entry-level courses to graduate and professional courses. Many of these men and women are well-credentialed and well-experienced professionals who bring the authority of both thought and practice to classrooms, and they do so for a fraction of the costs associated with the appointment of full-time faculty. Thus, the use of part-time faculty can become attractive not only for the skill and experience they bring to the campus but for the reduced costs in the cost containment times depicted in chapter six. However, use of part-time faculty is accompanied by the liability that these faculty are often not around to handle community matters of student advising and curricular design. Here is a mixed blessing, the dimensions of which have been debated in recent years and which will probably remain under engagement in future years.

MENTORS AND MODELS

The faculty of America's colleges and universities are entrusted with profoundly important elements of role and responsibility that include the following: (1) to seek truth in framing and engaging the central questions of our time in all spheres of human inquiry and understanding—science, technology, society, government, economy, philosophy, religion, and arts; (2) to disseminate and apply the findings of their scholarship and to critically review the answers disseminated and applied by others; (3) to teach, in the classroom and in the field, based on the best thinking, inquiry, and practice currently known, and in so doing, to inspire and guide students to the fullest measure of personal development and self-knowledge; (4) to construct and maintain the great bridges necessary to connect our cultural heritage with our current lives and thinking; to "speak truth to power," that is, to provide social and political critique with informed voices of reason and conscience; and (5) to apply knowledge and skill to the amelioration of human problems of every kind.

College and university faculty have the privilege and the joy, the duty and the responsibility of engaging in two activities that govern the center and the health of any society, certainly democratic societies: to search for truth and to develop human promise. How can colleges and universities encourage, cultivate, and sustain the best in their faculties and how can they call them to high standards of performance? How can they insist that faculty respond to their stewardship responsibilities? How can we honor differentiation of faculty role among different institutions and among disciplines within the same institution? These are daunting leadership questions, but not new leadership questions. These are perennial questions of intent, courage, and responsibility. College and university faculty in late twentieth century America find themselves faced with conflicting demands and expectations. There is, however, some contradiction between the manifest and latent philosophies that undergird expectations for individual choices and behavior in all vocations and walks of life in the United States. On the one hand, the manifest philosophy routinely expressed in many of our social institutions, including schools and universities, exhorts people to follow a personal value compass that is not directed solely by the aim for material gain and self-interest (Barber, 1992; Bellah, et al., 1985). This is a servant role and one that accents community. In contrast, the behaviors and attitudes too often and publicly rewarded in our society are those of competition, maximization of individual self-interest, and the successful exploitation for profit of human and natural resources.

Referring again to *The American Scholar* we have these reflections from Emerson:

> Men, such as they are, very naturally seek money, or power. Wake them and they shall quit the false good and leap to the true, and leave

governments to clerks and desks. The main enterprise of the world for splendor, for extent, is the upbuilding of man. The private life of one man shall be a more illustrious monarchy than any kingdom in history (1929, p. 31).

The upbuilding of man is indeed the work of the American scholar, the work of those faculty who hold our colleges and universities in trust.

CHAPTER 9

Academics and Athletics

The Arenas of Ideological and Physical Contest

Education or entertainment? Complementary or corrupting? Financial boon or financial drain? Character forming or character depraving? Which of these most accurately describes the mission and relationship of intercollegiate athletics in the life of American higher education? In chapter one we used an intercollegiate athletics illustration to emphasize American higher education diversity. Not only are intercollegiate athletic programs a manifestation of diversity, their presence is clearly one of the more distinctive features in American higher education heritage. Thus, whatever perspective one may embrace concerning the role and contribution of athletics, the centrality of athletics in the life of American colleges and universities is undeniable.

The "extracurriculum," those activities taking place outside the formal curriculum explored in chapters four and seven, is a unique feature of American higher education. Here we find a wide range of student organizations, both social and academic. Drama and debate, musicals and lecture societies, greek-letter organizations, and special interest groups—a wide array of student activities form the extracurriculum and contribute to the formation of character as well as intelligence, to the preparation of students as "citizens and persons as well as specialists and savants" (Brubacher and Rudy, 1976, p. 385). In addition to these more noble purposes, it may well be argued that the activities of the extracurriculum have also served to absorb and channel excess youthful energy. No part of the extracurriculum commands as much attention, creates as much emotion, or calls forth as much dissent as does intercollegiate athletics. Here is a collegiate activity that, some will assert, has engaged a disproportionate attention of campus presidents and has elicited the attention and comment of our nation's presidents. Here is an activity so contentious, so politically and economically complex that it may be debated whether any other issue has led to the unplanned and hasty departure of so many American college presidents. This activity is so emotionally contagious and commanding that even the most cerebral of personalities will yield to the call of celebration associated with victory over one's rival. Any book, therefore, that purports to treat the heritage and the promise of American higher education would be missing an important part should it fail to engage the relationship between the forum of ideological contest, which we cited in chapter two, and the arenas of physical/athletic contest. This relationship has been one characterized by debate and dissent from the very beginning; and it is the relationship to which we turn in this chapter.

We first briefly examine the evolution of intercollegiate athletics, an evolution that began as a student-oriented and initiated diversion in collegiate life but that now clearly involves major entertainment and commercial interests external to the campus, a commercialization of no small economic import as we shall soon see. Next, we explore the scope of the intercollegiate athletic enterprise, examining the three major national organizations that oversee athletics. Finally, we evaluate some of the contemporary issues that swirl about athletics on campus and speculate on the future of the relationship between the arenas of ideological and physical contest.

THE EMERGENCE OF "BIG-TIME ATHLETICS"

Certainly, the training of the body has been an accepted educational goal from earliest history. Physical education and games were important elements of education in antiquity, a devotion to the exercise of mind and body. In the early years of American higher education, however, physical exercise was relatively informal and spontaneous, and games were played for recreation and enjoyment—elements of mission not entirely lost in contemporary intramural programs of colleges and universities. In *Higher Education in Transition*, Brubacher and Rudy (1976) suggest that the emergence of big-time athletics began in the latter part of the nineteenth century. According to their report, the first intercollegiate football game, more a form of soccer or rugby, was played between Rutgers and Princeton in 1869 (p. 127). In England, intercollegiate sport in the form of cricket matches had been underway since the early part of the nineteenth century.

The competitive spirit gathered momentum quickly. In an 1891 letter, we find University of Chicago President William Rainey Harper, known for his intellectual contributions to higher education and to the university, calling on his newly appointed athletic director Alonzo Stagg as follows: "I want you to develop teams which we can send around the country and knock out all the colleges. We will give them a palace car and a vacation too"(Gould, 1951, pp. 122–23). Stagg had suggested that until athletics arrived on campus, the major student sport had been friendly bouts of drinking. An earlier and contrasting presidential view may be found in the remarks of Cornell President Andrew White. When Cornell was challenged by men from the University of Michigan to a football game on neutral ground in Cleveland, White is reported to have said "I will not permit thirty men to travel four hundred miles merely to agitate a bag of wind" (Sagendorph, 1948, p. 150). The role and contribution of athletics continues to draw conflicting opinion from American college presidents. In his annual report of 1892-93, President Charles Eliot of Harvard testified to an array of physical, moral, and spiritual benefits flowing from college athletics. He included among those courage, fortitude, perseverance, and self-control (Savage, et al. 1929, p. 294). Thus, among the acknowledged intellectual leaders of the late nineteenth century in American higher education history, there were highly visible advocates and equally visible critics. In the 1929 Carnegie report, Savage and others present the presumed advantages of sport, and then a few pages later call these into question as follows:

> College athletics, especially football, and other body-contact games, *inculcate* in participants such desirable qualities as courage, perseverance, initiative, uprightness, cooperation, and honesty. Thereby they contribute very essentially to the popular welfare, because these estimable qualities, once established in youth, persist into manhood as habits and thus benefit society and its members (p. 294).
>   . . . however strong may be the conviction that they inculcate or increase in young men courage, initiative, and other moral qualities, this remains to be scientifically established. More than a decade ago it was pointed out that excessive desire for victory has deprived us of one of the most important educational advantages of athletics, since coaching from the side-lines removes from the players the essential quality of initiative (p. 300).

If Savage and others found coaching from the side lines a serious distraction to individual initiative, they would be more distraught with the complex statistics, strategies, and technology applications that associate with development and execution of the "game plan" in contemporary athletics.

The tension between "winning at all costs" and responding to some sense of ethics is a tension that has challenged athletics from the beginning. In the early history of football, "tramp" athletes sold their services to the highest bidder, and according to historian Frederick Rudolph, "the football coach at Syracuse turned out to be the next season's captain at Cornell" (Rudolph,

1990, p. 374). At least current intercollegiate regulation seems to inhibit this swing of talent application.

Historians Brubacher and Rudy suggest that the danger and violence associated with the history of football in the early twentieth century (18 killed and 159 seriously injured in one season) was sufficient for President Theodore Roosevelt to call a special White House conference in 1905 to deal with this dark side of sport. Perhaps intercollegiate athletics is a civilized and modern alternative to war among cities and states. Whatever the mayhem and cost associated with big-time sports, these must be less formidable than a large scale social bloodletting.

Tales of unusual sporting events contributed spice to collegiate life, even in the early history of intercollegiate sport. According to Rudolph, the 1891 football game between Purdue and Wabash ended at Purdue 44, Wabash 0, when in the second half a frustrated and unhappy Wabash player ran from the field with the ball, and neither another player nor ball could be found to continue the contest.

More interesting in process and outcome was a 1916 game reported by Jim Paul in his book entitled *You Dropped It, You Pick It Up*. A hastily gathered team from Cumberland University in Lebanon, Tennessee, traveled to Atlanta to play Georgia Tech, coached by the now-famed John Heisman. The extent to which the gentlemen from Tennessee were outclassed is carried in the final score: Georgia Tech 223, Cumberland 0. The game and the score must appear in someone's book of bizarre sporting events. Some Cumberland players went AWOL, hiding outside the field, while another Cumberland player was found hiding on the Georgia Tech bench. A Cumberland back, Johnny Dog, fumbled the ball late in this bruising and humiliating contest and yelled to George Allen, the fullback, to pick it up. Moving quickly away from the ball to avoid collision with a huge Georgia Tech lineman approaching with the momentum of a freight train, Allen yelled back "You dropped it, you pick it up" (Paul, 1983, pp. 217–18).

The American preoccupation with sport is reflected in the attention and priority that it commands in our national life. Perhaps a third of most newspapers and a third of evening televison newscasts is taken with sports reporting. Casual conversation will be laced with the latest player and team statistics, and a lively speculation with the latest press reports on who is number one in any sport. Street and hallway exchanges will be heated by the armchair commentary of those who, in retrospect, could have made better decisions than the coach.

Early in the emergence of intercollegiate athletics, sports were quickly seen as a major public relations benefit to those campuses who were winning, though it may be argued that contests, like the aforementioned Georgia Tech-Cumberland game, can afford a certain notoriety as well. The pleasure of winning and the embarrassment of a solid drubbing remain welcome and painful public relations outcomes, respectively.

Historians of higher education also alert the reader to the importance and complexity of sport. Brubacher and Rudy (1976) devote a chapter to student-initiated extracurricular activities of fraternities and athletics, and Rudolph (1992) devotes an entire chapter to "The Rise of Football." Attention to athletics is not absent in Lawrence Veysey's *The Emergence of the American University* (1965) nor in Christopher Lucas' 1994 history, which contains a section on "Gridiron Loyalties."

When one can find an annual institutional intercollegiate athletic budget of perhaps $250,000 and another of $25 million and learn that both institutions are playing football, it becomes clear that something different in the way of athletic competition must be happening on these two campuses, and one could wager a safe bet that teams from these two campuses would not be meeting on the same field or in the same arena. Contemporary college and civic leaders can read in the newspaper the story of one state university ready to give up football because of deficits in its program (Mangan, 1996, p. A47–A48), while another state university has contracted with its football coach for a million dollar annual salary (Naughton, 1996, p. A37). In their morning newspaper, they may read an inspiring story of an athlete serving as both character and intellectual exemplar for the millions who watch him or her play each week.

There is something attracting and beautiful in the display of stellar artistic talent—whether that talent is musical, athletic, literary, or in visual arts. Anyone who has experienced the inspiring and mesmerizing performance of a college basketball player temporarily defying gravity, a football player evading the grasping hands of would-be tacklers, a gymnast demonstrating the most complex bodily aerobatics, or the spirit of an athletic team performing beyond any reasonable expectation of its talent knows how the human spirit resonates to the presence of such talent. Here indeed is a form of intelligence which we can admire, the kinesthetic intelligence suggested by Howard Gardner and to which we referred in chapter four.

In that same newspaper, however, academics and civic friends may read of well-known athletes forsaking their integrity in sordid scandals involving violence, sex, and money, often with the help of coaches, faculty, and alumni. Such disappointing fissures of character and behavior are as repugnant and repelling as the exemplary performance and character among athletes are attracting and admirable. Yes, here is a domain of collegiate activity where there is clear diversity in program scope, mission, and of opinion on whether athletics is complementary or corrupting to academia.

Earlier we commented on the 1905 role of President Theodore Roosevelt in convening a conference on football. More recently, the federal government has taken an assertive role in the oversight of intercollegiate athletics with the passage of the Student Right to Know and Campus Security Act of 1990. This act requires colleges and universities receiving federal aid to report graduation rates by sport, race, and gender to the secretary of education. The bill was introduced by Senator Bill Bradley, a former NCAA All-American basketball player from Princeton, who felt that players, parents, and counselors deserved candid information as they made choices in their selection of colleges (Bradley, 1992).

The enterprise of intercollegiate athletics is of sufficient scope and interest in its activity and performance that it now commands national legislative attention. Let us explore the scope of the enterprise.

ATHLETIC ORGANIZATION AND GOVERNANCE

Most intercollegiate athletic programs will be a member of one of three national governance and regulatory organizations. These governance organizations generally serve to create a "level playing field" by insuring fair competition. Frey reports on the origins of the call to fairness:

> The goals of the Harvard and Yale crews in 1852 combined pleasurable recreation with honorable competition. Harvard was answering a challenge from Yale to "test the superiority of the oarsmen of the two colleges." But despite the Harvard victory, the contestants enjoyed a week of "much good feeling." Institutional prestige, however, had assumed greater importance by the time of the rematch in 1855. At that time Yale questioned the eligibility of the Harvard cox, who had already graduated. Unfortunately, Yale had neither an arbiter nor a regulation to which it could appeal. Clearly some form of collective governance was in order (Frey, 1982).

National Collegiate Athletic Association (NCAA)

The oldest, largest, and perhaps the best-known governance organization is the National Collegiate Athletics Association. Any American who has the slightest addiction to television is likely see the NCAA seal featured in some intercollegiate athletic contest during any week of the year. The Intercollegiate Athletic Association of the United States, forerunner of the NCAA, was formed in 1906 just a few months after the previously described conference called by President Theodore Roosevelt to deal with the unhappy life and limb outcomes of the 1905 football season. The NCAA succeeded the IAAUS in 1910.

Table 9.1 reveals that the current membership in the NCAA stands at approximately 1,200, with this membership spread across three divisions

---

TABLE 9.1

NCAA MEMBERSHIP BREAKDOWN

	Division I				Div. II	Div. III	Grand Total
	1-A	**1-AA**	**1-AAA**	**Total**			
Active	114	122	82	318	262	393	973
Provisional	0	0	3	3	35	30	68
Conference							
Voting	11	11	11	33	21	37	91
Other	0	2	8	10	5	14	29
Affiliated							81
Corresponding							18
GRAND TOTAL							1,260

Note: University of Idaho is a Division 1-AA Institution electing to apply Division 1-A legislation.

Source: *The NCAA News*, September 13, 1999.

representing different levels of play. The criteria for membership in the three divisions include number of sports sponsored, football and basketball scheduling requirements, academic eligibility requirements, and financial aid limitations. In the case of Division I-A membership there is also a requirement for football attendance. The intent is to establish different competitive levels of play and to offer regulation that will guarantee the integrity of that competition.

In the realm of academic aptitude, in the 1960s, potential college athletes had to have a predicted freshman GPA of 1.6 to receive scholarship aid. In the 1970s, a student athlete had to have a 2.0 GPA on all high school subjects to receive scholarship aid. Currently, a high school athlete hoping to play for a Division I school must present a grade point average of 2.5 on 13 core curriculum units (mathematics, physical sciences, social sciences, English, and foreign language) and a score of 17 on the American College Testing entrance examination or 820 on the Scholastic Aptitude Test. Thus, in some cases, student athletes are held to a higher standard than other students gaining admission to a university. Academic eligibility for students aspiring to play for Division I or Division II is currently established by the NCAA Clearinghouse.

There are, unfortunately, too many instances where an athlete's academic credentials are falsified to help insure admission, a matter to which we will return in the final discussion. In addition, the framing of these and other academic policies affecting athletes is not without public rancor involving arguments of racial bias and the lofting of expository mortar shells from the ramparts of opposing camps.

The profile of financial activity for the two scholarship Divisions I and II is carried in Table 9.2. A wide swing in average revenues moves from just under $1 million for Division II schools without football to the average of $15.5 million for Division I schools. Football programs at Division I-A schools earned a net profit of almost $4 million on average in 1995. The range of income for big-time athletic programs may vary from just under $10 million to more than $40 million. Gate receipts will furnish a little more than a third of total revenue for these large schools whereas television and postseason revenue will furnish approximately 20 percent. Travel to a postseason bowl for football can mean formidable extra revenue, not only for the team attending, but is shared with other schools playing in the conference.

TABLE 9.2

AVERAGE REVENUE BY NCAA DIVISION 1995

Division	Average Total Revenue
I-A	$15,482,000
I-AA	4,012,000
I-AAA	3,042,000
II (with football)	1,350,000
II (without football)	838,000
II (with football)	NA
III (without football)	NA
FOOTBALL I-A	6,439,000

Source: Revenues and Expenses of Intercollegiate Athletic programs, NCAA, 1995

As an informing and important aside, the 1996 intercollegiate athletics budget for the University of Tennessee in 1996–97 was approximately $35 million, which was among the top five budgets in the nation. The budget for the University of Tennessee for 1999–2000 is $45 million. However, an analysis and report by an accounting professor at the university indicates that the athletic department also contributed more than $6 million to the other academic and student service programs of the university, including contributions to scholarships and library (Dickey, 1996). This is not a small financial matter in the general fund budget of the university and constitutes an exemplary act among peer institutions in the nation. Other institutions across the nation have also made contributions to general fund budgets from their intercollegiate athletic budgets.

In *Keeping Score* (1996), Richard Sheehan provides another look at the financial diversity of big-time college sports programs, with institutional profiles in 10 conferences such as Big Ten, Southeastern, Big Eight, Pacific Ten, and also independents. For 1994, net revenues indicate that in the Big West

Conference only three of seven schools had a positive income flow, with one school experiencing close to a million dollar deficit and the top school an approximate million dollar surplus. In the Big Ten, Michigan had the highest national net revenue at approximately $18 million. Five of the twelve teams in the Southeastern conference had net revenues among the top ten teams in the nation, with most of these running in excess of $10 million.

For NCAA-member schools, the typical Division I program will offer 10 varsity sports for men and 9 varsity sports for women. National championships in each of the major sports are held each year, with the exception of football in Division I-A. While at the moment the number one team in Division I-A football is determined by a national vote rather than a playoff, this may change very shortly when a playoff for the champion will be held. At present, the bowl alliance for postseason play in football is arranged to produce play between the number one and number two teams in the nation.

The NCAA has its headquarters in Kansas City, employs a staff of more than 250, and has an operating budget of in excess of $225 million, most of the revenue coming from a television contract with a major televison network, CBS Sports. An institution found in violation of important NCAA regulations, such as recruiting or athlete benefits, may be barred from television appearances and postseason playoffs or be subjected to other penalties such as loss of scholarship opportunities in major sports.

Examples of institutions holding membership in the three different divisions are instructive. As one might expect, some of the better-known universities in the nation hold membership in Division I-A, and their public relations spots appear frequently on the Saturday television game of the week—examples include Michigan, Stanford, California, Florida, Nebraska, Tennessee, Notre Dame, Penn State, and Ohio State. Other well-known institutions in the country—Harvard, Yale, Johns Hopkins, Chicago, Emory—will not be found in the highest competitive level, having selected another level of play for their athletic programs.

While most national attention is centered on the big-time athletic programs, there is a nonscholarship Division III in the NCAA where athletes are not given athletic grant in aids for participating in intercollegiate athletics. Here the student athlete suits up and plays for the fun of the game, or so the theory suggests. As we described in chapter one, attendance at a Division I football game may run over 100,000, while a few miles away attendance at a Saturday afternoon Division III football game may be a few hundred. For Division III teams, buses rather than jet planes will convey teams to the point of contest and there will be no 300-piece marching band to entertain television audiences, because with rare exception there will be no television coverage.

Not even Division III play escapes the temptation to enhance won-loss records via ethical shenanigans. Writing in an article entitled "Innocence Lost," Draper (1996) says that "Division III programs want it both ways: everyone wants to win, but no one wants to be judged on that basis. To admit that winning is the goal would collapse the philosophical distinction that supposedly separates Division III from Division I programs" (p. 49). Draper goes on to indicate how the tug of winning causes some folks at Division III schools to engage in creative, albeit shady approaches to determining need-based scholarships, which are allowed in Division III play.

In recent actions, the NCAA has established additional governance independence for each of its three divisions of play. The creation of three governance entities is designed to enhance the distinctive level of play and associated leadership challenges at each of the three levels.

National Association of Intercollegiate Athletics (NAIA)

The NAIA began in 1940 with the aspiration of finding a method for small colleges and universities to determine a national basketball championship, and indeed the original name of the association was the National Association of Intercollegiate Basketball (NAIB). In 1952, national championships were added in golf, tennis, outdoor track and field, cross country, baseball, swimming, and diving. Wrestling was added in 1958, soccer in 1959, bowling in 1962, indoor track and field in 1966, and men's volleyball in 1969. In the 1970s, two divisions in football competition were added, and in the 1980s championship events were added for women's sports. By the 1990s, every NAIA sport relied upon conference and regional tournaments to qualify for postseason play.

A council of institutional presidents governs the association and they elect a president and chief executive officer of the association, which has a membership of approximately 400 institutions, most of the institutions private. The association has an annual budget of approximately $4 million and a staff of approximately 30. The NAIA now sponsors scholarship and nonscholarship categories of play in its two divisions and championship playoffs in 24 sports (*History of the NAIA*, 1999).

National Junior College Athletic Association (NJCAA)

As we noted in chapter one, there are approximately 1,500 two-year colleges in this nation, and these colleges constitute an important and distinctive American invention. Approximately 40 percent of first-time enrollments are in these two-year colleges. While the admission policy of the NJCAA is less stringent than its senior institution counterparts, as one might expect for institutions designed to serve the mission of enhancing access, eligibility requirements may be more stringent for different regions and conferences. Some states, for example, operate their own conferences of two-year schools and establish their own operational regulations. The NCJAA is located in Colorado Springs, Colorado, has a membership of 540 institutions, a staff of 8, and an operating budget of approximately $500,000—also an important contrast to the staff and financial profile of the NCAA.

ABUSE AND REFORM IN INTERCOLLEGIATE ATHLETICS

> It is a useless enquiry to ask who were (sic) responsible for the development in the colleges of commercialized sports. The tendencies of the time, the growing luxury, the keen inter-college competition, the influence of well-meaning, but unwise, alumni, the acquiescence in newspaper publicity, the reluctance of the authorities of the university or the college to take an unpopular stand—all these factors have played their part.

The theme and tone of this passage would surprise no one familiar with the life of our colleges and universities as we move to the end of the twentieth century. What might surprise some readers is that this note can be found on page xx of the 1929 Carnegie report by Howard Savage and others earlier cited. Thus, issues related to the role of intercollegiate athletics in the life of the American college and university are not new issues.

Consider, however, the following headlines appearing in the local newspaper over a period of months in the community of a large state university: "Prostitute, Gun Cloud Bowl Trip"; "Attempted Murder Charge Against Athlete Reduced"; "Players Suspended from School for Brawl Involvement"; "Hearing on Athlete Rape Charge Set"; "Former University Stars Implicated in Payoff Scam"; and "University Cites 56 in Phone-Fraud Case." While extracted from the pages of a single newspaper, similar events have been chronicled for other sports programs over the country. Such stories cast a dark shadow over the earlier cited and presumed moral advantages of sport.

Readers interested in a far-ranging treatment of abuse in college sport will find *College Sports, Inc.* by Murray Sperber a painful reading if you are a fan of sport and confirm what you already believed if you are not. Section titles from the book anticipate the sad reports that may be found there: "Part I: Old Siwash in Red Ink: The Finances of College Sports"; "Part II: Greed City: College Coaches' Salaries, Perks, Deals, and Scams"; "Part III: Toxic Waste: Recruiting Wars & Athletic Scholarships"; and "Part IV: The NCAA: The Fox in the Henhouse."

Sperber points out that American intercollegiate athletics ". . . has created a situation that is unknown and unthinkable in other countries: To become a major league player in a number of sports, an athlete must pass through an institution of higher learning" (Sperber, 1990, p. 7). This, indeed, is a remarkable development. The path to possible professional employment, certainly in football and basketball, lies almost entirely in an athlete having first played at the collegiate level. At the end of any season, newspapers are filled with speculation as to whether star athletes will forgo another season of collegiate competition and enter the professional ranks to enjoy what is often a multimillion dollar salary package. There are arguments and rules concerning who can and should talk to an athlete during such decision periods. Such debates tip the scales in favor of athletics as entertainment and money rather than education and moral seasoning. The introduction to a 1991 special report on the reform of intercollegiate athletics, and sponsored by the Knight Foundation, opened with this commentary:

> At their best, which is most of the time, intercollegiate athletics provide millions of people—athletes, undergraduates, alumni and the general public—with great pleasure, the spectacle of extraordinary effort and physical grace, the excitement of an outcome in doubt, and a shared unifying experience. Thousands of men and women in the United States are stronger adults because of the challenges they mastered as young athletes. . . . But at their worst, big time college athletics appear to have lost their bearing. With increasing frequency they threaten to overwhelm the universities in whose name they were established and to undermine the integrity of one of our fundamental national institutions: higher education (*Keeping Faith . . .* , 1991, p. vii).

Chaired by two of the most respected and experienced collegiate leaders in the latter half of the twentieth century, President Ted Hesburgh of Notre Dame and President William Friday of the University of North Carolina, the work of the Knight Commission also involved some of the better-known collegiate, civic, and corporate executives in the country. Their report acknowledged the strident call for reform in athletics and offered a "one-plus-three" cluster of recommendations for reform. First among their recommendations was the insistence on presidential control, to be accompanied by accent on academic and fiscal integrity, and annual independent audit and certification of academic and financial matters related to athletics.

In 1993, the NCAA adopted a certification policy for all programs in Division I play. The Division I Athletics Certification Handbook, 1995–96, calls for a self-study and peer review visit that are similar in intent and process to the self-study and committee visits undertaken for regional accreditation as described in chapter five. Indeed the advantages of "self-awareness, affirmation, and opportunities to improve" are almost exactly the same as the advantages cited for institutional accreditation. Some institutions have elected to undergo regional accreditation and athletics certification visits at the same time. This is an interesting collaboration, since regional accrediting agencies have been criticized for not paying attention to abuse in athletics. Whether the certification process will lead to more exemplary performance in programs approved by the NCAA remains a matter open to question. History does not encourage a high degree of optimism.

For example, in the 1980s, 57 of 100 institutions playing at the NCAA's Division I-A level were censured, sanctioned, or on probation. What can we say about the integrity of big-time athletics if more than half of the teams competing have been caught cheating in one form or another over a 10-year period? The University of Florida football team was ranked number one in the nation for most of the 1996 season and its coach Steve Spurrier was awarded a contract with total annual earnings in excess of $1 million (Naughton, November 22, 1996, p. A37). Just a decade earlier, however, then President Dr. Marshall Criser fired the Florida football coach for massive NCAA rule breaking and stated that "with its moneymaking activities, its vast support by local boosters and its network of communications to alumni and fans, the football program became a power unto itself" (Sanoff, 1985, p. 62). Are presidents in control of their athletic programs, as the Knight Commission recommended? More than one college president has found himself on the light end of the power seesaw when attempting to hold the reins in check on intercollegiate athletics In the same year as Florida president Criser made his firing of the coach stick, then president of Clemson University Dr. William Atchley was forced to resign in a confrontation with his board of trustees over an athletic issue (Sanoff, 1985). When Clemson University's athletic program received visibility for its involvement in a drug scandal, Atchley tried to fire the school's athletic director and to reorganize the department. The trustees of the university fired Atchley for his efforts (Sanoff, 1985).

One of the best-known and nationally competitive programs in basketball, the University of Kentucky, was found guilty of engaging in a point shaving scandal in 1952 and was prohibited from participating in NCAA basketball competition the following year. In 1989, Kentucky again came under NCAA investigation for alleged cash offers to basketball recruits and falsified entrance examinations (Callahan, 1989). The Southeastern Conference subsequently stripped Kentucky of its conference basketball title for the 1988–89 year.

Well-regarded private universities cannot escape the emotion of alumni and supporters who want that winning reputation for their alma mater. In early 1996, Chancellor Joe Wyatt of Vanderbilt University came under fire from alumni who felt the administration was not giving enough support to the athletic program (Benavides, 1996). In the 1996 football season, the Vanderbilt Commodores threw scares into national powers Notre Dame, Florida, and Tennessee—each a nationally ranked team who managed only one-touchdown victories over Vanderbilt—but the intrepid commodores won no conference game. What pressures the institution and its administration may feel following this season remain unknown.

The heart of the matter is that in the minds of many, sport offers a number of benefits. It has been an important instrument in ameliorating the degrading and demeaning influence of bigotry and prejudice. Readers interested in a fictional account of this effect imbedded within a larger story will find Ernest Gaines' novel *A Gathering of Old Men* (1985) stimulating reading. It has been an instrument that has brought to common ground the cultures of East and West, the economic interests of socialist and capitalist.

In its best form, sport carries lessons about the values of courage, persistence, and self-knowledge. It teaches the importance of discipline and delivers lessons in work and sacrifice as bases of achievement. It commends the special joy of teamwork, in which the individual talents of each team member are multiplied in the chemistry of team play.

What does an athlete learn when he or she is bathed in the cheering adoration of fans following exemplary and winning performance, but later endures the booing and jeering of fans when a performance is not so stellar and wins are hard to earn? For one thing, that athlete is going to learn lessons that may not be found in a psychology, mathematics, or economics text. That athlete will learn that there are many side line and armchair critics ready to evaluate those who put their talent on public display but fewer who will suit up to play and subject their own personalities and talent to public scrutiny. When a team suffers a string of defeats, what will an athlete learn? If things work right, that athlete will learn about dogged persistence and develop a stalwart heart. And if by chance his or her team defeats a more-talented or more-favored opponent, in one of those lovely competitive moments we all enjoy, he or she will experience an emotional high that no cerebral or pedantic academic lesson could have matched. He or she will marvel at the power of human spirit and store in memory the joy of a moment that all men and women should be able to experience in any their lifetime.

Nobility in human behavior is neighbor to evil, and the beautiful often only a heartbeat or quick breath from the ugly. Thus, in sharp and ragged contrast to these benefits of sport are the growing commercialization of intercollegiate athletics, record of presidential and faculty indifference, absence of moral compass in some student athletes, and abuse of student athletes by uncaring or unprincipled faculty or staff.

Some coaches will have trouble controlling the behavior of well-meaning but misguided alumni, to say nothing of those alumni with a heart of darkness. Presidents often will have difficulty controlling coaches who may be the best-known personalities in a state and who command an intricate and widespread power base in a state. Faculty will vacate the campus on football weekends and often look the other way in the face of abuse. Governors will show up for board meetings and meddle in institutional matters when athletics is on board agendas, but cannot be found when questions of state support are on the table for discussion. When television revenue may make the difference between a highly successful season financially and a mediocre one, the most important question for institutional presidents and coaches may become not one of standards but "What time do you want us to play?" or "How about the value of a division playoff at the end of the season?" Athletic directors become chief executive officers of a multimillion dollar entertainment business whose goal is to win, where the difference between a 10 win-1 loss season and a 9 win-2 loss season may result in the firing of a football coach, if he has lost in consecutive seasons to a rival. A paraphrase of remarks from former coach Paul Dietzel (who coached at LSU, Army, and South Carolina) suggests that for football coaches the distance between the penthouse and the outhouse is short indeed. And this is a truth which Dietzel knew personally and painfully. Indeed, some football coaches—and college presidents—often exit their jobs the same way they entered. In a play on words, former president of the University of California Clark Kerr once referred to the entry-exit condition as "fired with enthusiasm."

Most every major report and study of intercollegiate athletics has championed the important role of the college president in terms of maintaining control and balance in athletics. The 1929 Carnegie report on *American College Athletics* (Savage et al., 1929) indicated that the integrity of a campus lay with the president and the faculty. And as we earlier noted, the 1991 Knight report recommended a stronger role for presidents. Being president of a university with a big-time athletic program may be likened to riding a tiger. If the president dismounts, with the intent of getting the animal under control, he or she runs the danger of becoming dinner for the tiger. It is safer, therefore, simply to ride the animal wherever it wants to run. If the teams are winning, if the budget is in balance, if there are no stories on the front page of the paper, the president is unlikely to be the recipient of warm and reinforcing praise from faculty, trustees or civic leaders. If, however, the teams are not winning, the budget is not balanced, and scandals pepper the press, the president can plan on a multifront assault.

In perhaps one of the most comprehensive and contemporary reviews of big-time intercollegiate athletics Murray Sperber (1990) chronicles in *College Sports, Inc.* the attempts by the American Council on Education and a Presidents' Commission to gain some control over the policies of the NCAA. In the book, he details a number of notable failures of policy changes suggested by presidents and notes in his preface that "This reliance on university presidents as the instrument of change in college sports is the central weakness of both the Knight Commission's and the NCAA Presidents' Commission's approach to reform" (Sperber, 1990, p. xiii).

The biographical sketches of some American college presidents make fascinating reading. In 1974, President Paul Hardin of Southern Methodist University was fired for exposing NCAA violations in the football program of the university, violations eventually leading to scandal and the "death penalty" by NCAA—a two-year ban on football at the university. Hardin later became the chancellor of the University of North Carolina, after enduring this bumpy journey.

"It is right and proper that members of the higher education community concern themselves with moral question about universities, not merely with gate receipts and the balance sheet. Otherwise, universities jeopardize their societal privileges as special institutions" (Thelin and Wiseman, 1989). This note from a monograph entitled *The Old College Try: Balancing Academics and Athletics in Higher Education* is quick and informing reading for one who wants to gain concise perspective on many of the issues related to athletics. Abuse in college athletics is but one of those factors that contribute to questions of public trust, and this is a theme to which we will return in the closing chapter of this book.

EDUCATION OR ENTERTAINMENT—A LOOK AT THE FUTURE

Opening the preface to his extended analysis of the policy and practice of American intercollegiate athletics, Sperber comes to the conclusion that ". . . intercollegiate athletics has become College Sports, Inc., a huge commercial entertainment conglomerate, with operating methods and objectives totally separate from, and mainly opposed to, the educational aims of the schools that house its franchises" (Sperber, 1990, p. vii). And in his concluding remarks, he recommends that we stop pretending that big-time athletics has any real or sensible connection to the mission of the university (Sperber, 1990, p. 333). We have not in this chapter engaged a host of other issues associated with current ferment over that role and responsibility. For example, as we noted in chapter three on governance, Title IX of the 1972 Education Amendments mandated equitable opportunity for women in education, and the meaning of that act for opportunity in intercollegiate athletics continues to unfold in interpretation in a series of court cases. Does the act require, for example, equivalence in spending and budget, and equivalence in number of athletes? While the answers to these questions are being hammered out in various proposals and court cases, it is clear that women's athletics is achieving more visibility in colleges and in the professional world. Witness, for example, the birth of two professional basketball leagues for women. Might we expect to find the salaries for these professional women athletes in basketball the same as men in the National Basketball Association? Well, as one female athlete about to enter one of these leagues commented "My salary will be pocket change to a male basketball player." On the other hand, she has now an opportunity to be paid for her talent that did not exist a few years ago.

Related to this issue is another question of whether college athletes should be paid. In the larger programs, their labor is at the heart of multimillion dollar revenue programs. Should the athletes participate in the fruits of their efforts, more than currently represented in their scholarship packages? Some argue that paying athletes would recognize that big-time sports programs are no longer truly amateur and that this would simply recognize that reality. Under this scenario, paid athletes would attend college if they qualified for admission, take whatever course load they could carry, have access to the same services, and meet the same standards as other students. Under this scenario, athletic programs as auxiliary enterprises would either earn their way financially or not, but there would be no creative accounting to buttress a program losing money.

This issue, of course, is also part of the larger question related to pay of coaches and associated staff. University of Florida football coach Steve Spurrier was awarded a $1 million contract in 1996. As a matter of comparative interest, the president of the University of Florida, Dr. John Lombardi, makes approximately $200,000 per year, and the 1996 October issue of *Academe* indicates that the average faculty salary for full professors at the university was $66,000.

Let us carry the inquiry further. If, for example, the athletics department is truly a part of the university, should the secretary to the football or basketball coach receive a "bonus" if the team plays in a postseason contest and brings in additional revenue . . . but the secretary in the physics or psychology department would never have the opportunity for such a bonus? Should the bonus, for both secretary and coaches, simply be counted as financial recognition for the extra work associated with the extended season, as a professor might earn additional or "extra service" pay for teaching an extra course or taking on a special assignment? When many may bemoan the half million or million dollar salary packages of a coach, why do we hear less outcry if a professor becomes a millionaire through a lucrative consulting opportunity or writing a best-selling textbook or novel? Questions of equity, performance, and opportunity in pay and benefits are not isolated to athletics.

Some have argued, Sperber among them, that colleges and universities should quit pretending that athletics is a part of the academic enterprise, that coaches are teachers, and that athletes are students. Their argument, suggested above, is that big-time athletic programs should be treated as the independent, entertainment, and commerical enterprises which the data suggest they are.

Thus, constructing the future of college athletics can take the form of "might be" or "should be" scenarios. It would be hard to envision a "might be" future for college athletics in which commercial interests will not continue to loom very large. One of the most probable scenarios is that intercollegiate athletics will continue to experience, at least among the larger programs in the country, a "rich-get-richer" picture, as the more successful teams enjoy the benefits of television revenue and thus are able to afford larger stadiums/arenas and more attractive programs. And larger stadiums/arenas beget larger gate revenues. If history is prologue, big-time athletic programs will continue to stretch the meaning of the word "amateur," and will continue, for football and basketball at least, to serve as farm clubs for professional sport franchises. This scenario, however, will not deny athletes, institutions, and their supporters that moment we earlier described in which a "David" institution with a net revenue half or a quarter of its "Goliath" competitor nevertheless leaves Goliath defeated and inert on field or arena, depositing into individual and institutional memory of the victor and fans a moment to be savored for years. In the fall 1996 football season, a down-and-out football team from the University of Memphis was picked to lose to the nationally ranked University of Tennessee football team by 26 points. Before a national television audience, however, the men from Memphis defeated Tennessee 21 to 17 for the first time in 15 games over 30 years. Emotional memories are created from such events. The men from Tennessee did not fade following this defeat, however, and went on to a 9-win 2-loss season, a national ranking in the top 10 and a victory over Northwestern in the Citrus bowl. It might be argued that persistence was honored by both teams. And that same persistence, it might be argued, played a role in the University of Tennessee winning the national football championship in 1998 with a 13-0 season, with a victory over Florida State in the Fiesta Bowl.

Nor should we lament the several levels of play currently found in the various divisions of the three national sport governing organizations. This is but a way to recognize and challenge different levels of talent and mission among our campuses. Fans and faculty of a team competing for a Division III or Division II championship will find as much joy, if less money and national recognition, as their larger and more expensively funded Division I counterparts.

Athletics is an art form, and we have in this nation different levels of artistic performance in many different expressions of human talent. The performance of the Knoxville Symphony Orchestra or the Memphis Symphony Orchestra may not reach, on average, the performance of the Philadelphia Symphony Orchestra or the New York Philharmonic. However, on a given evening, in a pinnacle moment, the performance of a second- or third-echelon orchestra may produce as much emotional excitement and pleasure as a mechanical and "just so" performance of a top-tier orchestra; and this "Division III" or "Division II" orchestra will enrich the cultural lives of those touched and served by these and other arts organizations at whatever level of talent and scope. Fans and faculty will continue to marvel at the athlete who can move down the court or the field with grace and power and still make a 3.5 GPA. And they will mourn the athlete who can move down the court or field with grace and power but who will find the most elementary college academic tasks a daunting task. Fans and faculty will continue to enjoy and support the spectacle, drama, and celebration of Saturday afternoon football and Wednesday night basketball. Fans and faculty will continue to wonder what the spectacle, drama, and celebration have to do with what takes place in their classrooms, laboratories, and studios on Monday morning. College and university presidents will continue trying to maintain some sense of sanity and control over big-time, multimillion dollar, star-coach empires. Profit-minded advertising executives, excited and meddling governors, assertive and one-issue board members, coaches without moral center, and eager but unthoughtful alumni will continue to make life interesting for these presidents. These presidents may experience premature and painful departure if sports coverage moves from the sport page to the front page; or they may, after a reasonable tenure and a sigh of relief, exchange places with a successor who will experience the exhilaration of riding the tiger of big-time athletics.

American intercollegiate athletics will continue to serve as a major and constructive instrument for establishing and nurturing a sense of community, which is essential to the cause of quality. Those athletic programs will continue to serve as exemplars of the principle "varieties of excellence," as we marvel at the richness of human artistic talent as expressed in different sports and different levels of competition. Most of our athletes, at whatever level of play, will earn their degrees. Some will take early exit of their own volition for professional sport opportunity; and others will, through lack of talent or discipline, experience academic frustration and become an apparent debit statistic in our retention efforts.

Education or entertainment? Complementary or corrupting? Financial boon or financial drain? Character forming or character depraving? There are multiple truths here for the role and responsibility of intercollegiate athletics. There is positive and negative valence in that role. The leadership challenges that come in accenting the positive valence and confronting the negative valance are entirely appropriate for our colleges and universities. The search for meaning in life is among life's most fundamental discovery journeys, and that search and journey belongs in the mission of our colleges and universities.

Our students deserve the opportunity of seeing us struggle with questions of what gives life meaning and nobility. In that struggle, would we pretend that we are not interested in winning any athletic contest or competition, in whatever sport or level of play? No! We play games to win and it would be foolish and dishonest to admit otherwise. The larger moral and educational question is whether we are willing to sacrifice and prostitute integrity in order to win. What price is victory? The price of discipline and devotion is a legitimate price. The price of duplicity and degradation is not an appropriate price. Is the meaning of life to be found in pay, power, and prestige? Athlete or not, take from any man or woman the gifts of health, friendship, love, and meaningful labor, and the answer to this question will quickly present itself.

Any art form, including the art form of athletics, is a legitimate and powerful instrument for learning about self and society, skills and values, and meaning and method. The leadership challenge of integrating the learning promise of both academics and athletics in colleges and universities is a legitimate and powerful instrument for both individual and institutional learning. The arenas of ideological and physical contest are not at variance with the fundamental mission of learning. In each of those arenas, the forces of both nobility and meanness will be at play. The facts which are the fruits of our curiosity will not emerge without accessories of emotion and value. In colleges and universities, the power of mind will be affected and accompanied by power of heart and spirit, and the ethics of means and ends will call us to decision agonies that let us know what it means to be human. These are not lessons or learning ventures to be hidden from our students, or from those friends external to the academy.

CHAPTER 10

Reform and Renewal
The Dance of Change and Tradition

I
n the late 1960s, American writer Norman Cousins asked some of the prominent minds of that time to construct essays on the theme "What I Have Learned," ultimately constructing a volume rich in ideological provocation. In that volume of essays is one entitled "First Glimpses of a New World" by Robert Hutchins (1968). Hutchins offers two thought nuggets that nicely launch the theme of our concluding chapter. When he served as president of the University of Chicago, Hutchins observed that

> The Great Depression conferred marked benefits on the university, for it forced a reconsideration of the whole enterprise. The first thing I had to contend with was the demand that I cut everything twenty-five per cent. This made no sense to me. I thought what was important should be supported and what was trivial should be dropped (p. 182).

Hutchins also mused that in times of crisis, those responsible for our colleges and universities cannot comfortably wander the halls of ivy with their academic oil cans and wrenches, simply tending to the machinery of higher education. For in times of crisis, someone is sure to ask whether the machinery is being put to proper work, or indeed whether we still need all the machinery being tended. Deciding what is trivial and what is important in higher education is not a small or inconsequential occupation. Identifying what is trivial and what is important would be difficult and delicate enough if engaged only by academicians—grist for the grinding mill of many a committee, task force, and study group. As we have noted in previous chapters, civic and political friends will want and deserve a place at the table for this conversation. If there has ever been a time when colleges and universities were accorded a polite and unquestioning deference by board members and civic/political leaders, that day is past. Deciding what is trivial and what is important is going to be a more complex conversation.

In previous chapters, we have celebrated American higher education as a unique institutional investment in the power of ideas and education. The genius of the American system of education, including its colleges and universities, is the intent to educate the discretion of everyone in our society, to call each talent to the far edge of its circle of promise and thereby create what Barber calls as "aristocracy of everyone" (1992, p. 5). We have claimed our colleges and universities as organizational instruments of our curiosity and wonder, as independent enclaves of thought and criticism where truth and wisdom are sought and cultivated. We have profiled colleges and universities as crucibles of dissent and discovery, as adversarial forums for the discovery and testing of truth. We have identified them as places where we advance on the enemies of ignorance and prejudice, as "ivory towers" of reflection. We have heralded them as repositories of value, beauty, and standard—calling student and society to excellence in the arts, sciences, and professions. We have marked them as engines of both cultural and economic development, as organizations helping both individuals and society realize their full potential. We have assigned to them the responsibility of putting knowledge and wisdom to work, grappling in the dirty trenches of the nation and the world to battle those problems that beset mind, body, and spirit. The proper engagement of our colleges and universities may embrace both soil and soul erosion.

These chapters have clearly indicated that challenge, criticism, and crisis are a lively occupation of faculty and administrators as we turn toward the twenty-first century. Higher education must not only contend with leadership challenges internal and external, but must acknowledge that there are those within and without battering at the castle walls, bringing hallowed traditions and principles under scrutiny and calling into question the vitality and efficacy of such principles. It should be apparent from the commentary of those chapters, and from the half-century-old reflections of Robert Hutchins, that this is not the first moment of presumed crisis for American higher education. Those who lived and served in American colleges through the economic depressions of the early 1800s, 1920s, and 1930s might, if alive today, find contemporary issues and challenges of light and simple burden.

Some scholars suggest that crisis in American education, including higher education, is a chronic condition. Where might we find an age or moment in which someone or some agency was not finding fault with our schools and colleges? The concept of "chronic crisis" is something of a contradiction, but we will leave that puzzle to other wordsmiths.

Nevertheless, the range, frequency, intensity, and source of contemporary critiques of the academy acknowledged in each of our chapters indicate that American higher education may be facing a breakpoint moment in this transition from the twentieth to the twenty-first century. A breakpoint moment is a moment of both danger and opportunity. It may become a moment when those responsible for colleges and universities struggle with greater intensity and determination but with less imagination and daring, leading our colleges to fossilize and atrophy. A breakpoint moment, however, may release fresh energy and thought, leading to new inventions of purpose and organization and creating a moment of reform and renewal.

For institutions that have the responsibility of honoring our heritage even as they assist us in reaching for the future, of conserving memory and knowledge of the past as they evaluate and critique that past as a basis of building a better tomorrow, the challenge of change is a particularly wrenching exercise. Among the organizations of human construction, colleges and universities are among the most stable and longer lived in this country and in other nations. That stability of place and focus must be considered important in the search for and conservation of truth.

What exactly in the occupation of the moment is trivial and what is important in the experience of colleges and universities? Who will decide what is important, and what precisely makes an element of current mission "trivial?" Is it as simple as recognizing that we may not be able to afford all that we have been trying to do? Thus, the issue may not be so much an issue of academic triviality and academic quality as it is an issue of economic and political reality.

How many contemporary industries and corporate enterprises have overlooked dramatically changing conditions and discoveries in their field and thus yielded place and position to fresher ideas and more assertive spirits? Those working within a particular field, intimate to its culture and accepted ways of doing business, are often confined by their vision of paradigm, their assumptions about how business is done. For example, it was the Swiss who invented quartz movements for watches and who rejected their own innovation. American electronics manufacturer Texas Instruments and Japanese manufacturer Seiko recognized the advantage of the technology, and subsequently made important inroads on the market share that had been controlled by Swiss watch manufacturers. A similar story may be told of American automobile manufacturers, who held a commanding world market domination when foreign competitors were hard at work on quality and market choice.

Writing in *Innovation and Entrepreneurship*, Peter Drucker said that "No better text for a *History of Entrepreneurship* could be found than the creation and development of the modern university, and especially the modern American University" (Drucker, 1985, p. 23). Drucker comments on the emergence of both public and private universities, and especially those serving metropolitan areas, and alludes to the enhancement of services that have made a college education available in a host of new times and places and that have attracted a new clientele in the older student. While he does not mention the American community college, this institution also represents a notable expression of educational entrepreneurship. In the closing moments of this chapter we consider the dance of change and tradition and the pressures being felt in the American college and university for change. Meanwhile, some degree of historic perspective is useful as one considers the dramatically changing profile and landscape of American higher education, a profile we have attempted to present in each of our chapters, and especially in chapter one.

For Drucker and perhaps other writers, the American college and university represents the fruits of our imagination and initiative; and at the moment, American higher education is widely recognized and respected over the world. Is this a moment for alertness, when some new expression of educational competition might render colleges and universities as we know them obsolete? Will some "outsider" bring together a fresh combination of ideas and technology, a new paradigm that will deliver on the purposes of higher education in a more effective and more efficient fashion?

On the other hand, management innovations from the corporate and profit sector have a way of making quick digestive passage through higher education, initially furnishing lively conversation and much heralded acronyms (PERT, PPBO, MBO, TQM, etc.) that promise a new way of doing business and rendering current ways obsolete and outmoded. It is not that these new philosophies and tools do not have a constructive impact on our colleges and universities, for in many cases they furnish advances and may leave behind helpful residue in the passing. However, the departmental structure of colleges and universities is so autochthonous that change tends to walk and crawl rather than run and leap. Given the cultural curator and cultural critic mission of higher education, this may not be all bad. There is something to be said for the andante majesty of higher education in its pace of change.

A college or university wavering in the wind to every political breeze, philosophical fad, or methodological whim in our society would not encourage our confidence in its stability of mission or thoroughness of method. After all, colleges and universities are not in business to make a profit, they are in business to nurture truth and human talent. These are eminently personal occupations. Students will remember the loving, the inspiring, and elevating touch of a teacher before they will remember computer capacity, financial ratios, or building utilization. Moreover, the work of nurturing truth and human talent is a long-term job, and the measure of that job's success is not to be found in a neat balance sheet for the current quarter. It is a work of faith.

A moment's discretion is appropriate here. We noted above that colleges and universities are not in business to make a profit. Well, of course, that is not the whole truth. For-profit or proprietary colleges in the nation are indeed in business to make a profit and constitute an emerging sector of national interest, as attested by an article by Winston appearing in the January/February 1999 issue of *Change Magazine* and by Ruch in the February 1999 issue of the *AAHE Bulletin*.

Whether serving the nonprofit or for-profit motive, it would be a mistake of some arrogance to assume that colleges and universities are immune from pressures of reform and renewal and that they should escape the pressures of change—social, technical, economic—being felt in other parts of our society today. Would we in higher education take as mission the education of men and women who have both the will and the competence for critical thought, who live with that energizing little word "why" hiding in mind and heart and simultaneously expect the abode of their intellectual incubation to be exempt from the scrutiny of those whom we have taught to be curious?

American higher education faces contemporary challenges of focus, trust, and accountability. Our vision of these leadership challenges is no more prescient than many others who are thinking along the same lines. But these three challenges—focus, trust, and accountability—seem to capture the mainstream of concern and criticism with which higher education must contend as we build bridges to the twenty-first century. What we want to do in this closing chapter is to examine briefly these challenges and then look at postures of thought and value that will allow us to honor the heritage even as we move to shape and accommodate the future, producing constructive patterns of reform and renewal.

THE CHALLENGE OF FOCUS

In good economic times, there is less inclination for any organization to ask serious questions about its mission, priorities, and focus. In a good deal of government enterprise there can be what one of the authors has previously identified as the "growth-progress syndrome" (Bogue, 1972). In government work, and more specifically in educational settings of all kinds, we can be easily drawn to measures of success and effectiveness that feature growth—in enrollments, budgets, programs, and faculty. If we add to these indicators the measures of athletic prowess in our won-loss records, it is possible to be happy and feel confident in our effectiveness. But crisis and melancholy can be induced quickly if these measures turn downward in trend. We can become timid and narrow philosophers if our measures of effectiveness are linked entirely to numbers, dollars, size, and growth. When state budgets admit pleasant increases in appropriations for public higher education and when enrollment demand and tuition elasticity encourage private higher education, both faculty and civic friends can rejoice in the growth of access for students, and the increased availability of programs. Chapters one and six make clear that this nation has made an extraordinary investment in both student access and program availability in the last half of the twentieth century. What is equally apparent is that the end of the century has brought a sober reality to the halls of ivy, especially for public institutions, as state revenue conditions have slowed or even reversed. What was an unquestioned expansion in previous years becomes a question of mission and focus in more difficult revenue times.

Writing many years ago in *The Affluent Society*, John Kenneth Galbraith remarked that "As a society becomes increasingly affluent, wants are increasingly created by the process by which they are satisfied" (Galbraith, 1958, p. 158). We should not be so surprised that an enhanced access to higher education has created a demand for more access.

The call for higher education to reexamine its focus and the character of its mission can be seen in a number of ways. In tight financial times, civic and political friends tend to become more interested in "unnecessary duplication." In good financial times, it will not trouble us overly much to have several programs within a state or region in several fields of study—engineering, medicine, educational administration, business administration—or at more advanced levels of study, such as doctoral study. For example, in 1950 only one state institution in Tennessee offered doctoral degrees, and that was the University of Tennessee. In 1990, all but three of the nine universities in the state offered doctoral degrees. In the early years of the community college movement in Alabama, more than 40 community and technical colleges were established. Now, in more challenging financial moments, there appears to be some conviction that with 18 senior schools and 32 community colleges, the state has more in place than it needs or can afford. However, taking a public college or university out of business is a difficult and almost impossible business, and the reason is not so hard to find.

College campuses become instruments of political pride, community cultural enrichment, and economic development. A state even remotely considering the closure of a campus site or a second medical school will encounter understandable, predictable, and notable political resistance from the area or community affected. Political and corporate leaders may urge retrenchment in general but find repugnant the elimination of a college in their district. If there is a need to reduce services, then by all means let us do that . . . but in someone else's backyard.

Given the political heat of terminating programs that might save large amounts of money and for which reasonable educational and economic arguments might be advanced in support, there is a tendency for political leaders to turn to smaller academic entities with less political fury attached, such as schools of education and social services. Here much sound and fury may be generated to give the appearance of serious retrenchment work, but the actual dollars saved may be trivial to modest.

Within campuses, a similar sound and fury may be produced. Much ado about termination of degree programs may be publicly proclaimed regarding academic programs that were already dead but no tombstone had been erected. Other program consolidations may be proclaimed but represent cosmetic changes at most. These are charades that may be enjoyed by both political and educational leaders.

In some states and on some campuses, however, revenue diets are of sufficient moment that more momentous changes can be seen as campuses eliminate programs and entire academic units. A few years ago, Emory University, a private research university, eliminated its dentistry school and program. Several state systems have eliminated or consolidated their schools of education and programs in teacher education, while others have terminated or seriously reduced programs in selected arts and sciences fields. Other universities are downsizing their doctoral programs.

A second manifestation of the call to reexamine higher education focus turns on expansion of campuses and facilities. Civic and political leaders often lament the entrepreneurial spirit of colleges in building/acquiring new campuses and facilities and yearn for stronger control by coordinating boards and governing boards to rein in this unbridled expansion. But some of these same civic and political leaders will be the first to don the symbolic hard hat and take shovel in hand to break ground for a new campus or building in their community. The paradox of public confidence and concern with higher education continues.

American academics contribute to this condition because too many have not yet learned how to take pleasure in limited mission. There are perhaps two or three generally accepted success models in American higher education. Generally speaking, the American community college has a clearly defined mission and one well recognized by campus and community together. Speak even quietly, however, about the possibility of a community college gaining four-year status, and community supporters will fall over one another in proclaiming the obvious benefits of this expansion in mission to the community and its citizens.

The second success model is the liberal arts college. Though many of our liberal arts colleges are private, a number of public institutions have adopted that prized but limited mission. However, when faced with declining enrollment pressures, one should not be surprised to find such colleges more interested in the obvious market advantages of programs in business, teacher education, nursing, computer science, and other professional fields of study holding enrollment promise. Older students desiring to study in the evenings and on the weekends will become welcome to their hallowed halls. And thus one should not be surprised to see them leave that romantic, ivy-covered campus to find new markets in the concrete jungles and shopping malls of nearby metropolitan areas.

A third success model is the research university, the large doctorate-granting university featuring nationally- and internationally-recognized faculty, extensively funded research programs, and wide-ranging graduate programs—the ultimate in higher education aspiration. The phenomenon of "bracket creep," the increase in doctoral and research universities, has taken place over the last 20 years or so. The movement of an institution from offering master's degrees to offering even one doctoral degree is cause for celebration. This is an "arrival" of some moment, the ultimate destination for the American university.

These models leave a goodly number of splendid but often confused institutions over the country. These are usually state universities often considered in a permanent state of academic adolescence. They may be located in urban settings and thus look something like a community college, which indeed they are. They will offer bachelor's degrees and perhaps master's degrees. They may even participate in joint doctoral programs with other research or doctoral universities in the state. Thus, they look something like universities, which they are. Given the unfortunate and inappropriate pecking order of prestige that Americans often assign to the pyramidal model of higher education—community colleges at bottom and research universities at the top—these campuses may be troubled about their image as a community college and frustrated in their inability to attain the coveted posture of awarding the doctorate. They are often unable to achieve a sense of identity and pleasure in their work. Some will see expanded football programs and stadiums as the key to enhanced status. Others see a change in name as the cure.

A third civic call to achieve a clearer sense of focus in higher education is the call to rethink commitment to the teaching, instructional, and learning mission of higher education. If one reviews any of the book-length critiques of higher education that have been issued over the last decade, one of the clearest themes is that higher education is neglecting its commitment to teaching, to what some call "the business of the business." Another evidence of this concern may be found in the character of the performance indicators now required by many states and profiled in chapter five on quality assurance. The number of sections taught by adjunct faculty and graduate assistants, graduation and retention rates, enrolled student and alumni satisfaction, licensure pass rates—these and other performance indicators often specified by state law reflect a public concern with teaching.

Among the more informing and provocative policy voices in American higher education are the *Policy Perspectives* publications of the PEW Higher

Education Research Program at the University of Pennsylvania. One of their earlier publications, the May 1989 issue, was entitled "The Business of the Business" and featured these comments:

> Outside the academy, however, teaching and learning have become focal points of a debate over the future of the American system of higher education. The public—or at least the public press—has compiled an expanding catalog of what is considerd to be wrong with the way institutions have come to do their business: (1) Too seldom is collegiate teaching viewed for what it is: the business of the business—the activity that is central to all colleges and universities; (2) Too many institutions attempt to be all things to potential customers; (3) Too few define their missions with precision or limit the scope of their enterprise to what they do best; (4) Too often teaching is seen as private, protected by academic freedom, and conducted in the classroom behind closed doors; (5) Too many professors still stand as tellers of truth, inculcating knowledge in students, and too many students sit and listen passively—or not at all; (6) Too many faculty, pursuing narrow specializations, teach at the periphery of their disciplines, resulting in curricula that are increasingly fragmented and atomized; (7) Too often teaching is an "open loop system," leaving faculty without feedback on what or how well their students are learning; and (8) Too often junior faculty are sent into the classroom untrained, ill-prepared, and without a sense of what it means to be a scholar-mentor (1989, p. 1).

The scope of the research enterprise is a fourth area in which questions of focus have arisen. What began as a federal effort to enhance research related to defense, health, and education in the late 1950s and 1960s has been transformed into a major multimillion dollar enterprise of research centers, parks of extensive and expensive facilities, faculty stars and entrepreneurs, and academic haves and have nots. A September 1991 issue of *Policy Perspectives* entitled "An End to Sanctuary" comments as follows:

> While the major research universities illustrate the theme in large scale, the skewing of purpose and value that results from multiple agendas can be seen in colleges and universities of every kind. Relatively few presidents of universities or colleges can claim comfortable rein over any part of their institution that has recourse to outside funding (p. 4A).

Complicating this picture is a change in research support sources. As federal government funds declined following the decline of cold war expenditures, business and industry have become sought-after partners. This is not all bad, but what constraints does a faculty member accept in conducting research for corporate sponsor and what ethical pressures may accompany such contracts? The complications of the research partnership can be extraordinary and the threats to the integrity of academic science equally extraordinary. What should we think, for example, of a study reported in a leading medical journal suggesting that a high percentage of men and women suffer from "sexual dysfunction" if we learn that the study's authors were paid consultants to a company manufacturing a new and highly touted drug to enhance male potency? The tension between truth and profit we have only begun to know here.

A fifth area representing curiosity on the focus of college life is the domain of intercollegiate athletics. Here too we may discern major evidence of "bracket creep." There are perhaps fewer than 100 big-time football powers in the nation—schools whose budgets, schedules, and won-loss records reflect a consistent presence in those competitive circles. There will be many others, however, in full pursuit of Division I play in football, anxious to add to the size of their stadiums, believing that this will launch them into more widely known academic circles. These schools will travel to play the leading schools, returning home frequently with richer pockets but with occasional battered athletic egos. It is a rare community, academic and civic, that can resist the siren call to enter what many perceive as a more prestigious appointment and reputation. Athletic budgets in the millions of dollars, often exceeding in size the budgets of many public colleges in a state and marking the athletic enterprise in many colleges as a multimillion dollar entertainment enterprise. Private universities struggle with competing issues of academic standards and athletic standard. Public universities struggle with the pressure to escalate their programs. Two-year colleges rush to establish programs and scholarship so that they can feed the university programs.

And in no phase of college and university life can we find integrity issues of greater frequency, leading to our second leadership issue of trust.

THE CHALLENGE OF TRUST

It is almost impossible to pick up any issue of the *Chronicle of Higher Education* without reading disappointing stories of faculty and administrators forsaking both personal and professional integrity—taking themselves, their students, and institutions in harm's way. College presidents are indicted for mismanaging or embezzling institutional funds. Deans are indicted for stealing financial aid monies or appearing in porn videos. Department chairs are indicted for falsely awarding academic credits. Faculty are indicted for selling degrees in exchange for lucrative consultant contracts. American colleges and universities are increasingly and unfortunately viewed as greedy and grubby places chasing the dollar, bending principles, abandoning integrity, and neglecting honor in acts of both personal selfishness and institutional aggrandizement.

And these acts and behaviors are occurring in an organization whose avowed purpose is the preparation of leadership for every sector of national life.

While the spectacular and sensational stories of folks in corporate, civic, and collegiate America traveling on the shallow and shady side of morality might lead one to conclude that there is a pervasive meanness and duplicity in our national life and in our colleges and universities, we affirm that these aberrant behaviors do not reflect the dominant reality in any sector of national life. However,the specter of tabloid journalism does haunt academia. Goodness is quiet and evil is loud. There is a reality of goodness and nobility in our colleges and universities, a reality represented in quiet and unheralded stories of faculty and administrators who exhibit care, concern, sacrifice, and service in daily acts of leadership.

The difficulty is that just one departure from the path of nobility, from our responsibility to exemplify integrity is one too many; and each departure diminishes public trust in our colleges and universities. In chapter five on quality, we presented several unhappy adventures and deviations from the path of educational quality, unworthy and unexpected departures for colleges and universities. These too invite a diminution of public trust. Faculty claiming conditions of overload and overwork, who are found moonlighting for other campuses or engaged in extensive away-from-campus consulting do not encourage a public portraiture of integrity nor do they encourage the public trust. College presidents busy feathering their own financial nests with large salaries and retirement perks, with lavish life styles and unbridled ambitions— while their faculties languish in difficult salary posture because of revenue reductions and retrenchment requirements—do not encourage a happy view of leadership integrity. Well-known private colleges engaging in price fixing, which is only supposed to be done by greedy corporate folks interested in ripping off the government, hardly helped. Scholars charged with faking data on research projects do not encourage public belief that we are really in search for truth. Parents pay tuition and states make appropriations with the expectation of caring concern for students entrusted to colleges and universities. Placing inexperienced graduate assistants and foreign students with limited language skills in leading positions for teaching our undergraduates does not encourage the idea that learning and teaching occupy principal positions in our educational priorities.

We have used the word integrity in these reflections. In the minds of most, the term implies both nobility of behavior and a certain consistency, a link between value and behavior. Consider this situation: A small liberal arts college of less than 2,000 has an average faculty salary of $35,000, as verified in the American Association of University Professors' publication of academic salaries in *Academe*. Its president has an annual salary of $120,000.

During a recent year, the board of trustees for the college mentioned above, affiliated with and supported by a Christian fellowship, offered its faculty a 2 percent average raise, amounting to approximately $700 for each faculty member, while it approved in executive session a raise of $10,000 for its president and similar percentage increases for four other executive-level administrators. The faculty for this institution is in a momentary state of wonder about whether the president, chief administrators, and board members have recently reviewed New Testament admonitions about chiefs being servants and about the relationship between leading and servanthood. At the moment they are curious but docile. Whether the "integrity" of this policy act will leave them in passive posture remains to be seen.

Not 500 hundred miles away a public doctoral university's administration engaged in a similar behavior, with the president approving a token and modest percentage raise for his faculty and then awarding more exuberant percentage raises for several administrators. In this case, the local newspaper caught the scent of his behavior and the entire affair appeared in grand display in the morning newspaper. The faculty were not in a docile mood. While the president escaped being hanged in effigy, he was treated to rude exposure in the newspaper and to scathing inquiry by the faculty. He subsequently reversed his decision on the administrators, as an uninformed and uninvolved board of trustees waited to get him in executive session at their next board meeting.

In yet another disappointing display of values, a major state university and its medical center were found admitting patients for heart transplant surgery, with the full knowledge that the probabilities of these surgeries actually taking place were virtually zero. Those aware of this cruel charade included selected medical staff, the dean of the medical school, and upper-level administrators in the university.

Here we are not talking about the mismanagement of research data or the plagiarization of a report. We are talking about a callous disregard for human life and dignity in a profession and institution whose purposes are to revere and enhance human life and dignity.

We may pass more quickly, but with no less disappointment and anger, over the behavior of both board and president at Adelphi University simply because the situation there enjoyed so much national press coverage (*The Chronicle of Higher Education*, February 27, 1997). The New York Board of Regents removed all but one of Adelphi's trustees for neglect of duty in failing to properly oversee President Peter Diamandopoulos—who had been granted an annual salary approaching a million dollars, a million-dollar New York apartment, and an expensive Mercedes. The antics of this board and president generated disbelief and anger across the nation.

The aforementioned incidents are reasons enough for civic, corporate, and political observers to believe that the dominant disease of contemporary collegiate leaders is that they simply don't stand for anything. They have severed the precious links between mind and heart. Or as we noted in chapter four, competence has been divorced from conscience.

The unhappy conclusion to these occasional and disappointing pathologies of the academy is forcefully carried in the following note:

> What does matter—what makes these charges stick—is an end to the public perception of the college campus as a place of sanctuary, a place where values other than the purely financial might prevail, where commitment to the freedom of expression and truly unfettered inquiry guarantees a standard of conduct exceeding that observed by the population at large. The message is that whatever their claims to a special calling, these institutions are no different, no better, no longer exempt from public scrutiny and caricature. . . . The loss of sanctuary means, among other things, that the public, in the form of regulators, budget officers, state and federal legislative staffs, higher education commissions, accrediting bodies, and emboldened boards of trustees, will want a seat at the table. In some states and at some institutions, they may even insist that they own the table ("An End to Sanctuary," 1991, p. 6A).

The concerns regarding the integrity of higher education programs, personnel, and the loss of public trust associated with departures from nobility of behavior and clarity of purpose take us to our final leadership challenge, the growing expectations of accountability. Mistrust breeds suspicion. And suspicion breeds control.

THE CHALLENGE OF ACCOUNTABILITY

Consider the following: In 1994–95, 24 states conducted studies of faculty workload; and in 1995–96, 21 states did so. In 1994–95, 20 states had laws or policies requiring public campuses to assess student learning; and in 1995–96, 24 states had such assessment requirements. In 1995–96, 18 states had some form of performance funding/budgeting in which some portion of higher education appropriation was linked with meeting state goals (*Chronicle of Higher Education Almanac*, September, 1995, p. 10; *Chronicle of Higher Education Almanac*, September, 1996, p. 12). These policy trends, when taken with the performance indicator policy trends cited in chapter five, place the locus of accountability on issues of quality and performance.

As with the term "crisis," in some ways "accountability" is a tired term, one perhaps used too much and too often. Yet it is an accurate descriptor of current climate and context for higher education. Among the more obvious and dramatic changes in the social, political, and economic environment of American higher education in the latter part of the twentieth century is the more aggressive posture of agencies external to the campus—boards, coordinating commissions, legislators, accrediting agencies—insisting on a more public engagement of quality and performance issues. We have already reported the growing number of states now requiring forms of assessment and performance indicator reporting by public campuses. In regional accreditation, and in some cases in specialized or professional field accreditation, there has been a clear transition from a "process" approach to accreditation to an accent on institutional and program effectiveness, an examination of evidence demonstrating the extent to which program and institutional goals are being accomplished.

And within higher education there has been a range of campus initiatives that may be seen as a leadership response to the challenge of accountability. Campuses developing competency-based educational programs and assessments to insure the mastery of knowledge, skill, and value have certainly engaged the issue of accountability. Some campuses and systems have begun to present periodic accountability reports to their boards and/or legislatures. As acknowledged in chapter five, one can find examples of colleges and universities in every Carnegie classification making informed and innovative use of assessments, Total Quality Management (TQM), and performance indicators. The American Association for Higher Education has presented a national forum on assessment for each of the past few years, reflecting the national level of interest. Similar meetings may be found at both the regional and state level. The state of South Carolina, for example, annually holds a forum on assessment. In 1979–80, higher education in Tennessee adopted a performance funding policy that linked educational performance on several indicators to the financial allocation process for colleges and universities in that state, as referred to in chapter six.

That the term "accountability" is not a new term is evidenced in the monograph Accountability in Higher Education, by Kenneth Mortimer and published in 1972. Mortimer suggested that "Accountability accentuates results—it aims squarely at what comes out of an educational system rather than what goes into it. It assumes that if no learning takes place, no teaching has taken place" (Mortimer, p. 6). This view affirms the change in perspective we just presented—a shift in perspective and paradigm from assuming that the presence of a qualified faculty, a carefully developed library, a well-equipped physical plant, and an adequate financial resource base are guarantors of quality to the question of whether students really learned and changed in the presence of these resources.

This transition from the resources and reputational model of quality and performance to the results model of quality and performance must also be counted one of the more interesting changes in perspective in American higher education in the latter years of the twentieth century.

What further meaning and implications might we attach to this concept? We are inclined to see accountability as a formally expressed expectation—a campus or board policy, state or federal law, or formal standard of another agency such as an accrediting agency—that (1) requires evaluation of both administrative and educational services; (2) asks for public evidence of program and service performance; (3) encourages independent/external review of such performance evidence; and (4) requests information on the relationship between dollars spent and results achieved. The concept of accountability implies a formal curiosity with effectiveness, efficiency, and productivity of both administrative and educational services.

A July 1995 issue of *Policy Perspectives* suggests that the idea of accountability stresses the need for colleges and universities "to pay more attention to those they teach and to those that provide their funding" (*A Calling to Account*, p. 1). Calling for a more effective partnership among boards, presidents, and faculty, authors of this issue nicely place the dangers of extremes in perspective:

> Indulging the ideal of the academy as a place of quiet contemplation designed principally to support faculty scholarship invites the withdrawal of public support on which the academy depends. Remaking the enterprise as a business complete with a bottom line and a president cast as an 'in-charge, take-no-prisoners' chief executive invites a prolonged confrontation over governance that detracts from an institution's ability to fulfill its core purposes (pp. 4–5).

Thus, neither complete autonomy nor complete accountability constitute worthy or practical goals. The concept of partnership, we believe, is a helpful one. Candid and open conversation among all the stakeholders in the mission and performance of our colleges and universities is essential.

A parenthetical note on partnership may be appropriate here. Partnership is not possible without strength among all parties, academics within and civic friends without. Neither arrogance nor ignorance is a friend of partnership. Those of us in higher education may not ignore the validity of criticism being lofted at the academy nor delay in responsive action. Nor may we target our society and culture with the probing light of our scholarship and remain unwilling to turn that light on the house of intellect. In the same spirit, civic and corporate friends looking down the barrel of the criticism cannon at higher education should make sure they are not living in glass houses. The financial, personal, and civic costs of duplicity disasters such as the savings and loan debacle and insider trading scandals offend our sense of decency and justice, sear the public conscience, and create a climate of cynicism dangerous to democracy.

Profit is a human motive and impulse engine of notable power. This is one real world. Service is a human motive and a constructive force of equally majestic import. This is also a real world. In a democratic society, these two motives and these two worlds are essential and complementary. Neither can exist without the other. And public accountability on issues of quality and integrity is central to the real but different worlds of profit and service.

However, the motives and methods of civic and collegiate accountability interests are sometimes contentious and adversarial. The differences tend to create two cultures:

- Improvement versus stewardship
- Peer review versus regulation
- Process versus results
- Enhancement versus compliance
- Consultation versus evaluation
- Trust versus evidence

There are sobering realities to be entertained as we think about how to bring political and academic accountability cultures closer together. The first of these realities is that no accountability system will negate the unhappy fruits of poor economic and revenue conditions in a state, region, or nation. Second, there is no accountability policy that will negate the attitudes of some political officers who may not value higher education. Third, there is no accountability system that will negate the positions and perceptions of those who do not want to be bothered by the facts. It has been said that under carefully controlled conditions human beings will behave as they please. A variant of this law is that in the face of incontrovertible scientific proof human beings will believe what they wish.

Nor is there an accountability system that will compensate for dark motives, shallow standards, courage deficits, and insensitive conscience in some academic administrators and faculty members. Finally, we would be wise to understand in advance that favorable trend lines, factual evidence, and statistical portraits many not alter cherished beliefs or flawed character in either political or academic leaders. Though limited in effect, complex in construction, delicate in balance, and challenging in operation, a well-crafted system of accountability can serve internal, external, academic, and political accountability purposes. In chapter five, we presented design principles important in the architecture of a system of quality assurance. Perhaps the most important tactic, as previously suggested in this discussion, involves the recognition and promotion of a spirit of partnership and collaboration, the joining of academic and political leaders in the design of such an accountability system. To this point, this has been the case too infrequently. It is always easier in human affairs to talk about someone rather than with someone when there are difficult routes to chart.

THE DANCE OF CHANGE AND TRADITION

Some of the variables in a climate less friendly, and sometimes downright hostile, to higher education include: cost containment pressures and reduced revenue regimens; political leaders expecting sharper mission focus and less across-the-board mentality in dealing with fiscal retrenchment; parents and students expecting their college tuition investment to yield a good paying and satisfying job upon graduation; policy makers relying increasingly on market mechanisms to define public goals and priorities; dramatic expansions in the educational promise of technology; civic dissatisfaction with attention to teaching; competitive pressures from an emerging privatized sector; impressions of organizational obsolescence and recalcitrance to change; egalitarian discomfort with higher education as a haven for a protected and privileged class; and public disaffection with values modeled in higher education. It is no longer a question of whether institutions must change but of who will control that recasting—the nation's colleges and universities, or an increasingly competitive market for postsecondary education that holds little sympathy for institutional tradition? ("Double Agent," 1996, p. 1).

How do we cherish the call of tradition and embrace the call for change in American higher education? An observation attributed to Dr. Samuel Johnson says that when a man knows he is to be hanged in the next day or so, this knowledge has the effect of concentrating thought and forcing his attention to first things. A softer version is that folks in tight places find themselves more inventive, that we become swift when pursued. Perhaps a useful first reaction to current criticism and pressures for change is that they may call us to a more imaginative and inventive consideration of our enterprise. After all, the current rich profile of American higher education institutions, programs, and services is not exactly the product of timid spirits or empty minds. As Drucker noted, no sector of our national life better represents a historic entrepreneurial spirit than American colleges and universities.

A second useful attitude may be found in advice offered by Ralph Waldo Emerson:

> Our strength grows out of our weakness. The indignation which arms itself with secret forces does not awaken until we are pricked and stung and sorely assailed. A great man is always willing to be little. Whilst he sits on the cushion of advantages, he goes to sleep. When he is pushed, tormented, defeated, he has a chance to learn something. . . . The wise man throws himself on the side of his assailants. It is more his interest than it is theirs to find his weak points (Emerson, 1929, p. 161).

In an organization that prospects for truth in adversarial forum, holding that we have not understood a truth unless we have contended with its challenge, we could hardly feel comfortable if our policies and practices, our assumptions and ways of doing business went unchallenged. The mind of the scholar, therefore, is hospitable to dissent and disputation—and should be so hospitable when the dissent and disputation targets the heart of the collegiate enterprise. At the very least, we may expect to more fully understand our work as a result of the call for change; and at the outset, we may expect a better idea to birth from the contention. When one's occupation is to search for truth, we would hardly run in fear if a prepared and persistent mind finds a more effective way to pursue truth.

Third, we must recognize that a college or university, whose principal work is to assault the limitations of common sense, may itself come under assault. Today's truth was yesterday's heresy, and the harbingers of new truth, whether individuals or institutions, are not always greeted with friendly and warm embrace. As the invention of the automobile did little to advance the welfare of the horse and buggy industry, there lies hiding in the fertile mind of some thinker or tinkerer—and not necessarily within a college or university—a replacement transportation idea for the automobile. The point is simple. If there is an organization whose occupants have the principal work of looking to displace comfortable ways of knowing and doing, we should not be surprised that this organization should itself come under scrutiny.

Fourth, college educators may find cause for celebration that Americans have made such a magnificent philosophic and financial investment in such an organization, that Americans are willing to pay for an organization to be critical of the social, cultural, economic, educational, political status quo.

Fifth, it should not be offensive to our collegiate and civic common sense that the quality and range of public criticism, including criticism of the academy, is a performance indicator of higher education's success—a pleasure measure of some importance and validity. The enhancement of access to college and university education produces more minds equipped for and inclined to criticism. Higher education faculty want their graduates to think critically. Did these educators believe that students might think critically about every organization in society except for colleges, their intellectual homes? Gibran (1973) reflects that "I have learned silence from the talkative, toleration from the intolerant, and kindness from the unkind; yet strange, I am ungrateful to these teachers" (p. 58). It is easy to be ungrateful to the critics—but one should resist that impulse.

A sixth and final posture that will allow us to bridge past and future and honor heritage and change is to embrace those values that should mark the mind of the scholar. We have already mentioned a hospitality to dissent and disputation as a mark of the educated mind. Such dissent and disputation are inevitable and welcome outcomes of our inclination to curiosity, which is perhaps the most fundamental value of the educated mind. Accompanying that curiosity should be the values of courage and persistence that enable a good mind to stay the course. Such a mind does not run and hide at the first sign of disappointment, failure, challenge, or criticism. The mind of the scholar also salutes the power of contradiction and paradox and is open to the promise of mistakes and imperfections. Tender strength, irreverent devotion, and guerilla goodness are not strange or surprising combinations. Planned and structured inquiry resulting in failure of theory may be the first glimpse of a new paradigm. A servant and steward attitude is a value that keeps us from the arrogance that can often afflict those who think they know more than others. Those who know more owe more. Finally, a compassionate and empathetic heart establishes the basis for placing knowledge in service of noble purpose and undergirds the morality of the academic enterprise. Compassion is also companion to creativity.

THE INSTRUMENT OF OUR WONDER

A beautiful line found in Gibran's *Sand and Foam* observes that "Your mind and my heart will never agree until your mind ceases to live in numbers and my heart in the mist" (Gibran, 1973, p. 30). A captivating dimension of the inner life of the American college and university is that here are places where some minds live in numbers and some hearts live in the mist—and there are truths to be found in both places. Here are expressions of nobility and beauty—of art, music, poetry, literature—that furnish inspiration to elevate and enrich our lives. Higher education is the home of our hope—enclaves of social and physical science and engines of search for solutions to those pains and problems that rob men and women of their promise, dignity, and joy. Here is the cradle of leadership development—professional schools attempting to link technical and ethical and delivering men and women who will in every field of human endeavor serve us not so much with direction and structure as by calling us to responsibility for our own actions and values, who in both solitude and teamwork seek to enlarge our repertoire of ideas and perspective. Here also are places of encounter where lifelong friendships are forged. Here are found the dreamers of day, faculty men and women living in the interrogatory mood and exemplifying colleges and universities as the ultimate instruments of our humanity, as the instruments of our capacity and inclination for wonder. Honoring the heritage of American higher education is to recognize and celebrate the energizing power of our curiosity.

REFERENCES

"Across the USA, News From Every State." *USA Today*, no. 183 (June 2, 1994): 7A.

Adelman, C. *Tourists in Our Own Land: Cultural Literacies and the College Curriculum*. Washington, D.C.: U.S. Department of Education, October 1992.

Alinsky, S. *Rules for Radicals*. New York: Random House, 1971.

Allmendinger, D. *Paupers and Scholars: The Transformation of Student Life in Nineteenth-Century New England*. New York: St. Martin's Press, 1975.

"Almanac Issue." *The Chronicle of Higher Education*, no. 42 (September 1, 1995): 1.

"Almanac Issue." *The Chronicle of Higher Education*, no. 43 (September 2, 1996): 1.

"Almanac Issue." *The Chronicle of Higher Education*, no. 45 (August 28, 1998): 1.

An American Imperative: Higher Expectations for Higher Education. A Report of theWingspread Group on Higher Education. The Johnson Foundation on Higher Education, 1993.

Anderson, J. *The Education of Blacks in the South, 1860–1935*. Chapel Hill: University of North Carolina, 1988.

Anderson, M. *Imposters in the Temple*. New York: Simon & Schuster, 1992.

Anderson, R., and J. Meyerson (eds.) *Financing Higher Education: Strategies After Tax Reform. New Directions for Higher Education*. San Francisco: Jossey-Bass, n. 58, Summer 1987.

The Assembly on University Goals and Governance. Cambridge, MA: The American Academy of Arts and Sciences, 1971.

Astin, A. *Achieving Educational Excellence*. San Francisco: Jossey-Bass, 1985.

———. *Assessment for Excellence*. Phoenix: American Council on Education/ Oryx Press, 1993a.

———. *Four Critical Years*. San Francisco: Jossey-Bass, 1997.

———. *What Matters in College?: Four Critical Years Revisited*. San Francisco: Jossey-Bass, 1993b.

Baker, G., ed. *A Handbook on the Community College in America*. Westport, CT: Greenwood Press, 1994.

Banning, J., and L. Kaiser. "An Ecological Perspective and Model for Campus Design," *Personnel and Guidance Journal*, vol. 52, no. 6 (1974): 370–75.

Banta, T., et al. *Assessment in Practice*. San Francisco: Jossey-Bass, 1995.

———, and Associates. *Making a Difference*. San Francisco: Jossey-Bass, 1994.

———, et al. *Making a Difference: Outcomes of a Decade of Assessment in Higher Education*. San Francisco: Jossey-Bass, 1993.

———, et al. "Performance Funding Comes of Age in Tennessee." *Journal of Higher Education* vol. 67, no. 1 (January/February 1996): 23–45.

Barak, R. *Program Review in Higher Education: Within and Without*. Boulder, CO: National Center for Higher Education Management Systems, 1982.

———, and B. Breier. *Successful Program Review: A Practical Guide to Evaluating Programs in Academic Settings*. San Francisco: Jossey-Bass, 1990.

Barber, B. *An Aristocracy of Everyone*. New York: Oxford University Press, 1992.

Barker, R. *Ecological Psychology: Concepts and Methods for Studying the Environment of Human Behavior*. Stanford, CA: Stanford University Press, 1968.

Barr, R., and J. Tagg. "From Teaching to Learning—A New Paradigm for Undergraduate Education." *Change* vol. 27, no. 1 (November/December 1995): 12–25.

Barzun, J. *The House of Intellect*. New York: Harper and Row, 1959.

The Basic Fund Accounting Training Package. Washington, D.C.: National Association of Colleges and University Business Officers, 1987.

Baum, S. R., and S. Schwartz. "Equity, Envy, and Higher Education." *Social Science Quarterly* vol. 67, no. 3 (September 1986): 491–503.

Baxter Magolda, M. *Knowing and Reasoning in College: Gender Related Patterns in Students' Intellectual Development*. San Francisco: Jossey-Bass, 1992.

"Beginning the Dialogue." *Policy Perspectives* (March 1992): 1B–6B.

Bell, D. *The Reforming of General Education*. New York: Columbia University Press, 1966.

Bellah, R., et al. *Habits of the Heart*. Berkeley: University of California Press, 1985.

Benavides, L. "Vanderbilt Faculty Under a Lens." *The Nashville Tennessean* (April 7, 1996): D1–D6.

Benjamin, R. "Looming Deficits: Causes, Consequences, and Cures." *Change* vol. 30, no. 2 (March/April 1998): 12–17.

Bennett, W. *To Reclaim a Legacy: A Report on Humanities In Higher Education.* Washington, D.C.: National Endowment for the Humanities, 1984.

Berdahl, R. *Statewide Coordination of Higher Education.* Washington, D.C.: American Council on Higher Education, 1973.

Bergmann, B. "Bloated Administration, Blighted Campuses." *Academe* vol. 77, no. 6 (1991): 12–16.

Berman, P., ed. *Debating P.C.: The Controversy Over Political Correctness on College Campuses.* New York: Bantam Doubleday Dell, 1992.

Blackburn, R., and F. Conrad. "The New Revisionists and the History of U.S. Higher Education." *Higher Education* vol. 15, no. 3–4 (1986): 211–30.

Block, P. *Stewardship.* San Francisco: Berrett Koehler, 1993.

Bloom, A. *The Closing of the American Mind.* New York: Simon & Schuster, 1987.

Bloom, B. *Taxonomy of Educational Objectives: Handbook I, Cognitive Domain.* New York: David McKay, 1956.

Blumenstyk, G. "10 States Receive $75 Million from NSF to Improve Teaching of Science and Math." *Chronicle of Higher Education*, vol. 37, no. 36 (May 22, 1991): A19–A20.

Bly, R. *Iron John: A Book About Men.* New York: Vintage, 1990.

Bogue, E. *A Journey of the Heart.* Bloomington, IN: Phi Delta Kappa, 1991.

———. "Alternatives to the Growth-Progress Syndrome." *Educational Forum* vol. 37, no. 1 (November 1972): 1, 35–43.

———, and W. Brown. "Performance Incentives for State Colleges." *Harvard Business Review* vol. 60, no. 6 (1982): 6.

———, J. Creech, and J. Folger. *Assessing Quality in Higher Education: Policy Actions in the SREB States.* Atlanta: Southern Regional Education Board, 1993.

———, and R. Saunders. *The Evidence for Quality.* San Francisco: Jossey-Bass, 1992.

———, and W. Troutt. *The Performance Funding Project.* Nashville: Tennessee Higher Education Commission, 1980.

Bok, D. *The Cost of Talent.* New York: The Free Press, 1993.

Bolman, L., and T. Deal. *Reframing Organizations.* San Francisco: Jossey-Bass, 1997.

Bowen, H. *Investment in Learning: The Individual and Social Value of American Higher Education.* San Francisco: Jossey-Bass, 1978.

———, and J. Schuster. *American Professors: A National Resource Imperiled.* New York: Oxford University Press, 1986.

Bowles, F., and F. DeCosta. "1952 to the Present." In *Between Two Worlds: A Profile of Negro Higher Education*. Carnegie Commission on Higher Education. New York: McGraw Hill, 1971.

Boyer, E. *College: The Undergraduate Experience in America*. New York: HarperCollins, 1987.

————. *Scholarship Reconsidered: Priorities of the Professoriate*. A Report of the Carnegie Foundation for the Advancement of Teaching. San Francisco: Jossey-Bass, 1990.

————, and A. Levine. *A Quest for Common Learning*. Washington, D.C. : The Carnegie Foundation for the Advancement of Teaching, 1981.

Bradley, B. "The View From the Hill." In *Monitoring and Assessing Intercollegiate Athletics*, edited by B. Mallette, and R. Howard. New Directions in Institutional Research. San Francisco: Jossey-Bass, 1992.

Brewster, K., Jr. "On Tenure." *AAUP Bulletin* vol. 58, no. 4 (winter 1972): 381–83.

Brubacher, J. *On the Philosophy of Higher Education*. San Francisco: Jossey-Bass, 1977.

————, and W. Rudy. *Higher Education in Transition: A History of American Colleges and Universities, 1636–1976*. New York: Harper and Row, 1976.

Burke, J. "The Proof Is in the Performance." *Trusteeship* vol. 2, no. 3 (May/June 1994): 25–29.

————, and A. Servan, eds. *Performance Funding for Public Higher Education: Fad or Trend?* New Directions for Institutional Research No. 97. San Francisco: Jossey-Bass, Spring 1998.

"The Business of the Business." *Policy Perspectives* vol. 1, no. 3 (May 1989). Philadelphia: Institute for Research on Higher Education.

Caen, H. "Gamut: From Ho to Hum." *San Francisco Chronicle* (August 25, 1993): 6.

Cahn, S. *Saints and Scamps: Ethics in Academia*. Totowa, N.J.: Rowman & Littlefield, 1986.

Callahan, T. "You Do It Until You Get Caught." *Time* vol. 133, no. 2. (January 9, 1989): 43.

Callan, P. *Public Purposes and Public Responsibilities*. San Jose: California Higher Education Policy Center, 1994.

"A Calling to Account." *Policy Perspectives* vol. 6, no. 2 (July 1995). Philadelphia: Institute for Research on Higher Education.

Campus Life: In Search of Community. Princeton, N.J.: Carnegie Foundation for the Advancement of Teaching, 1990.

Caplow, T., and R. McGee. *The Academic Marketplace*. New York: Basic Books, 1958.

Carnegie Commission on Higher Education. *The Purposes and the Performance of Higher Education in the United States Approaching the Year 2000*. New York: McGraw-Hill, 1973.

Carnochan, W. *The Battleground of the Curriculum: Liberal Education and American Experience.* Stanford, CA: Stanford University Press, 1993.

Cartter, A. *An Assessment of Quality in Graduate Education.* Washington, D.C.: American Council on Education, 1964.

Chait, R. "Thawing the Cold War Over Tenure: Why Academe Needs More Employment Options." *Chronicle of Higher Education* vol. 43 (February 7, 1997): B4–B5.

———, T. Holland, and B. Taylor. *The Effective Board of Trustees.* Phoenix: American Council on Education/Oryx Press, 1993.

Cheit, E. *The New Depression in Higher Education: A Study of Financial Conditions of 41 Colleges and Universities.* New York: McGraw-Hill, 1971.

Cheney, L. *50 Hours: A Core Curriculum for College Students.* Washington, D.C.: National Endowment for the Humanities, October 1989.

Chickering, A. *Education and Identity.* San Francisco: Jossey-Bass, 1969.

———, and L. Reisser. *Education and Identity.* San Francisco: Jossey-Bass, 1993.

Church, R., and M. Sedlack. *Education in the United States: An Interpretive History.* New York: Free Press, 1976.

Clark, B. *The Academic Life.* Princeton, NJ: The Carnegie Advancement of Teaching, 1987.

A Classification of Institutions of Higher Education: 1994 Edition. Princeton, NJ: The Carnegie Foundation for the Advancement of Teaching, 1994.

College and University Business Administration. Washington, D.C.: National Association of College and University Business Officers, 1992.

Commission on Colleges. *Report of the Committee on Institutional Integrity* (draft). Atlanta: Commission on Colleges, Southern Association of Colleges and Schools, 1998.

Community Colleges: Core Indicators of Effectiveness. Washington, D.C.: American Association of Community Colleges, 1994.

The Condition of Education, 1995. Washington, D.C.: U.S. Department of Education, National Center for Education Statistics, NCES 95–273.

The Control of the Campus: A Report on the Governance of Higher Education. Washington, D.C.: Carnegie Foundation for the Advancement of Teaching, 1982.

"Coping with the Cutbacks." *AAHE Bulletin* (March 1991): 3–6.

Cordes, C. "Academe's Pork Barrel." *Chronicle of Higher Education* vol. 40, no. 48 (August 3, 1994): A19–A21.

———. "Budget Office Proposes New Limits on Overhead Costs." *Chronicle of Higher Education* vol. 37, no. 36 (May 22, 1991): A19, A24.

Crosby, P. *Quality Without Tears.* New York: McGraw-Hill, 1984.

Cross, K. *Accent on Learning: Improving Instruction and Reshaping the Curriculum.* San Francisco: Jossey-Bass, 1981.

————. *Adults as Learners*. San Francisco: Jossey-Bass, 1981.

Davies, G. "The Importance of Being General: Philosophy, Politics, and Institutional Mission Statements." In *Higher Education: Handbook on Theory and Research, Volume II*, edited by John Smart. New York: Agathon Press, 1986.

————. "The Influence of Public Policy on the Quality of Higher Education." In *The Uneasy Public Policy Triangle in Higher Education*, edited by D. Finifter, R. Baldwin, and J. Thelin. New York: American Council on Education/Macmillan Publishing Company, 1991.

Del Valle, C., E. Schine, and G. McWilliams. "A Lot Less Moola on Campus." *Business Week*, no. 3286 (October 5, 1992): 114–15.

Delworth, U., G. Hanson, and Associates. *Student Services: A Handbook for the Profession*. San Francisco: Jossey-Bass, 1989.

Deming, W. *Out of the Crisis*. Cambridge, MA: Massachusetts Institute of Technology, 1986.

DePalma, A. "Short of Money, Columbia Weighs How Best to Change: Tough Choices on Campus, A Special Report." *The New York Times* (May 25, 1992): 1, 25.

Dewey, J. *Democracy and Education*. New York: Macmillan Publishing Company, 1916.

Dickey, D. "A Report to the UT Athletics Board on Sports Contributions to Academic Funding." *Context*, The University of Tennessee, Knoxville, vol. 14, no. 5 (December 1966).

Dobbins, C., and C. Lee. *Whose Goals for Higher Education?* Washington, D.C.: American Council on Education, 1968.

"Don't Put Pork First." *The Christian Science Monitor* (March 8, 1993): 20.

"Double Agent." *Policy Perspectives* vol. 6, no. 3. Philadelphia: Institute for Research on Higher Education, University of Pennsylvania, 1996.

Doucette, D., R. Richardson, Jr., and R. Fenske. "Defining Institutional Mission." *Journal of Higher Education* vol. 56, no. 2 (March/April 1985): 190–205.

Draper, A. "Innocence Lost: Division III Sports Programs." *Change* vol. 28, no. 6 (November/December 1996): 46–49.

Drucker, P. *Innovation and Entrepreneurship*. New York: Harper and Row, 1985.

DuBois, W. *The Souls of Black Folk*. Millwood, N.Y. : Kraus-Thomson Organization Limited, 1973.

Durant, W. *The Story of Civilization: Part I, Our Oriental Heritage*. New York: Simon & Schuster, 1954.

Dykes, A. *Faculty Participation in Academic Decision Making*. Washington, D.C.: American Council on Education, 1968.

Eble, K. *Professors as Teachers*. San Francisco: Jossey-Bass, 1972.

Eddy, E. *Colleges for Our Land and Time*. New York: Harper and Bros., 1956.

Eells, W. *Degrees in Higher Education.* New York: The Center for Applied Research in Education, 1963.

Emerson, R. "Compensation." In *The Complete Writings of Ralph Waldo Emerson, Volume I.* New York: Wm. H. Wise and Company, 1929.

"An End to Sanctuary." *Policy Perspectives* no. 4. Institute for Research on Higher Education, (September 1991): 4, 6A.

Erwin, T. *Assessing Student Learning and Development.* San Francisco: Jossey-Bass, 1991.

Etzioni, A. *The Spirit of Community.* New York: Crown Publishing, 1993.

Ewell, P. *The Self-Regulating Institution: Information for Excellence.* Boulder: National Center for Higher Education Management Systems, 1984.

―――. *Using Student Outcomes Information in Program Planning and Decision Making.* Volume 1. Boulder: National Center for Higher Education Management Systems, 1985.

―――. "Outcomes, Assessment, and Academic Improvement: In Search of Usable Knowledge." In *Higher Education: Handbook of Theory and Research,* vol. 4, edited by J. Smart. New York: Agathon Press, 1988.

―――, J. Finney, and C. Lenth. "Filling in the Mosaic: The Emerging Pattern of State-Based Assessment." *AAHE Bulletin* vol. 42, no. 8 (April 1990): 3–5.

"Fact File: 460 College and University Endowments." *The Chronicle of Higher Education* vol. 42, no. 23 (February 16, 1996).

Feldman, K., and T. Newcomb. *The Impact of College on Students.* San Francisco: Jossey-Bass, 1973.

Fifteenth Annual Status Report on Minorities in Higher Education. Washington, D.C.: American Council on Education, 1997.

Flexner, A. *Universities: American, English, and German.* New York: Oxford University Press, 1930.

Folger, J., ed. *Financial Incentives for State Colleges.* New Directions for Higher Education, No. 48. San Francisco: Jossey-Bass, 1984.

Forum for College and University Governance. *State Incentive Funding: Leveraging Quality. Briefings.* College Park, MD: Forum for College and University Governance, University of Maryland, 1990.

Frey, J., ed. *The Governance of Intercollegiate Athletics.* West Point, N.Y.: Leisure Press, 1982.

Gaff, J. *General Education Today.* San Francisco: Jossey-Bass, 1983.

Gaines, E. *A Gathering of Old Men.* New York: Alfred A. Knopf, 1985.

Gaither, G., ed. *Performance Indicators in Higher Education: What Works, What Doesn't and What's Next.* Proceedings from the Pre-conference Symposium. College Station, TX: Texas A & M University System, June 1996.

―――, B. Nedwek, and J. Neal. *Measuring Up: The Promises and Pitfalls of Performance Indicators in Higher Education.* ASHE-ERIC Higher Education

Report No. 94-5. Washington, D.C.: School of Education and Human Services, George Washington University, 1994.

Galbraith, J. *The Affluent Society*. Boston: Houghton Mifflin, 1958.

Gardiner, L. *Planning for Assessment*. New York: Lion F. Gardiner, 1989.

Gardner, H. *Frames of Mind*. New York: Basic Books, 1983.

Gardner, J. *Excellence*. New York: W.W. Norton, 1984.

Garvin, D. *Managing Quality*. New York: Free Press, 1988.

General Education in a Free Society. Cambridge, MA: Harvard University Press, 1945.

Geyelin, M. "Court Rejects Scholarship Aid for Blacks Only" (Law). *The Wall Street Journal* (February 5, 1992): B1–B5.

Gibran, K. *Sand and Foam*. New York: Alfred A. Knopf, 1973.

Gilligan, C. *In a Different Voice: Psychological Theory and Women's Development*. Cambridge, MA: Harvard University Press, 1982.

Gillis, A. "Program Choice/Resource Compaction." *Planning for Higher Education* vol. 10, no. 3 (spring 1982): 33–38.

Gilmour, J. "Participative Governance Bodies in Higher Education: Report of a National Study." In *Faculty in Governance: The Role of Senate and Joint Committees in Academic Decision Making*, edited by R. Birnbaum. New Directions for Higher Education Report No. 75. San Francisco: Jossey-Bass, 1994.

Glassick, C., M. Huber, and G. Maeroff. *Scholarship Assessed: Evaluation of the Professoriate*. San Francisco: Jossey-Bass, 1997.

Goals for Education: Challenge 2000. Atlanta: Southern Regional Education Board, 1988.

Goldberger, M., B. Maher, and P. Flattau, eds. *Research Doctorate Programs in the United States: Continuity and Change*. Washington, D.C.: National Academy Press, 1995.

Goleman, D. *Emotional Intelligence*. New York: Bantam, 1995.

Gould, J. "William Rainey Harper and the University of Chicago." Unpublished Ph.D. dissertation, Syracuse University, 1951.

Graff, G. *Beyond the Culture Wars*. New York: W.W. Norton, 1992.

Graham, P., R. Lyman, and M. Trow. *Accountability of Colleges and Universities*. New York: Columbia University, 1995.

Graubard, S., ed. "The Embattled University." *Daedalus* vol. 99, no. 1 (1972): xiv.

Gross, F. *A Comparative Analysis of the Existing Budget Formulas Used for Justifying Budget Request or Allocating Funds for the Operating Expenses of State-Supported Colleges and Universities*. Knoxville, TN: University of Tennessee, Office of Institutional Research, 1973.

Grossman, H. "Rebirth of the Ivy Cartel" (Rule of Law). *The Wall Street Journal* (January 26, 1994): A15.

Gruber, K., ed. *Encyclopedia of Associations—1985*. Detroit: Gale Research Company, 1985.

Guaspari, J. *I Know It When I See It: A Modern Fable About Quality*. New York: AMACOM, 1985.

Guernsey, L. "Is the Internet Becoming a Bonanza for Diploma Mills?" *The Chronicle of Higher Education* vol. 44, no. 17 (December 19, 1997): A22–A24.

Gumport, P., and B. Pusser. "A Case of Bureaucratic Accretion: Context and Consequences." *Journal of Higher Education* vol. 66, no. 5 (September/October 1995): 493–520.

Guskin, A. "Restructuring the Role of Faculty." *Change* vol. 26, no. 5 (September/October, 1984): 16–25.

Gutman, A. "What Counts As Quality in Higher Education?" In *The Uneasy Public Policy Triangle in Higher Education*, edited by D. Finifter, R. Baldwin, and J. Thelin. New York: American Council on Education/Macmillan Publishing Company, 1991.

Hackney, S. "Reinventing the American University." *Teachers College Record* vol 95, no. 3 (spring 1994): 311–16.

Halfond, J. "Too Many Administrators." *AAHE Bulletin* vol. 43, no. 7 (March 1991): 7–8.

Harari, O. "Ten Reasons Why TQM Doesn't Work." *Management Review* vol. 82, no. 1 (January 1993): 33–38.

Healy, P. "Activist Republican Trustees Change the Way Public Universities Seek Presidents." *Chronicle of Higher Education* vol. 42, no. 48 (August 9, 1996): A19–A20.

Henry, W. III. *In Defense of Elitism*. New York: Doubleday, 1994.

Higher Education for American Democracy, Volume I. A Report on the President's Commission on Higher Education. Washington, D.C.: U.S. Government Printing Office, 1947.

"Higher Education: How Unruly Aspirations Built a System Alabama Can't Afford." Alabama: *Mobile Register* (July 9, 1995).

"Higher Education, Part II. After Decades of Growth, Now a Search for Quality." Alabama: *Mobile Register* (November 21, 1995).

Highet, G. *The Immortal Profession*. New York: Weybright and Talley, 1976.

Hines, E. *Higher Education and State Governments: Renewed Partnership, Cooperation of Competition?* ASHE-ERIC Higher Education Report No. 5. Washington, D.C.: Association for the Study of Higher Education, 1988.

Hirsch, E., Jr. *Cultural Literacy: What Every American Needs to Know*. Boston: Houghton Mifflin, 1987.

History of the NAIA. Tulsa: National Association of Intercollegiate Athletics, 1999.

Hofstadter, R., and R. Smith, eds. *American Higher Education: A Documentary History*, Volume 1. Chicago: University of Chicago Press, 1961.

Holland, D. and M. Eisenhart. *Educated in Romance: Women, Achievement, and College Culture*. Chicago: University of Chicago Press, 1990.

Horowitz, H. *Campus Life: Undergraduate Cultures From the End of the Eighteenth Century to the Present*. New York: Alfred A. Knopf, 1987.

Hsu, S., and M. Tousignant. "Making Allen the Bad Man on Campus: Students, Faculty Rally Against Proposed Cuts." *The Washington Post* (January 30, 1995): B1, B5.

Huber, R. *How Professors Play the Cat Guarding the Cream*. Fairfax, VA: George Mason University Press, 1992.

The Humanities in American Life. Berkeley: University of California Press, 1980.

Hutchins, R. "First Glimpses of a New World." In *What I Have Learned*, edited by Norman Cousins. New York: Simon & Schuster, 1968.

———. *The Higher Learning in America*. New Haven, CT: Yale University Press, 1936.

Ingram, R. and Associates. *Governing Public Colleges and Universities: A Handbook for Trustees, Chief Executives, and Other Campus Leaders*. San Francisco: Jossey-Bass, 1993. See also companion volume, *Governing Private Colleges and Universities*.

Joint Commission on Accountability Reporting. Washington, D.C.: American Association of State Colleges and Universities, 1994.

Kaplan, W. *The Law of Higher Education*. San Francisco: Jossey-Bass, 1985.

Kaplin, W., and B. Lee. *The Law of Higher Education*. San Francisco: Jossey-Bass, 1995.

Keeping Faith With the Student-Athlete: A New Model for Intercollegiate Athletics. Report of the Knight Foundation on Intercollegiate Athletics. Charlotte, N.C.: Knight Foundation, March, 1991.

Keeton, M. *Shared Authority on Campus*. Washington, D.C.: American Association for Higher Education, 1971.

Keller, G. *Academic Strategy*: Baltimore: Johns Hopkins University Press, 1983.

———. "Shotgun Marriage: The Growing Connection Between Academic Management and Faculty Governance." In *Governing Tomorrow's Campus*, by J. Schuster, L. Miller and Associates. New York: American Council on Education/Macmillan, 1989.

Kennedy, D. *Academic Duty*. Cambridge, MA: Harvard University Press, 1997.

Kerr, C., and M. Gade. *The Guardians: Board of Trustees of American Colleges and Universities*. Washington, D.C.: Association of Governing Boards of Universities and Colleges, 1989.

Knefelkamp, L., C. Widick, and C. Parker, eds. *Applying New Development Findings*. New Directions in Student Services, No. 4. San Francisco: Jossey-Bass, 1978.

Kohlberg, L. "Stage and Sequence: The Cognitive-Developmental Approach to Socialization." In *Handbook of Socialization Theory and Research*, edited by D. Goslin. Skokie, IL: Rand McNally, 1969.

Kolb, D. *Learning Styles Inventory Technical Manual*. Boston: McBer, 1976.

Komives, S., and D. Woodard. *Student Services: A Handbook for the Profession*. San Francisco: Jossey-Bass, 1996.

Kors, A., and H. Silvergate. *The Shadow University*. New York: The Free Press, 1998.

Kuh, G. *Student Learning Outcomes Outside the Classroom: Transcending Artificial Boundaries*. ASHE-ERIC Higher Education Report No. 94–8. Washington, D.C.: Graduate School of Education and Human Development, George Washington University, 1994.

————, E. Whitt, and J. Shedd. *Student Affairs Work: A Paradigmatic Odyssey*. Alexandria, VA: American College Personnel Association, 1987.

Kuhn, T. *The Structure of Scientific Revolutions*. Chicago: University of Chicago Press, 1962.

Kurian, G. *Datapedia of the United States 1790–2000*. Lanhan, MD: Bernan Press, 1994.

Land, G., and B. Jarman. *Breakpoint and Beyond*. New York: Harper Business, 1992.

Lee, J. "Beyond the Pale: How Student Aid Cuts Hurt Access." *Educational Record* vol. 67, no. 2–3 (spring/summer 1986): 20–24.

Lempert, D. *Escape From the Ivory Tower*. San Francisco: Jossey-Bass, 1996.

Levine, A. *Handbook on Undergraduate Curriculum*. San Francisco: Jossey-Bass, 1978.

Levine, D. *The American College and the Culture of Aspiration, 1915–1940*. New York: Cornell University Press, 1986.

Levine, L. *The Opening of the American Mind*. Boston: Beacon Press, 1996.

Lewis, R., and D. Smith. *Total Quality in Higher Education*. Delray Beach, FL: St. Lucie Press, 1994.

Licata, C. "Post-Tenure Review." *AAHE Bulletin* vol. 50, no. 18 (June 1998): 3–6.

Lindsley, P. "On the Failure of the American College, 1832 and 1848." In *American Higher Education: A Documentary History, Volume One*, edited by R. Hofstader and W. Smith. Chicago: University of Chicago Press, 1961.

Lipset, S. "Political Correctness, Historically Speaking." *Educational Record* vol. 73, no. 1 (winter 1992): 5–11.

Lucas, A. *Strengthening Departmental Leadership*. San Francisco: Jossey-Bass, 1994.

Lucas, C. *American Higher Education: A History*. New York: St. Martin's Press, 1994.

————. *Crisis in the Academy*. New York: St. Martin's Press, 1996.

Mager, .R. *Mastering Instructional Intent*. Belmont, CA: Lear Siegler/Fearon Publishers, 1973.

Magner, D. "Beyond Tenure." *Chronicle of Higher Education* vol. 41, no. 45 (July 21, 1995): A13, A16.

———. "The New Generation." *Chronicle of Higher Education* vol. 42, no. 21 (February 2, 1996): A17–A18.

———. "Tenure Re-examined." *Chronicle of Higher Education* vol. 41, no. 29 (March 31, 1995): A17–A18.

Malcolm Baldrige National Quality Award Pilot Criteria, 1995. Gaithersburg, MD: United States Department of Commerce, December 1994.

Mandell, R. *The Professor Game*. New York: Harold Matson Company, 1977.

Mangan, K. "U. of Houston Considers the Unthinkable for a Texas University: Ending Its Sports Program." *Chronicle of Higher Education* vol. 43, no. 2 (September 13, 1996): A47–A48.

Marchese, T. "Bye, Bye, CAI For Now." *Change* vol. 28, no. 3 (May/June 1996): 4.

———. "Costs and Quality." *Change* vol. 22, no. 3 (May/June 1990): 4.

———. "TQM: A Time for Ideas." *Change* vol. 25, no. 3 (May/June 1993): 10–14.

Marsden, G. *The Soul of the American University*. New York: Oxford University Press, 1994.

Mason, H. *College and University Government: A Handbook of Principle and Practice*. New Orleans: Tulane University, 1972.

May, H. "Ex-Students Sue Universities Over Quality of Education." *Chronicle of Higher Education* vol. 42, no. 4 (August 16, 1996): A9.

May, W. *Ethics and Higher Education*. New York: Macmillan, 1990.

McGuinness, A. Jr. *A Framework for Evaluating State Policy Roles in Improving Undergraduate Education*. Denver: Education Commission of the States, 1994.

———, R. Epper, and S. Arredono. *State Postsecondary Education Structures Handbook, 1994*. Denver: Education Commission of the States, 1994.

Meeth, R. *Quality Education for Less Money*. San Francisco: Jossey-Bass, 1974.

Meiklejohn, A. "Should Communists Be Allowed to Teach?" *New York Times Magazine* (March 27, 1949): 10, 64–66.

Mercer, J. "A Gift Transforms a College." *Chronicle of Higher Education* vol. 42, no. 15 (December 8, 1995): A29–A31.

Metzger, W. "Academic Governance: An Evolutionary Perspective." In *Governing Tomorrow's Campus*, edited by J. Schuster, L. Miller, and Associates. New York: American Council on Education/Macmillan, 1989.

Miller, J. *State Budgeting for Higher Education*. Ann Arbor: Institute of Public Administration, University of Michigan, 1964.

Milton, O., and J. Edgerly. *The Testing and Grading of Students*. Washington, D.C.: Change Magazine, 1976.

Mingle, J., and Associates. *Challenges of Retrenchment*. San Francisco: Jossey-Bass, 1981.

Mortimer, K. *Accountability in Higher Education*. Washington D.C.: American Association for Higher Education, February, 1972.

———, and T. McConnell. *Sharing Authority Effectively*. San Francisco: Jossey-Bass, 1978.

Mouritsen, M. "The University Mission Statement: A Tool for the University Curriculum, Institutional Effectiveness, and Change." In *Crisis Management and Higher Education*, edited by H. Hoverland, P. McInturff, and C. E. Tapie Rohm. New Directions for Higher Education (fall 1986): 45–52.

Myers, C. "Lawmakers' Earmarking Called an Ineffective Way to Allot Funds" (Government & Politics). *Chronicle of Higher Education* vol. 37, no. 36 (May 22, 1991): A27.

Myers, I. *Gifts Differing*. Palo Alto, CA: Consulting Psychologists Press, 1980a.

———. *Introduction to Type*. Palo Alto, CA: Consulting Psychologists Press, 1980b.

National Education Association. Educational Policies Commission. *Higher Education in a Decade of Decision*. Washington, D.C.: National Education Association of the United States and the American Association of School Administrators, 1957.

The National Education Goals Report: Building a Nation of Learners. Washington, D.C.: National Education Goals Panel, 1991.

Naughton, J. "Who Runs College Sports? A Million Dollar Contract for a Football Coach in Florida Raises That Question." *Chronicle of Higher Education* vol. 43, no. 13 (November 22, 1996): A37–A38.

Newman, F. *Choosing Quality*. Denver: Education Commission of the States, 1987.

Newman, J. *The Idea of a University*. Notre Dame, IN: University of Notre Dame, 1982.

Newsom, W., and C. Hayes. "Are Mission Statements Worthwhile?" *Planning for Higher Education* vol. 19, no. 2 (winter 1990–91): 28–30.

"Not Just the Yacht" (Editorial). *The Washington Post* (January 12, 1992): C6.

Ogilvy, J. *Living Without a Goal*. New York: Doubleday, 1995.

Ostling, R. "Big Chill on Campus." *Time* vol. 139, no. 5 (February 3, 1992): 61–63.

———. "The Tuition Game: Advisors Offer Perplexed Parents Clever College-Aid Schemes. But Where's the Line Between Working the System—and Cheating It?" *Time* vol. 140, no. 19 (November 9, 1992): 60, 65.

Palmer, P. "Community, Conflict, and Ways of Knowing." *Change* vol. 19, no. 5 (September/October 1987): 20–25.

————. *The Courage to Teach*. San Francisco: Jossey-Bass, 1998.

————. "The Heart of a Teacher: Identity and Integrity in Teaching." *Change* vol. 29, no. 6 (November/December 1987): 14–22.

Parini, J. "Tenure and the Loss of Faculty Talent." *Chronicle of Higher Education* vol. 41, no. 42 (July 14, 1995): A40

Parr, S. "Polarized Campuses." *Liberal Education* vol. 77, no. 4 (September/October 1991): 23–25.

Pascarella E., and P. Terenzini. "Designing Colleges for Greater Learning." *Planning for Higher Education* vol. 20, no. 3 (spring 1992): 1–5.

————. *How College Affects Students*. San Francisco: Jossey-Bass, 1991.

Patterson, D. *When Learned Men Murder*. Bloomington, IN: Phi Delta Kappa, 1996.

Paul, J. *You Dropped It, You Pick It Up*. Baton Rouge: Ed's Publishing Company, 1983.

Perkins, L. "The Impact of the 'Cult of True Womanhood' on the Education of Black Women." *Journal of Social Issues* vol. 39, no. 3 (1983): 17–28.

Perry, W. *Forms of Intellectual and Ethical Development in the College Years: A Scheme*. Troy, MO: Holt, Rinehart and Winston, 1970.

Peters, R. "Some Sharks are Boojums: Accountability and the Eno(s) of Higher Education." *Change* vol. 26, no. 6 (November/December 1994): 16–23.

Pirsig, R. *Zen and the Art of Motorcycle Maintenance*. New York: Morrow, 1974.

Poch, R. *Academic Freedom in American Higher Education: Rights Responsibilities and Limitations*. ASHE-ERIC Higher Education Report No. 4. Washington, D.C.: School of Education and Human Development, George Washington University, 1993.

Postsecondary Opportunity vol. 78. Oskaloosa, IA: December 1998.

Principles of Good Practice for Assessing Student Learning. Washington, D.C.: American Association for Higher Education, 1992.

Putka, G. "Academic Barter: A Professor Swapped Degrees for Contracts, University Suspects." *The Wall Street Journal* vol. 218, no. 9 (June 12, 1991): A1.

Rand, A. *Atlas Shrugged*. New York: Random House, 1957.

————. *The Fountainhead*. New York: Bobbs-Merrill, 1968.

Ravitch, D. *The Troubled Crusade*. New York: Basic Books, 1983.

Renewing the Academic Presidency: Stronger Leadership for Tougher Times. Washington, D.C.: Association of Governing Boards of Universities and Colleges, 1996.

Rice, R. *Making a Place for the New American Scholar*. Inquiry no. 1, American Association for Higher Education Forum on Faculty Roles and Rewards. Washington, D.C.: American Association for Higher Education, 1996.

Richardson, J. "Centralizing Governance Isn't Simply Wrong; It's Bad Business, Too." *Chronicle of Higher Education* vol. 45, no. 23 (February 12, 1999): B9.

Roche, G. *The Fall of the Ivory Tower*. New York: Regnery Publishing, 1993.

Ruch, R. "For Profit Application of the Corporate Model to Academic Enterprise." *AAHE Bulletin* vol. 51, no. 6 (February 1999): 3–6.

Rudolph, F. *The American College and University, a History*. Athens, GA: University of Georgia, 1990.

Ruppert, S. *Charting Higher Education Accountability: The Roots and Realities of State-Level Performance Indicators*. Denver: Education Commission of the States, 1994.

Sagendorph, K. *Michigan: The Story of the University*. New York: E.P. Dutton, 1948.

Sanford, N. *The American College*. New York: Wiley, 1962.

————. *Self and Society: Social Change and Individual Development*. New York: Atherton Press, 1966.

Sanoff, A. "Almost Anything Goes: Hard-Pressed Schools Are Cutting Deals to Land Students They Want." *U.S. News & World Report* vol. 115, no. 14 (October 11, 1993): 93–96.

————. "It's Cleanup Time for College Sports." *U.S. News and World Report* vol. 99, no. 5 (July 1, 1985): 62–64.

Sapp, M., and M. Temares. "A Monthly Checkup: Key Success Indices Track Health of the University of Miami." *NACUBO Business Officer* vol. 25, no. 9 (March 1992): 24–31.

Savage, H., et al. *American College Athletics*. New York: The Carnegie Foundation for the Advancement of Teaching, 1929.

Schlesinger, A. *The Disuniting of America*. New York: W.W. Norton & Company, 1992.

Schuster, J., L. Miller, et al. *Governing Tomorrow's Campus*. Washington, D.C.: American Council on Education/Macmillan, 1989.

————, et al. *Strategic Governance: How to Make Big Decisions Better*. Phoenix: American Council on Education/Oryx Press, 1994.

Seldin, P. *The Teaching Portfolio*. Bolton, MA: Anker Publishing, 1997.

Senge, P. *The Fifth Discipline: The Art and Practice of The Learning Organization*. New York: Doubleday, 1990.

Seymour, D. "The Baldrige Cometh." *Change* vol. 26, no. 1 (January/February 1994): 16–27.

————. *On Q: Causing Quality in Higher Education*. Phoenix: American Council on Education/Oryx Press, 1992.

————, and Associates. *High Performing Colleges*. Maryville, MO: Prescott Publishing Company, 1996.

Shared Responsibility: Strategies to Enhance Quality and Opportunity in California Higher Education. San Jose: The California Higher Education Policy Center, 1996.

Sheehan, R. *Keeping Score: The Economics of Big-Time Sports.* South Bend, IN: Diamond Communications, 1996.

Shurden, W. "The Southern Baptists' Educational Holy War: A Review Essay." *Planning for Higher Education* vol. 19, no. 2 (winter 1990–91): 31–39.

Slaughter, S., and L. Leslie. *Academic Capitalism.* Baltimore: Johns Hopkins University Press, 1997.

Smith, P. "Beyond Budgets: Changing for the Better." *Educational Record* vol. 72, no. 1 (spring 1991): 26–28.

Smith, P. *Killing the Spirit.* New York: Viking Press, 1990.

Solomon, L., and P. Taubman. *Does College Matter? Some Evidence on the Impact of Higher Education.* New York: Academic Press, 1973.

Solomon, R., and J. Solomon. *Up the University: Re-creating Higher Education in America.* New York: Addison Wesley Publishing Company, 1993.

Spann, M., Jr., and S. McCrimmon. "Remedial/Developmental Education: Past, Present, and Future." In *A Handbook on the Community College in America,* edited by George Baker. Westport, CT: Greenwood Press, 1994.

Sperber, M. *College Sports, Inc.: The Athletic Department vs. The University.* New York: Henry Holt and Company, 1990.

"Sports-Event Tax Is Opposed." *The New York Times* (July 29, 1992): D3 (L).

Spurr, S. *Academic Degree Structures: Innovative Approaches.* New York: McGraw-Hill, 1970.

SREB Fact Book on Higher Education. Atlanta: Southern Regional Education Board, 1994–95.

St. John, E. *Rethinking Tuition and Student Aid Strategies.* New Directions for Higher Education, No. 89. San Francisco: Jossey-Bass, 1995.

"Statement on Government of Colleges and Universities." *Academe* vol. 52, no. 4 (1966): 375, 379.

"Statutes of Harvard, ca. 1646." R. Hofstadter and W. Smith, eds. *America Higher Education: A Documentary History, Volume One.* Chicago: University of Chicago Press, 1961.

Sternberg, R. *The Triarchic Mind.* New York: Viking Press, 1988.

Straight Talk About College Costs and Prices. Report of the National Commission on the Cost of Higher Education, February 1998.

Strange, C. "Student Development: The Evolution and Status of an Essential Idea." *Journal of College Student Development* vol. 35, no. 6 (November 1994): 399–412.

Strong Foundations: Twelve Principles for Effective General Education Programs. Washington, D.C.: Association of American Colleges, 1994.

"Student Personnel Point of View," In *Points of View*. Washington, D.C.: National Association of Student Personnel Administrators, 1937.

Student Poll. Vol. 1, no. 1 (fall 1995).

"Sweezey v. New Hampshire V354." *U.S. Reports* (1957): 234. Petition for Rehearing Denied, 355, U.S. 852.

Sykes, C. *Profscam*. Washington, D.C.: Regnery Gateway, 1988.

Task Force on Faculty Decision Making and Governance. American Association for Higher Education, 1967.

Tewksbury, D. *The Founding of American Colleges and Universities Before the Civil War*. New York: Columbia Teachers College, 1965.

Thelin, J., and L. Wiseman. *The Old College Try: Balancing Academics and Athletics in Higher Education*. ASHE-ERIC Higher Education Report No. 4, 1989. Washington, D.C.: School of Education and Human Development, George Washington University, 1989.

Thomas, L. *The Medusa and the Snail*. New York: Viking Press, 1974.

Thompson, D., ed. *Moral Values and Higher Education*. Albany, NY: State University of New York Press, 1991.

Thwing, C. *A History of Higher Education in America*. New York: Appleton & Company, 1906.

Toole, J. *Confederacy of Dunces*. Baton Rouge: Louisiana State University Press, 1982.

Trachtenberg, S. "Political Correctness: Can It Ever Be Politically Incorrect? *The College Board Review*, no. 105 (winter 1992–93): 6–26.

Trower, C. *Tenure Snapshot*. Inquiry no. 2 of the AAHE form 7 on Faculty Roles and Rewards. Washington, D.C.: American Association for Higher Education, 1996.

Trustees and Troubled Times in Higher Education. Washington, D.C. Association of Governing Boards of Universities and Colleges, 1993.

The Tuition Puzzle: Putting the Pieces Together. Washington, D.C.: Institute for Higher Education Policy, February 1999.

Tully, S. "Finally, Colleges Start to Cut Their Crazy Costs." *Fortune* (May 1, 1995): 110–13.

Vaughn, G. *The Community College in America: A Short History*. Washington, D.C.: American Association of Community and Junior Colleges, 1985.

Veblen, T. *The Higher Learning in America*. New York: B.W. Huebsch, 1918.

Veysey, L. *The Emergence of the American University*. Chicago: University of Chicago Press, 1965.

Waggaman, J. *Strategies and Consequences: Managing the Costs in Higher Education*. 1991 ASHE-ERIC Higher Education Report No. 8. Washington, D.C.: George Washington University School of Education and Human Development, 1991.

Wallace, T. "Maintaining Student Afford Ability and Access in a New Fiscal Reality." *Educational Record* vol. 74, no. 4 (fall 1993): 24–31.

Webster, D. "America's Highest Ranked Graduate Schools, 1925-1982." *Change* vol. 15, no. 4 (May/June 1983): 14–24.

———, and T. Skinner. "Rating Ph.D. Programs: What the NRC Report Says . . . and Doesn't Say." *Change* vol. 28, no. 3 (May/June 1996): 22–50.

Westmeyer, P. *A History of American Higher Education.* Springfield, IL: Charles C. Thomas Publishers, 1985.

Whalen, E. *Responsibility Center Budgeting.* Bloomington: Indiana University Press, 1991.

Whitehead, A. *Adventures of Ideas.* New York: The Free Press, 1933.

———. *The Aims of Education.* New York: The Free Press, 1957.

Wildavsky, A. *Speaking Truth to Power: The Art and Craft of Policy Analysis.* New York: Transaction Publishers, 1979.

Wilson, L. *American Academics: Then and Now.* New York: Oxford University Press, 1979.

Winston, G. "For-Profit Higher Education: Godzilla or Chicken Little?" *Change* vol. 31, no. 1 (January/February 1999): 12–19.

Wyatt, J. "Pork barrel science: Top colleges enrich lobbyists" (Column). *The New York Times* (October 12, 1993): A23 (L).

"The Yale Report of 1828." R. Hofstadter and W. Smith, eds. *American Higher Education: A Documentary History, Volume One.* Chicago: University of Chicago Press, 1961.

Young R. *No Neutral Ground.* San Francisco: Jossey-Bass, 1996.

Zemsky, R., and W. Massy. "Cost Containment: Committing to a New Economic Reality," *Change* vol. 22, no. 6 (November/December 1990): 16–22.

INDEX

by Kay Banning